4th EDITION

Senior Savvy

How to
Make the Most of
Your Life Savings
Before and After
You Retire

By
Kenneth A. Stern

CAREER PRESS
3 Tice Road
P.O. Box 687
Franklin Lakes, NJ 07417
1-800-CAREER-1
201-848-0310 (NJ and outside U.S.)
Fax: 201-848-1727

SENIOR SAVVY

Cover design by Suzanne Bennett

Printed in the U.S.A. by Book-mart Press

To order this title, please call toll-free 1-800-CAREER-1 (NJ and Canada: 201-848-0310) to order using VISA or MasterCard, or for further information on books from Career Press.

Library of Congress Cataloging-in-Publication Data

Stern, Ken, 1965-
    Senior savvy : how to make the most of your life savings before and after you retire / by Kenneth A. Stern. -- 4th. Ed.
        p.   cm.
    Includes index.
    ISBN 1-56414-352-X
    1. Aged--Finance, Personal.   2. Retirement income--United States--Planning.   3. Retirement--United States--Planning.   4. Savings and investment--United States.   5. Social security--United States.
    6. Medicare.   I. Title.
    HG179.S8352   1998
    332.024'0565--dc21   98-14307

Praise for Ken Stern's *Senior Savvy*

"I am sure that everyone who reads this book will benefit from Ken Stern's expertise in financial, estate and long-term planning matters."
—Rabbi M. Robert Syme, Temple Israel

"This is a must-read for anyone facing the maze of regulations and missed opportunities in their retirement years."
—Edward V. McVey
Senior Vice President,
Franklin Templeton Distributors, Inc.

"*Senior Savvy* is an informative, highly readable account that provides an excellent tool for anyone in or preparing for retirement."
—Jack Hellbron,
Chairman, Centurion Counsel

"Ken's got the answers to the questions everyone asks. Finally, straight talk about the tragic long-term care crisis. Invaluable."
—Jerry G. Bishop,
KPOP AM 1360, San Diego

"For most of us, money is confusing. Ken Stern cuts right to the core to provide concise, practical, and beneficial help on money (keeping more of it) and organizations (how to get them to work for you)."
—Dr. Karen Hayter,
Host of the nationally syndicated Southern
Baptist Christian Cable Network special, *COPE*

"Ken Stern has championed the cause of older Americans. He has witnessed the crises faced by many seniors and tackled these problems head-on."
—George Chamberlain,
KNSD-TV Financial Specialist
and host of "Money in the Morning"

"Information like this will come in handy sooner than I realize!"
—Katie Couric, *The Today Show*

Acknowledgments

In 1993 the first edition of *Senior Savvy* was published. The inspiration for this project was all of you, my readers and radio and television audiences. Your questions and thirst for knowledge inspired me to provide you with this resource. Now, *Senior Savvy* is in its fourth edition, and thousands of readers later, it promises to be filled with the most useful knowledge yet. Enjoy!

Senior Savvy could never have been completed without the incredible team I had the pleasure of working with, and I would like to thank all of them: my family for their support and my wife and best friend, Susan. Although I don't believe it, she said I get testy at times when working on projects such as *Senior Savvy*. If it's true, I'm glad she is so patient.

Also deserving of credit are the partners in my advisory firm Asset Planning Solutions. I want to thank Bill Scott for running the show, Rebecca Frankhouser for her creative input, and Steven Boyer for his technical advice.

—Kenneth A. Stern

Contents

Financial Freedom During Retirement

I would like to congratulate you on taking this important step toward making sure your retirement years will be the best of your life. In retirement, most people encounter more financial obstacles and pitfalls than they ever did as working individuals—and this happens during a time when they'd rather be enjoying their free time! To survive financial challenges brought about by political changes and economic cycles, withstand governmental changes in Medicare and Medicaid, and avoid the risk of a long illness depleting your life savings, it is critical to know how to protect your assets. You need to make sure your money lasts through constant market fluctuations, interest rate swings, tax law changes, and soaring inflation. You must keep your money safe from investment scandals, banking and insurance failures, and other problems with "guaranteed" investments.

Finally, provided you overcome these obstacles, you need to stay well-informed in order to avoid unnecessary costs and fees associated with probate, estate taxes, and capital gains taxes, and to make sure you are prepared for the responsibility of managing your estate without a spouse.

If any of this sounds gloomy, it shouldn't. People fail financially for two reasons: procrastination and lack of knowledge. This book will give you the knowledge; it's up to you start *now* to *control, maximize,* and *preserve* your assets. If you accomplish these three tasks, you can experience the happiest years of your life during your retirement.

Part I

The Financial Plan

Chapter 1

Why Creating a Plan Increases Wealth

What's the big deal? Why waste a great deal of time and energy to create a nebulous plan anyway? Because it's not a waste of time; rather, it's a terrific investment. Do you know for absolute certain:

♦ That your budget has no waste in it?

♦ That you are saving every dollar possible in taxes?

♦ How much interest you need (not *want*) on your money to ensure that you do not run out of money?

♦ What your expenses will be in 10 years?

♦ If the stock market drops, how much your investments will drop?

♦ How much you are making on your investments now?

♦ How you will avoid going broke if a major health care catastrophe occurs?

Not knowing the answers to these questions is akin to driving at night without headlights: One unexpected curve and you could be in for a nasty accident! A plan will insulate your finances from unexpected surprises.

Your Road Map

If you were getting ready to drive across the country, you probably would not start without a map and an idea of where you were going. In the same way, if you try to manage your money without a plan, you will spend too much time, waste money, and endure unnecessary aggravation—all because of mistakes that could have been avoided.

The mature American must prepare now for an extended life span, unexpected hyperinflation, higher taxes, and economic uncertainty. The unfortunate truth is that when you retire, public and private retirement programs will not pay the majority of your bills, and you will be left carrying the burden. The average person needs 80 percent of his or her annual pre-retirement income to maintain the same life style during retirement—and this estimate does not take inflation into account! Figure 1 shows how $40,000 has shrunk to barely $10,000 in buying power over the past 20 years because of inflation.

Figure 1:
The Purchasing Power of $40,000 Over 20 Years

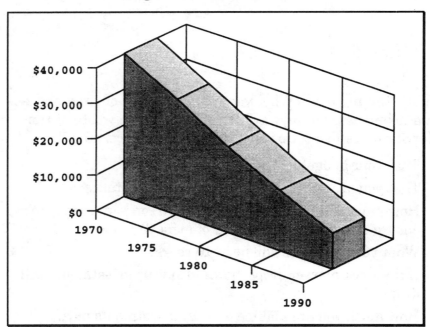

Most people do not plan for retirement, mainly because they are misinformed about the true extent of the retirement gap. A common myth is that Social Security and pensions will take care of the retiree. Unfortunately, Social Security and pensions usually do not account for even *half* of the required retirement income. This leaves the average retiree with the burden of coming up with the other half of his or her living expenses from personal savings. Furthermore, in the current economic environment, people are experiencing cuts in retirement benefits and reduced medical coverage, either one of which could unexpectedly result in increased expenses.

I am baffled when I hear that someone retires and invests money not knowing what he or she needs or wants to accomplish. Without this fore-knowledge, many retirees take either too much or too little risk, invest too much or too little, or select investment options that do not accurately reflect their needs and desires. In order to know how to prepare for your retirement, you need to know what you want from your retirement. Here are some steps to help you get started.

Step 1: List Your Goals

First and foremost, it is imperative that you make a list of your goals. *Never* do any investing until you know what you are trying to accomplish! Be sure your list of goals has a mix of financial, personal, and recreational issues, and both short- and long-term goals. Your list of goals might look like this:

- ♦ I will not outlive my money, and I will make sure my family is well-provided for.
- ♦ I will gift money to my grandchildren.
- ♦ I will not lose control of my estate because of probate and medical costs.
- ♦ I will make certain that if my spouse and I ever need to use our life savings for a medical crisis, my spouse will be well provided for.
- ♦ I will notify my family that in the event of a terminal illness, I do not wish to be kept alive on life-support systems.
- ♦ I will pay less in both income and estate taxes. I will make certain that my money is protected should I have to enter a nursing home.
- ♦ I will visit Europe.
- ♦ I will shoot under an 80 for 18 holes of golf.

Now that your goals are in place, work backwards. What must you do to make sure these goals can be accomplished?

Suppose I asked you, "What rate of return do you need on your money so that regardless of any situation, you are sure you will never outlive your money?" Many people do not know the answer. If you're one of them, I have a set of very important questions for you:

1. How did you decide where to invest if you didn't know the rate of return you needed?

2. Are you taking too much risk?

3. In any given year, how much could your portfolio lose? How much can your portfolio *afford to* lose?

4. Is your portfolio being maximized? Could you pay less in taxes in order to keep more of your money? Could you be getting the same return in a less risky investment?

5. If you live another 40 years, will the money you currently have run out? What interest rate or dividend do you need to earn to be certain your money will not run out?

6. How will inflation affect your income?

7. Are your assets protected from probate?

8. If you or your spouse passes on, can the other manage the portfolio? Will there be any delays or costs because of a death?

Step 2: Determine How Much Money You'll Need

What percent of your current earnings will you need during retirement? The rule of thumb is that, on average, retirees will need 70 to 80 percent of their preretirement earnings to maintain the life styles they are accustomed to. Part of the financial plan you create determines what you are going to need in today's dollars for retirement and what that will cost you when you actually retire and for all the years of retirement. Remember, just because you retired on a fixed income does not mean your expenses are fixed. To figure out what you'll need during retirement, start writing down everything you spend your money on. After a few months of this, subtract what you don't think will be an expense when you retire. However, add in new expenses, such as more greens fees, travel to see the kids, etc. To determine how much your costs will increase every year, see the Inflation Factor chart (Figure 5) in Chapter 2. You could also consult a financial planner or get a computer program.

Step 3: Determine Your Net Worth

Determining your net worth is a relatively simple task, but it can be very revealing. Your net worth can be figured in many different ways. For example, if you die and you own life insurance policies, the death benefits will most likely be figured into the gross value of your estate. If your estate is over a certain size, you will have to pay estate taxes. In that case, it might be advisable to lower your net worth by making certain that you don't own insurance policies. On average, an estate valued at more than $625,000 will pay from 37 to 55 percent in taxes!

For our purposes, we are going to use your net worth to size up your retirement nest egg. The first thing to look at is the value of your combined assets, including your home, investments, pensions, and savings. At the same time, you have to appraise your liabilities, such as mortgages and installment loans. When you subtract what you owe from what you own, this is your net worth. Net worth, in essence, is a like-it-or-not snapshot of your personal wealth.

To prepare your personal net worth statement, you need the following information.

Cash Reserve Assets

Add up your cash or near-cash resources such as checking accounts, savings accounts, and money market funds. These are your "liquid" assets because they can be liquidated quickly without penalties.

It's also possible to include the cash value of a life insurance policy, as well as a bank certificate of deposit (CD); these are liquid to the extent that it's possible to tap into them in an emergency. However, doing so may result in penalties for early withdrawal—or, as in the case of borrowing from the cash value of a life insurance policy, it may trigger interest and change the value of the loan.

In my opinion, between 15 and 20 percent of your total assets should be liquid, and there should be enough ready cash to cover your living expenses for a minimum of three months, but preferably six.

Equity/Retirement Assets

Generally, the most valuable asset in your portfolio is the equity in your home. But ideally, you will also have a combination of other investment assets, including stocks and options, mutual funds, taxable and tax-free bonds, Treasury bills, annuities, investment property (not your residence), and equity in a business.

Retirement assets also include IRA/Keogh Plans, 401(k)s, vested pension plans, and employee savings and stock option programs. All together, these should represent 50 to 60 percent of your total assets. Keep in mind that if you sell off investment assets, this will more than likely trigger tax liabilities and possibly penalties for early withdrawal.

To establish the values of these assets, ask your insurance agent, stockbroker, Realtor, and certified financial planner for assistance. You can also refer to recent price quotes in the newspaper. Although establishing values for real estate, limited partnerships, and vacation time-shares is complicated, for the purpose of this exercise, it's acceptable to place the value at the price you paid. Finally, to determine the value of your 401(k) or other company benefit programs, ask your employee benefits department to provide the calculations. As for personal property, such as clothing, furs, jewels, cars, and furniture, appraise the value by estimating how much money the item would generate if it were sold today.

Once you have compiled a list and the value of your assets, it's imperative to examine which ones can be converted into cash and/or income-producing investments. In essence, you need to figure out where you can generate more than 50 percent of your annual "salary."

Liabilities

Liabilities are the outstanding balances on your mortgage(s), installment loans, cars, and credit cards, and your projected state and federal tax bill. Normally, your liabilities should represent no more than 30 to 50 percent of your total assets. In retirement, however, I urge clients to carry as light a load as possible with respect to debts. They add significantly to monthly living expenses at a time when income may be fixed and limited.

In addition, the interest on car loans, credit cards, and installment loans is no longer deductible. Furthermore, with banks charging 18 percent interest (in Florida, it can be up to 21 percent), but only paying 6 to 7 percent on savings, it doesn't take an accountant to tell you that installment debt is a raw deal.

If you do not have a current net worth statement, fill out Worksheet 1 on page 24. If you need help, consult your financial planner or accountant.

Why Know Your Net Worth?

It is essential to know your net worth for several reasons. Your net worth will determine how much income you can earn from your investments. If your net worth grows, so should your discretionary income. If your investments shrink as a result of either inflation, excess spending, health care costs, or poor investments, your income will shrink. Thus, you should monitor your net worth like you monitor your blood pressure: regularly and with serious concern. Another important reason to figure net worth is so you can plan for estate taxes upon your death. After an estate reaches $625,000 in assets, the tax levied on the estate is very high. For many people, talking of estates valued at more than $625,000 sounds extremely high. But is it really?

Suppose a couple retires with an estate worth $350,000, including their home, car, and other personal assets. They have been very conservative with their investments. After taking the income they need, the estate is earning only 6 percent per year. Let's assume that 20 years later both spouses die. The growth on $300,000 at 6 percent per annum for 20 years has produced an estate valued at $1.25 million. But, wait! Add up all the life insurance polices—the wife had $50,000 and the husband had $100,000. The estate that was originally $300,000 has increased to more than $1,273,000! Let me thank this couple on behalf of Uncle Sam for the high estate taxes they will pay!

Every person or married couple is entitled to a onetime estate tax exclusion. In 1998, that exclusion equals $625,000, rising every year until it reaches $1 million in 2006 (see the chart in Chapter 7, on page 83). But after that, estate taxes are among the highest and most expensive taxes in existence—ranging from 37 percent to a high of 55 percent.

Let's say a person's estate is worth $2 million. Subtract the allowed $625,000. The tax burden on the remaining $1,375,000 is more than $625,000! This is not a negotiable sum or a figure you can ignore. Estate taxes must be paid within nine months after your death. How many beneficiaries can write a check for $625,000? Real estate or stocks will have to be sold to pay this tax. If the beneficiaries cannot come up with the money, the IRS will be delighted to liquidate the assets.

Figure 2:
Elements of Your Net Worth

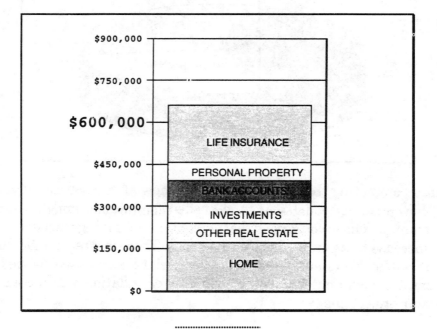

Depending on the year of your death, if your net estate, including your life insurance, is more than $625,000, estate taxes of 37 to 55 percent may be owed.

As you will learn, many easy strategies exist to lower your "paper" net worth. For example, consider that one of the largest assets of your net worth consists of insurance benefits that won't be paid until your death. A good way to get around this is simply to not own your own life insurance—have another person or entity own the life insurance, to remove the death benefit proceeds from your estate when you die.

Plan your net worth now. As you would prepare for a favorable net worth if your were trying to get a loan, plan for a small net worth upon your death.

Step 4: Determine Your Sources of Retirement Income

To understand your portfolio better, it is essential to know all the sources of your income. A good exercise for you to do is compute your total monthly or yearly income and its sources. Once you know your total, change it to percentages. Know how much comes (or will come) from Social Security, your retirement plan through work, and your investments.

Figure 3:
Sources of $50,000 Annual Retirement Income

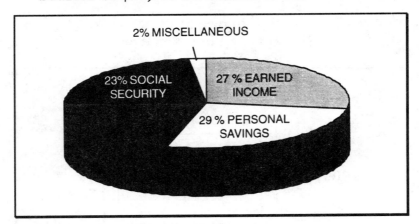

After completing this exercise, you will know all the sources of your income, how much of your savings is needed for income, and the interest rate required. Once you know the percentage of savings needed for income, increase this percentage by 10 percent. There is a reason for this 10-percent buffer: You never know whether Social Security will be reduced, your employer will cut retirement benefits, or inflation will increase beyond your projections.

When considering Social Security, it is important to note that taxes on Social Security benefits historically rise faster than income taxes. Newly proposed legislation may tax benefits even more, lowering your true Social Security benefit. Do not rely entirely on Social Security!

Step 5: Find Your Required Rate of Return

Now that the first four steps of building a financial plan are complete, the next step is to find your required rate of return. Your required rate of return is defined as the percentage of return you will need to receive on your investment portfolio in order to avoid outliving your money. Always allow for the worst-case scenario. Start with this rule of thumb: Retirement will cost 80 percent of your preretirement income, increasing each year with the cost of living. Assume that inflation will average much higher than you expect (at least 5 percent), and assume that you will be retired for at least 40 years (you might retire at age 60 and live to be 100). Although this may sound farfetched, living until 100 years of age is increasingly common. In fact, the fastest growing age group in America is people over the age of 85. Next, discount Social Security as a source for secure retirement income.

This is what I call *bulletproofing* your portfolio. If you can still retire comfortably after making the above assumptions, chances are you will be successful in retirement. You won't have to worry about investments, interest rate swings, recessions, or living past your expected life span. You are covered! Now when your head hits the pillow at night, all you should be thinking about is tomorrow, your hobbies, or your grandchildren—not worrying about your finances!

Now that you know the parameters, you are on your way to finding your required rate of return. Based on the above assumptions, if you know that all you need to earn is 8 percent to accomplish your goals, should you take any unnecessary risks? Should you invest in aggressive mutual funds, stocks, commodities, or anything where you could lose substantial amounts of money? If you can reduce your risk by avoiding these investments, you will not have to allow for losses from bad investments. This will increase, or secure, your return with less risk. Consider the following scenarios.

Scenario #1

You made $80,000 during your last year of employment, and you retire at age 65. You will need at least $64,000 per year in the first year of retirement. At 5 percent per year for inflation, in 10 years you will need $79,000, in 20 years you will need about $100,000, and so on. Further, assume that you will need to receive *about $30,000 per year from your employee retirement plan and $11,000 in Social Security.*

This means you will need to generate $23,000 per year out of your pocket, rising at 5 percent per year. Now, divide $23,000 by 8 (assuming 8 percent is your required return). This will tell you the dollar amount you will need in order to generate $23,000 per year without touching principal. That number is almost $290,000. If you assume that after the first year you will need 5 percent more in income to maintain your standard of living in order to keep up with inflation, you will now need to begin using principal. The bottom line is that your principal will be spent in about 40 years if the value of (or interest on) your money doesn't rise. (See Appendix A)

This plan is close to bulletproof. However, it counts on Social Security, no extra medical expenses, and leaves little room for error. If you calculated the same numbers using 9 or 10 percent as your required return, you would need less to invest. However, if you used higher, perhaps unreasonable percentages, you would need to consider riskier investment options, which should never be something you count on for retirement. Be aware that not many people earn 10 percent on their entire portfolio.

Scenario #2

Take a different look by assuming, instead, that you have $300,000 in savings and only need to generate $23,000 every year for income. Your numbers will be different. At an 8-percent interest rate, the income on $300,000 is higher: $24,000 per year. If the extra $1,000 of income is reinvested until needed, in an effort to keep up with inflation, your money should not run out for more than 50 years. The power of compounding interest is unbelievable. Investing any amount, no matter how small, could make a major difference in your retirement life style.

In Appendix A, you can see how the present value of a dollar compounds at different interest rates. Furthermore, if you continually add to your investment, the return on your money will appear almost overwhelming.

To be completely bulletproof, have an extra 10 percent more than the original $290,000. Conversely, to be absolutely sure, do the same calculations on only 90 percent of your assets, holding back 10 percent. With this 10 percent, you have spending money to spoil yourself occasionally. You could exceed your budget, tour the world, help *your children, or try to earn more money in certain investments with a higher degree of risk. Of course, you could also keep this money absolutely safe and use it as your safety net. Regardless of what you do with the extra 10 percent, you know that if you lose every penny of it, it will not affect your life style.*

Why not find a hobby that you enjoy and that might earn you some money? Many retirees purchase rental property as a hobby, and often they make a great deal of profit at it by becoming experts in the "business" of their hobby.

Putting It in Writing

Upon having completed this chapter, you should be able to come up with specific answers to the following questions.

1. What is the rate of return I need to retire?
2. How much money will I need to have saved?
3. What should my yearly budget be?

With careful, proper planning, higher inflation and fluctuating interest rates should not affect your golden years.

Now that you have figured your personal needs and understand what is required, you can review Chapters 15 and 16 to see how to invest. Chapters 8 and 11, the estate planning chapters, discuss how to hold title to your assets, protect those assets, and distribute them.

Worksheet 1: Your Net Worth Statement

Assets

Cash Reserve Assets

Checking accounts/cash	$ _____
Savings accounts	$ _____
Money market funds	$ _____
Certificates of deposit	$ _____
Life insurance (cash value)	$ _____

Equity/Retirement Assets

Time deposits (T-bills)	$ _____
Stocks and options	$ _____
Retirement savings (IRAs/Keoghs)	$ _____
Annuities (surrender value)	$ _____
Pensions (vested interest)	$ _____
Profit-sharing plans	$ _____
Collectibles	$ _____
House (market value)	$ _____
Other real estate/limited partnerships	$ _____
Business interests	$ _____
Personal property (automobiles, jewels, etc.)	$ _____
Loans owed you	$ _____
Other assets	$ _____

Total Assets $ _____

Liabilities

Mortgage or rent (balance due)	$ _____
auto loan (balance due)	$ _____
Credit cards	$ _____
Installment loans	$ _____
Annual tax bill	$ _____
Business debts	$ _____
Student loans	$ _____
Brokerage margin loans	$ _____
Home equity loans/2nd or 3rd mortgages	$ _____

Total liabilities $ _____

Total net worth (assets minus liabilities) $ _____

Chapter 2

Fabulous Formulas

How can you not love easy formulas, especially when they can provide so much valuable information? Formulas can teach you how long it will take to double your money, how long your money will last, and how inflation affects your buying power. The best part about using formulas and numbers is that the numbers don't lie. Numbers show facts, and with those facts you can begin framing a wonderful plan.

The Rule of 72

One very easy, yet effective, formula is the *rule of 72*. For planning purposes, you may want to know when your money will double. This is easy to determine: Simply divide 72 by the interest rate. For example, assume that you expect to earn 10 percent. Thus, 72 divided by 10 percent equals 7.2 years. Then, look at the different interest rates. For instance, 72 divided by 3 percent equals 24 years, and 72 divided by 5.5 percent equals 13.09 years.

The Rule of 72

To find out the length of time required for doubling your money, divide 72 by the interest rate.

72 / 10 (interest %) = 7.2 years

How Far Will Your Retirement Dollars Go?

Once you've created a net worth statement (Chapter 1), and added your Social Security and pension benefits to the mix, you'll know the size of your nest egg. The next pressing matter is figuring out how long these funds can be expected to last.

To estimate the strength of your retirement account, look at the total amount of funds you're starting with. Refer to Figure 4 to see how many years the money will last.

Figure 4:
How Much Money Can You Withdraw?*

Size of nest egg	If you withdraw this each month for the following number of years, you'll have "0" balance.					If you withdraw this amount each month, you won't be touching your nest egg.
	10 years	**15 years**	**20 years**	**25 years**	**30 years**	
$15,000	$174	$134	$118	$106	$99	$59
$25,000	$290	$224	$193	$176	$166	$118
$50,000	$580	$448	$386	$352	$332	$285
$80,000	$928	$718	$620	$564	$532	$467
$100,000	$1,160	$896	$772	$700	$668	$585

*Figures based on 7-percent net annual growth (after taxes).

As Figure 4 clearly illustrates, even a fairly large sum of money can be used up quickly in retirement. If you're like most individuals, you may find an alarming gap between what you think you need for a comfortable retirement and the amount of money you will actually have on hand, given your current savings plan. Use Worksheet 2 on page 27 to determine your retirement income needs. Refer to Figure 5 to determine the correct inflation factor in filling out the worksheet.

Figure 5:
Inflation Factor

Age in 1998	25	30	35	40	45	55	60	61	62
Year of retirement at age 62	2035	2030	2025	2020	2015	2005	2000	1999	1998
Inflation factor	4.8	3.95	3.24	2.67	2.19	1.48	1.22	1.17	1.12

Worksheet 2:
Your Personal Income Needs

A. Estimate the monthly income you will need at retirement:
1. Enter current monthly income   _____
2. Multiply by 75%   _____
3. Multiply by inflation factor (See Figure 5)   _____
   = monthly retirement income needed   _____

B. Estimate the actual retirement income you will receive:
1. Enter Social Security benefit   _____
2. Multiply by inflation factor (Figure 5)   _____
3. Add estimated monthly company retirement benefits   _____
4. Add anticipated monthly income from your
   IRA and other investments   _____
   = monthly retirement income received   _____

C. Calculate your retirement income gap:
1. Enter monthly income needed (see A above)   _____
2. Subtract monthly income received (see B above)   _____
   **= estimated monthly retirement
   income gap at age 62**   _____

D. Monthly investments needed to fill your   _____
retirement income gap. Use the following chart to
determine the amount you'll need to invest monthly to
close your retirement income gap.

Age	If your monthly retirement income gap is approximately:					
	$500	**$1,000**	**$2,000**	**$3,500**	**$5,000**	**$10,000**
25	$2.57	$49.14	$98.28	$171.99	$245.7	$491.4
30	35.81	71.61	143.23	250.65	358.07	716.15
35	52.86	105.73	211.45	370.04	528.63	1057.26
40	79.61	159.73	318.45	557.28	796.12	1592.24
45	123.8	247.6	495.2	866.61	1238.01	2476.02
50	203.47	406.93	813.87	1424.27	2034.67	4069.33
55	372.6	745.2	1490.4	2608.19	3725.99	7451.98
60	900.81	1801.61	3603.22	6305.64	9008.05	18016.1

To compute your taxable equivalent yield, apply the following steps (assume we are using a tax-free bond yielding at 5 percent):

1. Determine your federal and state tax bracket. For this exercise, let's assume it is 31 percent.
2. Subtract your tax bracket from 100 (100 – 31 = 69).
3. Divide the tax-free return by 69 (5 divided by 69 = .07246 or 7.2 percent).

Magic of Compound Interest

Once you truly understand the magic of compounding interest, you will agree that it *is* the eighth wonder of the world.

For instance, if two people had $10,000 each to invest, and one put the money in an account that paid simple interest of 8 percent annually, and the other put the $10,000 that also paid 8 percent in interest, but compounded it annually, what would be the difference in their return after 15 year?

The owner of the first account, the one paying only simple interest, would receive $800 annually ($10,000 x 8%). After 15 years that comes to $12,000 dollars. Add that to the original principal and it comes to a total of $22,000. Not bad, right? Maybe, until you look at what the second account has done.

In the first year, the compound interest account also earned $800. But in the second year, interest was earned on the original amount plus the $800, so interest earned in the second year was $864. Now that amount is added to the $10,800 (for a new total of $11,664), and interest is earned on that amount. As you can see, after 15 years this can add up to quite a bit of money—$21,700 in interest, for a total worth of $31,700. That's $9,700 more than the simple interest account. It must be magic, right? No, it's compound interest, a very powerful way to increase your wealth.

Chapter 3

The Effect of Inflation on Your Retirement

It has been suggested that 1997 was one of the lowest inflation years in post World War II history. I find this hard to believe for several reasons: I paid more for my cereal than for a round of golf, airline tickets reached all-time highs, and car prices were up. It seems one of the only things that didn't go up was the amount Social Security paid to recipients. Therein lies the crux of the problem.

Social Security increases with inflation; however, Social Security benefits have recently been increasing by barely 2 percent. Increases are measured by the Consumer Price Index (CPI), which is supposed to consist of a representative basket of goods and services and measure the increase in the cost. I don't believe the basket is "representative"; I believe it is intentionally not representative so that the government would not be obligated to shell out more money to Social Security recipients.

During retirement, inflation will increase faster than your income. If inflation is perceived "low" now, all the more reason to believe high inflation is around the corner.

> *Over the last 20 years, inflation has averaged about 5.5 percent annually.*

Based on 5.5-percent inflation, if you need $1,000 per month today, 10 years from now you will need $1,700; 15 years from now you will need $2,232. The longer you live, the more of a threat inflation becomes.

From 1969 to 1979, there was a 50-percent loss in purchasing power. Although that sounds drastic, it was nothing compared to the 20-percent loss of purchasing power caused by inflation in the two years from the beginning of 1980 to the end of 1981. Today, it takes $1 to buy what 29 cents bought in 1970, and what 12 cents bought in 1945.

Inflation is caused by too much money competing to buy the goods and services available in the marketplace. For example, you and many other Americans eat cereal every morning and have no intention of quitting this practice. Unfortunately, if the farm belt is hit with a nasty frost and only a portion of the crops survive, the cereal makers will still need the product, but there won't be enough to go around. So the farmers will raise the price of the wheat. In order for the cereal makers not to lose money, they will increase the price of the cereal they sell. Thus inflation begins.

I am under the impression that if you rely on the low inflation figures provided by the media, you will find those figures inaccurate when applied to the life style of the typical retiree. As mentioned previously, to arrive at the inflation numbers the government reports, a typical market basket of goods is used, but the typical retiree's basket of goods is usually quite different from that of a working family. The mature American spends the bulk of his or her money on household goods, travel, recreation, and health care. The cost of these items is increasing rapidly, in part because of supply and demand. More people are retired than ever before and recreational activities are in high demand. As a result of the strong demand, the price of these activities is rising. The same is true of travel and health care. It is interesting to note that although the price of these services continues to rise, the overall inflation rate, based on the CPI, shows that in recent years (1994 to 1998) inflation remains low, with 1998 registering an inflation rate of 2.1%—one of the lowest inflation rates in recent history. How can this be? I believe that the reason for this is that the basket of goods that comprises the CPI is not representative of what normal retirees spend.

If you retired 20 years ago with $40,000 to invest, that amount would have had to increase to almost $120,000 just to keep pace with inflation. Today the average retiree has an expected post-retirement life span of more than 22 years. Using this average number, it is difficult to keep up with the pace of inflation—and in 10 years, this life span could increase to more than 30 years.

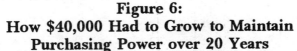

Figure 6:
How $40,000 Had to Grow to Maintain
Purchasing Power over 20 Years

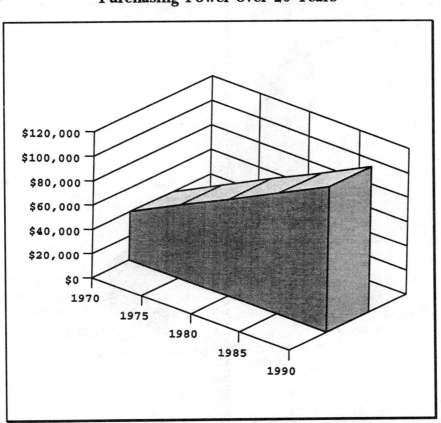

Consider your financial circumstances: Add together all of your investments, bank accounts, and certificates of deposit. Are you earning 8 percent? If you are like most of us, the answer is probably no. However, even if you are earning 8 percent, based on historical tax and inflation rates, your true, real rate of return would only equal 1.15 percent (see Figure 7). Can you afford this low rate of return with the length of time you will probably live?

The bottom line is that inflation is a serious concern. While you may be currently retiring in a low inflationary environment, don't lower your guard. If you do not respect the real possibility of hyperinflation, you may ruin your retirement plan. You must prepare for the unexpected.

Figure 7:
Effects of Inflation and Taxes on Investment Returns

(Assume that you are starting with $20,000; annualized real return over 20 years after inflation and taxes is 1.15 percent; gross return is 8 percent.)

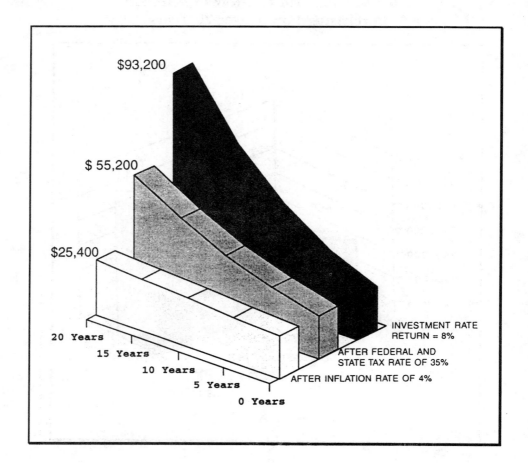

Chapter 4

Maximizing Your Retirement Benefits

When most employees retire, they need to decide how to take their retirement benefits. Usually, the two main choices include:

1. Taking a lump sum (specific dollar amount).
2. Taking a specified income for a specified time period.

The second option is called an "annuity payout." If you choose this option, typically even more choices will arise. You will need to choose if you want the income guaranteed for your lifetime; for you and a spouse; or for a specific number of years, regardless of whether you are alive or not. All of these very important questions will be explored in this chapter

Advantages of Annuitization

Annuitization is defined as taking a fixed amount of both principal and income for a specific period of time. Usually the period of time is a specific number of years or the remainder of someone's life, at least one principal and interest payment a year.

Say, for example, that you are 60 years old and have $50,000 in an annuity. The annuity company will offer you an option of forfeiting your

$50,000, in lieu of which you will receive $4,000 a year for 25 years. Even if you die before the 25 years are concluded, the $4,000 will continue to be paid to a beneficiary of your choice.

Although it may be rather traumatic to forego the $50,000, this could result in still further benefits. For instance, because you no longer have the asset, your estate taxes would be reduced. And although a factor of the remaining value would be included in your estate, if you need to qualify for Medicaid, the original $50,000 is no longer considered a part of your estate. This may increase your chances of passing the asset test for Medicaid qualifying purposes. (See Chapter 14 for more on Medicaid.)

If you annuitize your income, you will never have to worry about your money, because the check will come regularly. This is especially attractive if you do not wish to manage your money and you are certain the monthly income will be more than sufficient for the rest of your life.

Which Annuity Option Should You Take?

Should you decide to take the income option (annuity), you will most likely have three options:

1. Take the option on the highest income, but only for your lifetime (after your death income stops).
2. Take joint lifetime income (income payable to you and your spouse).
3. Take income for a guaranteed number of years.

This is a difficult decision, and the answer is different for every plan. For example, option one will pay the highest amount (say $500), but it's risky; and if you die, payments stop. Your spouse or beneficiaries will not receive any money. In option two, the benefit is lower (for our purposes we'll say it's $300), but it is guaranteed for as long as you and your spouse live.

Let's take a closer look at option one. If you take option one, use $300 for living expenses and invest the remaining $200 at an 8 percent return, and you live for 15 years, your account will end up worth $70,000. When you die (after 15 years), your spouse can draw more than $450 per month, without touching the principal (assuming the account earns an 8 percent interest rate).

Another popular strategy is to take the extra money from option one and buy a life insurance policy. Check to see how much insurance you can buy for the extra income under option one. Of course, be certain you can qualify for insurance before choosing this option. Also, be sure at this age that the insurance rate is permanent and will not rise annually.

Disadvantages of Annuitization

Although the monthly income sounds wonderful, there are some major drawbacks to electing the income if you're concerned with maximizing your money. Technically, when annuitizing your money, you not only lose your access to the principal, but also your ability to change your selection once your decision has been made. If you are concerned that you may one day need an emergency lump sum distribution, or if you are unsure the company from which you are retiring will be around longer than you, this inflexibility could be dangerous.

Remember, everyone is in business to make money, so your pension company is not going to give you an income so high that they will not earn money, too. Work the numbers carefully.

Scenario #1

You retire at age 60 and have a choice of taking a lump sum deposit of $100,000 or a monthly income of $835. You figure that by forfeiting the $100,000, you will receive $300,600 over 30 years. Doesn't that sound great? But do you realize that this does not even equal an annual return of 4 percent? Your annualized return is less than 4 percent, and you never get your $100,000 back!

Scenario #2

You take the lump sum retirement of $100,000 and roll the funds into an Individual Retirement Account (IRA). Inside the IRA, you are given the opportunity to invest in a U.S. Government bond earning 8 percent. You will receive $860 per month—only $175 less a month than if you had taken the annuity) and get your $100,000 back at the end of 30 years, guaranteed by the government. This is arguably one of the safest investment vehicles in the world!

Scenario #3

Is it possible to work the numbers a different way so that you can take the income option and still maximize your return? Take the $835 monthly income from Scenario #1 and invest the difference between that monthly payment and the $660 you would receive if you took the lump sum and invested it at 8 percent. This difference is $175. If you decided to invest that $175 per month for the next 30 years at 8 percent, at the end of 30 years that money would be about $245,000. Obviously that is much more than the $100,000 that you would have received should you have taken the lump sum.

Is Your Company Going to Outlive You?

If your company is responsible for providing your monthly income, are you sure the pension is properly funded and insured? Are you willing to take chances on this matter? What if the obligation of paying your income is that of an insurance company? How strong and solvent is that company? Almost all major pension plans are regulated and guaranteed through the Pension Benefit Guaranty Corporation (PBGC). This is the insurance company to the pension funds much like the FDIC is to banks.

All participants in the PBGC contribute a specified amount of money in their pension plan to pay the agreed-upon amounts to the retired employees. If several companies do not have sufficient funds, the PBGC acts as insurance, providing emergency funds if a shortfall exists. But if several companies default at once, PBGC may not have enough funds to pay everyone that may be affected, resulting in certain retired employees losing their monthly checks. It has been said that the PBGC could be operating at a deficit as high as $10 billion!

These numbers are both *real* and *scary*. Many of the large corporations' pensions are underfunded. This means they are probably using their current employees' money to pay the retirees, but there is a current shortfall. As workers continue to retire, almost $40 billion in benefits by corporate pension plans will likely turn out to be underfunded!

Chapter 5

Social Security and Retirement

The Social Security system was created by an act of Congress in 1935, and Social Security benefits now account for 20 to 30 percent of the average retiree's income. Although many people think of Social Security only as "old-age" benefits, it really is much more complex. The principal topic for this discussion is the Old Age and Survivors' Insurance Program, which provides monthly benefits to retirees, widows, dependents, spouses, and eligible divorced spouses. Medicare, which is also a function of Social Security for which you will become eligible when you reach the age of 65, is covered in Chapter 13.

If you plan to rely on Social Security for the majority of your retirement needs, think again. In the coming years, Social Security will cut retirees' benefits by taxing them more and reducing benefits to those who work during retirement. For those who have not retired yet, these trends in Social Security legislation mean many of us will not receive benefits prior to age 68 or 70.

As a result of longer life spans, the average retiree will receive more in Social Security benefits than the system was originally designed to distribute. Many people consider Social Security similar to a Ponzi Scheme, a fraudulent investment practice. What happens is that existing investors in a Ponzi Scheme are paid extremely high amounts of money, which is taken from the principal of new investors who are, in turn, paid off by the next level of new investors. Sooner or later, almost every Ponzi Scheme collapses under its own weight. That is what many people fear will eventually happen to Social Security, because those working now are paying for current retirees. When all the baby boomers retire, the coffers will be depleted.

Contacting Social Security

There are two critical times when you should contact Social Security: when planning for retirement, and again three months prior to retiring.

1. When Planning for Retirement

You will need to know how much Social Security is planning on paying you to try and figure out your retirement plan. Years prior to retiring, contact the Social Security Administration (SSA), and ask for your Personalized Earnings and Benefits Statement (PEBS). This will tell you how much in Social Security benefits you are entitled to and how the number was derived. I strongly urge you to check this amount, even if you are already retired and receiving benefits. Are you sure you are receiving the right amount? The Social Security Administration processes millions of W-2 tax forms and benefit amounts every year. Don't you think there is a chance they made a mistake? Isn't there a chance they missed an earning year for you or typed in the wrong amount? Check the amount you are going to receive or are receiving to make sure it is accurate.

2. Three Months Prior to Retiring

Benefits are not paid until you file. It is important to file at least three months prior to the time you are eligible to receive benefits. This is true for both income benefits and Medicare. Also, remember that the Social Security Administration is not always correct. If you feel there is an error in computing your benefits, it is your right to dispute the decision and have your case reviewed. Frequently, Social Security makes errors and corrects these in your favor. It will cost you nothing to have your case reviewed, and you do not need to hire an attorney. Many senior centers have attorneys on staff who will meet with you free of charge. Call your local Area for the Aging agency to find out about the availability of this service.

How to Contact Social Security

There are two main ways to contact the Social Security Administration. You can either go to your local Social Security office (look in the yellow pages or call a local agency for the aging for assistance—see Appendix B), or you can call the Social Security Administration's toll-free number: (800) 772-1213. I have used this number several times and have found it useful and the representatives who answer the phone to be fairly knowledgeable. You can use this number to request your Personal Earnings and Benefits Statement and to request the forms necessary to begin receiving your Social Security benefits.

A person eligible for Social Security benefits must choose between taking full benefits at 65 years of age, or taking a reduced amount beginning at age 62. My philosophy is that it usually makes sense to take benefits early, especially if you won't need the money for a few years. The following section explains why.

When to Take Your Social Security Benefits

Most mature Americans think it is better to wait until they are 65 to begin receiving their Social Security benefits. If you don't need the money right away and will get more money by waiting until age 65, why not do so? Consider the following scenarios.

Scenario #1

Let's assume you have the option to begin receiving either $800 per month at age 65 or $640 per month (about 80 percent) by electing to receive benefits at age 62. Take the $640 per month and put it into an investment that pays 8 percent. In three years when you turn 65, you will have more than $26,000.

Then, at age 65, if you wish to start using your Social Security, you will still be receiving your $640 (increased, of course, because of inflation). In addition, you can start drawing interest on the $26,000 you saved at 8 percent, which is about $170 per month, giving you a total that is higher than the $800 you would have received by waiting. What's more, you have an extra $23,000 of principal in your pocket for your retirement savings! Can you imagine the difference if you earned 9 percent on your money, or if you compounded Social Security benefits until you were 70? Personally, I like the fact that the money would be in my pocket, not in Uncle Sam's. Remember, however, that risk is involved whenever you are investing. You may or may not be able to earn 8 percent. Be absolutely sure you understand the risks before you make your decision.

Scenario #2

Now consider for a moment that you may need the money immediately and cannot invest it until you reach age 65. You will be receiving about $23,000 over those three years. It would take about 12 years to make that amount with the extra $160 per month you *would have received by waiting until you were 65. Assuming you did not invest, I suppose there is an argument for waiting to take the money until you reach age 65, but I would not wait just because I did not need the money. I would rather have the $23,000 than leave it in the hands of Social Security.*

Note: When you read Chapter 14 you will find an argument for showing lower monthly income.

Earnings Limitations

Many people ask, "If I keep working, will I receive Social Security benefits and will my benefits be taxed?" If your income exceeds the Social Security earnings limitations, your benefits may be reduced. The earnings limitation test applies only until you reach age 70; after age 70, you are entitled to earn any amount of money without benefits being reduced. Before age 70, if you earn more than the allowable amount set by the earnings limitation test, Social Security will reduce your benefits.

In 1998, if you were less than 65 years of age, your benefits are reduced by $1 for every $2 you earned over $8,640. If you were between the ages of 65 and 69, the reduction in Social Security benefits is $1 for every $3 of earnings over $13,500.

For instance, if you are 65 years old and earn $20,000 per year from your employer, you are allowed to earn $13,500 before your Social Security benefits are reduced. In this case you are vulnerable to the amount of $6,500 (subtract $13,500 from $20,000). Your benefits will be reduced by $1 for every $3 (about 33.3 percent). Now, 33.3 percent of $6,500 equals $2,164. That is the amount by which your Social Security benefits will be reduced.

In calculating your total earnings for this income test, it is important to note that many sources of income are not included in the earnings limitation test. These are pension payments, dividends and interest from investments, possibly annuities or certain trust funds (as long as they are not considered earned income), rental income, and lottery winnings. Payments for certain tax-exempt trust funds, such as profit sharing purchases or annuities may also be excluded.

Note: This is not a complete list and you should consult with a Social Security expert regarding questions on this matter.

Taxation of Social Security Benefits

Call it unconstitutional, call it robbery, call it the way it is—but Social Security is going broke. Instead of our lawmakers finding better ways to

invest the trust funds, or coming up with better solutions to avoid bank-
rupting Social Security, they tax us more. They are raising the amount of
tax working people are paying into Social Security, and they are taxing
people who receive benefits should they make too much money.

Currently, up to 85 percent of your Social Security Benefits could be
subject to federal income tax. The rules are as follows.

Single People

Single people include single individuals, widows and widowers, and
married couples filing separate returns and not living together. If you are
single, 50 percent of your benefits over the first threshold ($25,000 in
yearly income) will be taxed, and an additional 35 percent over the second
threshold ($34,000 in yearly income).

Married People

Married people include married persons filing joint returns or married
couples filing separately but living together. Married persons can have
$32,000 in yearly income before 50 percent of benefits are taxed, and the
second threshold is $44,000, over which an additional 35 percent of bene-
fits will be taxed.

What Is Considered "Income"?

Social Security is tricky when figuring your gross income. People who
own tax-free bonds and bond mutual funds, for example, might think they
are exempt because the tax returns show a lower adjusted gross income
(AGI). But in fact, "tax-free" bond interest *is* added into your gross income
to determine it for Social Security taxing purposes.

To figure out how much of your benefits will be taxed, Social Security
determines your AGI. However, you must realize that the AGI for Social
Security purposes is different from the AGI on your tax return. Social Security AGI is figured by using what is known as your preliminary adjusted gross Income (PAGI). Your PAGI is determined by adding all your
earnings, pensions, dividends, and interest from all investments or other
sources *including* tax-free bonds. In addition, 50 percent of your Social
Security benefits are added into your total income to arrive at your PAGI.

Once you have determined your PAGI, compare those numbers to the
thresholds. Fifty percent of any excess over the first threshold, plus 35
percent of any excess over the second threshold, is included in the AGI.
This amount cannot exceed 85 percent of the benefits or 50 percent of the
benefits plus 85 percent of any excess over the second threshold, which

ever is the smaller amount. Consider the following example of a married couple in 1998:

Preliminary adjusted gross income	$55,000
Tax-free bond interest	+ 5,000
50% of Social Security benefits ($20,000)	+ 10,000
Modified adjusted gross income	$70,000
Excess income over the first threshold ($32,000)	$38,000
Excess of income over the second threshold ($44,000)	$26,000
1. 50% of excess over first threshold, plus 35% of excess over the second threshold (.50 x $38,000 + .35 x 26,000)	$28,000
2. 85% of benefits (.85 x $20,000)	$17,000
3. 50% of benefits, plus 7% of excess over second threshold (.50 x $20,000+.85 x $26,000)	$32,100

In this example, the smallest of the three figures is $17,000. This would then be added to the PAGI of $55,000, thus giving the true AGI for figuring out Social Security tax: $72,000.

Lower Your AGI for Social Security Purposes

Many people collect their Social Security benefits, pay the taxes, and think nothing of it. Chances are that from the money you save on this Social Security tax you could enjoy a wonderful trip. Here are two ideas for reducing your AGI for Social Security purposes.

1. Instead of owning investments (such as stocks, bonds, or mutual funds) that pay dividends, look for investments that appreciate so you will have a lower income. Obviously, you will not realize as much income, but figure out how much income you really need. Why have more income than you need, simply to pay taxes on it? If you do need some extra money during the year, consider selling some of your original shares. If done properly, this should not increase your adjusted gross income.

2. Try keeping money inside of tax-deferred vehicles for a longer period of time. You can keep funds inside of your Individual Retirement Account (IRA), or you can create annuities and other nonqualified tax-deferred vehicles. As long as the funds stay inside the account, regardless of how much is made, you are not taxed on any of the income or gains until you withdraw the money.

Social Security Benefits After the First Death

Although many restrictions apply, if the widow(er) is over age 60 and not entitled to a Social Security benefit higher than the deceased spouse, the survivor files an application for widow(er) benefits. If the couple was married for at least nine months prior to the death, the surviving spouse will usually be entitled to benefits. The nine-month period may be waived if the spouse dies accidentally rather than from natural causes.

The widow(er) is entitled to receive reduced Social Security benefits between the ages of 60 and 64, or may wait until age 65 and receive the full retirement benefits. The amount would equal 100 percent of what the deceased spouse would have received. However, if the widow(er) takes the reduced payment before 65, he or she is not entitled to the full benefit at age 65.

The formula is as follows: The benefit is reduced by 19/40 (almost half) of 1 percent for each month that the widow(er) is under age 65 when the benefits begin. Therefore, check your formula—if you take the benefits at 62, you should be receiving roughly 82.9 percent.

If the widow(er) remarries after the age of 60, the benefit should not be reduced. If the survivor is entitled to Social Security as well as the deceased's benefits, the survivor will have to choose which benefits to take. You cannot get both. For a more complete guide to Social Security, including how to figure your benefits, understanding Social Security's role in disability, and more, read my book *Comprehensive Guide to Social Security and Medicare*.

Chapter 6

Milking Your IRA for All It's Worth

Individual Retirement Accounts (IRAs)—what an incredible concept. The right to contribute to an IRA was first established as a means to provide incentives to those individuals saving for their own retirement. Coincidentally, this great incentive was passed just around the time our lawmakers realized that the Social Security system would fall short of the average retiree's expectations.

As great as the IRA concept is, it is extremely confusing (as is anything the government is involved in). This confusion can lead to missed opportunities, the possibility of additional taxes, and stringent IRS penalties. This chapter will help you work through the maze of IRS regulations so that you can maximize the value of your IRA.

Prior to the Tax Reform Act of 1997, an IRA would typically fall into one of two categories: tax-deductible and not tax-deductible. Regardless of whether the original contributions were considered tax-deductible, both types of accounts had the ability to grow their earnings tax-deferred. This is an exceptional advantage for the long-term investor in that it allows the IRA earnings to compound much quicker. However, there are contribution limits, income limits, and there will ultimately be taxes to pay.

Contribution Limits

There are limits on the amount that can be contributed to an IRA in any given year. Contributions are limited to the lesser of $2,000 or earned income for that year. This means that an individual can contribute up to $2,000 of his or her earned income to an IRA account and that a married couple filing jointly can each contribute $2,000 per year of earned income to their respective accounts for an aggregate total of $4,000.

Recent legislation has enhanced the contribution levels for the benefit of a nonworking spouse. Under prior law, a working spouse could contribute $2,000 to his or her own IRA account and $250 to the account of a nonworking spouse. The new provision allows for a full contribution on behalf of both individuals as long as combined income is below $150,000 and the source of the contribution is from the earned income of the working spouse. In essence, this means that a married couple can make full contributions to their respective accounts as long as one spouse is working.

Income Limitations

The amount of income that you earn and whether you are covered by an employer-sponsored retirement plan will largely determine whether the contributions you make to an IRA will be considered tax-deductible. An individual not covered by an employer-sponsored retirement plan can make a full contribution to an IRA regardless of income. Individuals covered by an employer-sponsored plan may still qualify for a tax-deductible contribution if they fall within the applicable income range. Figure 8 shows the new income ranges that limit the amount of a deductible IRA contribution that can be made by individuals who are active participants in an employer-sponsored retirement plan.

Figure 8:
IRA Contributions

For Individual Returns			For Joint Returns		
	Minimum	Maximum		Minimum	Maximum
1997	$25,000	$35,000	1997	$40,000	$50,000
1998	$30,000	$40,000	1998	$50,000	$60,000
1999	$31,000	$41,000	1999	$51,000	$61,000
2000	$32,000	$42,000	2000	$52,000	$62,000
2001	$33,000	$43,000	2001	$53,000	$63,000
2002	$34,000	$44,000	2002	$54,000	$64,000
2003	$40,000	$50,000	2003	$60,000	$70,000
2004	$45,000	$55,000	2004	$65,000	$75,000
2005	$50,000	$60,000	2005	$70,000	$80,000
			2006	$75,000	$85,000
			2007	$80,000	$100,000

Individuals or married couples with income below the minimum qualify for a full deduction, and those with incomes in the range qualify for a partial deduction, while those above the range will not receive a deduction.

Strategies for Diversifying Your IRA

Your IRA account will be one of your primary sources of future retirement income; therefore it should be considered a long-term accumulation account geared for long-term growth. It is probably not the place for your most speculative investments, because should your speculative investments turn sour you will not be able to take the tax deduction for the loss. For example, assume that you are already retired and that you have enough income, and do not need any more. You will still need to diversify your investments. Consider investing in nonincome-producing investments and investments that only pay capital gains for assets held outside your IRA. This should lower your taxable income.

If for no other reason than diversification, you will still need income-producing assets, investments that pay dividends, and interest. This may include certificates of deposit (CDs) and stocks and mutual funds that pay dividends. Consider placing these investments inside the IRA.

Planning Tip: None of this income will show on your taxes until the money is withdrawn. Your taxes should be lower as a result.

Where Should You Hold Your IRA?

All IRAs need to be held through a qualified custodial account. Some individuals will hold IRAs at the bank, brokerage accounts, mutual fund companies, or in trust deeds. Regardless of what type of investments you make with your IRA account, I recommend having no more than one or two custodians—perhaps a bank and a brokerage firm. Most institutions charge an annual fee that could range from $10 to $50 per account. If you can find a custodian that has the ability to hold your certificates of deposit, stocks, mutual funds and bonds, you will be able to reduce your annual fees dramatically.

When Can You Withdraw from Your IRA?

Our lawmakers intended the IRA to be a long-term retirement savings account and, as such, they imposed restrictions on the amount of access you would have to the account prior to age 59½. Accessing an IRA account prior to age 59½ could result in a 10-percent premature withdrawal penalty tax. The only exceptions to this stiff penalty are as follows:

1. **First-time home owner.** If you have not owned a primary personal residence in the preceding two years, you would be considered a first-time home buyer and would be eligible to withdraw up to a lifetime limit of $10,000 to be used for the sole purpose of buying a home. Although this withdrawal avoids the 10-percent penalty, income taxes are still due on the amount you withdraw.

2. **Death or disability.** In the event of your death, your beneficiaries will not be subject to the 10-percent penalty even if they are under age 59½.

3. **Medical expenses.** If your medical expenses exceed 7.5 percent of your adjusted gross income, you can use a portion of your IRA to pay the medical bills. Again, although you avoid the 10-percent penalty, income taxes will have to be paid.

4. **Periodic and equal payments.** The IRA owner can start to receive income from the account prior to age 59½ by utilizing IRS code 72(t). This provision allows distributions from an IRA account prior to age 59½ if those distributions are set up as equal period payments based on the account owner's life expectancy, which must continue for at least five years and until the IRA owner reaches age 59½.

Required Distributions

Our lawmakers did not intend for us to reap the benefits of the IRA forever. In fact, they require that we start to deplete our IRAs when we reach age 70½. Just how much of the account we will be required to deplete will depend on the type of planning done to that point. The IRS mandates that we start to take a required minimum withdrawal or a required minimum distribution from the account no later than April 1st of the year following reaching the age of 70½.

In subsequent years, you must take your distributions by December 31st of each year. As previously discussed, many individuals hold IRAs at more than one institution. What is often misunderstood is that the required minimum distribution is not required to be taken from each of the IRAs, but rather based on the whole value of the IRAs. For instance, if you have two IRAs, each worth $50,000, and the required distribution for a particular year is $10,000, you can take that $10,000 out of either account, as long as the amount withdrawn is based on the value of all your IRAs combined.

Planning Tip: It is recommended that you take all of your IRA distributions from one account. This will allow you to allocate one account for the short-term. The investments will be safer and receive a lower return. The remaining investments will still be able to grow with a longer-term time horizon with the potential of realizing higher returns with longer-term, more growth-oriented investments. Of course, higher growth means more volatility and risk.

How Much Are You Required to Withdraw?

If you have an IRA, you will be required to withdraw money—this much is clear. The next section on methods of distribution will outline how much you are required to withdraw depending on your mode of distribution. The amount that you are required to withdraw from your IRA and the planning strategies that are involved is an issue that is crucial to your overall planning and where mistakes are rarely forgiven. Check the amount of your required minimum distribution carefully. Make a mistake and the IRS will impose a 50-percent tax penalty on the amount not taken.

Methods of Distribution

There are several options to choose from when deciding how to take your required distributions. These include lump sum, annuity payout, the reduction method, and the recalculation method.

Lump Sum

Lump sum distribution means that money in the IRA is taken all at once, rather than annuitized. This is usually not recommended because it results in the highest tax. When the money comes out of an IRA, it is considered to be income for that year and taxed accordingly. Depending on the value of the IRA, the distribution could push you into the highest tax bracket, exposing your hard-earned savings to even more taxes.

Annuity Payout

An annuity means that you will receive a payment from your IRA for a guaranteed number of years. You may take your IRA and convert it to an annuity. This is equivalent to the pension payments one might receive from a company-sponsored pension plan. To create an annuity, the payout must be paid at least annually for a specified number of years, not to extend your estimated life expectancy based on mortality tables. The benefit to this method is the assurance that you would never outlive your money. Usually, the payments will last until the death of the account holder. Of course, the negative issues associated with this distribution method are that the income you receive may not live up to your expectations and the choice is irrevocable.

The Reduction Method (also known as Term Certain)

This method spreads your payments over your life expectancy, or your and your beneficiary's combined life expectancy, as determined by IRS tables. (Examples of the life expectancy tables used by the IRS for this method are provided in Appendix A.) This method of payout is available for both spouse and nonspouse beneficiaries. For example, if an owner's life expectancy is 15 years and the owner's spouse has a life expectancy of 18 years, it is possible that the joint life expectancy under IRS tables of the husband and wife (the period during which at least one of the two will survive) might be 20 years. Suppose the fund to be distributed was $30,000. If the distribution is patterned on the basis of the individual's life expectancy alone, the annual required payout would be $2,000 ($30,000/15). If joint life expectancy is used, however, the annual distribution would only be $1,500 ($30,000/20). The results are reached by simple arithmetic: dividing the principal by the number of life expectancy years. Unfortunately, many financial institutions do not offer this method, and if they do you may have to specifically request it.

The reduction method is much safer than the recalculation method (see below). It allows for the distributions to continue, at the same rate, after both spouses die. That means that your beneficiaries can continue to take money out over time and not get hit with one big tax penalty

Recalculation Method

This method is available for both the owner or the owner and a beneficiary when the beneficiary is a spouse. The recalculation method is popular because it allows for the least amount of withdrawals for a husband and wife. However, there are consequences. Under the recalculation method, a new life expectancy would be determined for each passing year, the reasoning being that as each year passes the chances for continued survival increase. (Examples of the tables used by the IRS for this method are provided in Appendix A.) For example, under the IRS tables, the life expectancy of a 70-year-old individual is 16 year (to age 86); however, once that individual reaches age 80, his or her life expectancy is nine-and-a-half years (to age 89½). And again, upon reaching age 90, such individual would still have a remaining life expectancy of five years (to age 95).

Although the recalculation method does provide for smaller required minimum distributions, the plan could backfire. Should the IRA owner's spouse predecease the owner, the IRA owner will then be required to take future distributions based on his or her life expectancy alone. This could result in substantially higher forced distributions.

There is a further little-known tax trap associated with this method as well: When the surviving spouse dies, everything has to be paid out within a year. That could pose a serious tax penalty if a sizable balance still remains. To avoid this, after the first spouse dies, the surviving spouse may transfer the proceeds of the IRA into his or her own IRA. At this point the new IRA holder can recalculate the distributions.

Choosing The Right IRA Beneficiary

Whom you choose as a beneficiary to your IRA is a crucial decision. Most married people list their spouse as their primary beneficiary so that when one spouse dies, the surviving spouse can roll over the full amount of the deceased spouse's IRA to his or her own account, thus avoiding adverse tax consequences. However, individuals should consider listing someone other than a spouse as beneficiary for a number of reasons. Among those reasons are children from a prior marriage, an estate that is subject to estate taxes, or the fact that they are not in need of the IRA income and would like to minimize the forced distribution from the IRA.

Individuals who wish to minimize their required minimum distributions and have evaluated the pros and cons of listing their spouse as the primary beneficiary could consider listing someone younger than them as the primary beneficiary. The results of a combined life expectancy with a younger beneficiary could dramatically lower required distributions. However, it's important to note the limitations. If your beneficiary is a non-spouse, then the total deduction in the joint life expectancy cannot exceed 10 years. That is, even if you place a grandchild as beneficiary, you can only increase your life expectancy for IRA purposes by a maximum of 10 years. If the beneficiary is your spouse, however, you are not limited to the 10-year maximum.

Another strategy involves a little-known rule whereby you can have your IRA paid out to your children over *their* life expectancies. This could drastically reduce the taxes normally due upon the IRA owner's death.

If you have several beneficiaries, it may make sense to hold separate IRAs for each of them. Usually it is the oldest beneficiary's mortality table that is used if the accounts aren't separate. This could cause for higher than necessary distributions.

Choosing the right beneficiary is an important decision, one that should be carefully considered and made only when all the facts are clearly understood.

The W-9 and Other IRS Forms

When you receive income from your IRA, chances are the taxes will automatically be withheld. You can choose not to have any taxes withheld, but you must request this in writing on form W-9 and specify that you are not subject to backup withholding. Do not wait until a withdrawal is made, because it is not easy to change this procedure. The withdrawals made from your IRA will be considered ordinary income and should be reported as such on your tax forms. Any distributions you receive from your IRA will be reported on the 1099-R tax form, which both you and the IRS receive. Be sure your withdrawal records match the amount on your 1099-R form.

If you have made any nondeductible contributions to your IRA, you are required to file Form 8606 with your tax return when you take a distribution. This form can be obtained from your tax advisor or the IRS.

IRA Transfers and Rollovers

If you have an IRA and wish to change the custodian holding the investment, you can do this either by a transfer or a rollover.

IRA Transfer

An IRA transfer is when you never actually take possession of the money. Instead, you instruct the new IRA custodian (the institution to which you are transferring funds) to transfer the funds. The new custodian will then notify the current custodian and have the funds transferred. You are allowed to transfer IRAs as often as you wish.

IRA Rollover

An IRA rollover is slightly different in that it involves taking possession of your money. The custodian (a bank, for example) will roll the money over to you after filing an IRA distribution form (make sure you give instructions not to withhold taxes). Once you have the funds, you will have 60 days to roll them over into another IRA. If you do not roll the funds over, you will be obligated to pay income tax on the full amount you received. An IRA rollover is only allowed once a year.

When you rollover funds, you will receive a 1099-R tax form from the previous custodian. You will not owe taxes as long as you prove the funds were reinvested into another IRA within 60 days.

Transferring Pension Plan Funds to an IRA

Much talk has centered around the 20-percent withholding tax, a tax that is applicable if you are rolling over a pension or other qualified

(IRS-sanctioned) pension plan to an IRA. If you take possession of the funds (from the pension), even though you are still planning to roll the benefits into an IRA, an automatic 20-percent withholding tax will be levied. Fortunately, if you understand your rollover rights, you can avoid this tax. To do so, you will need to select a direct rollover of your benefits. In other words, instruct your pension institution to send the funds directly to the custodian of your IRA.

Avoiding Taxes on Your IRA at Death

If you want to save thousands of dollars in taxes on your IRA at the time of your death, you need to make two decisions right now: who the beneficiary will be, and how to take your distributions. If you don't make these decisions, your heirs could very likely lose 20 to 40 percent immediately in taxes on the IRA they inherit from you. But if a plan is established to stretch out the IRA benefits, it can potentially save you and your family thousands of dollars.

How to Build a Nearly Neverending IRA

You have done well, contributing to and growing your IRA. It is now worth $100,000 and you would like your children to inherit it. But when you die, the IRA is liquidated and the proceeds are added to all of your other income in the year you die. Assume you had $40,000 in regular income the year of passing. That $40,000 is added to the $100,000 (assuming most of the money is pre-tax contributions), and you now have $140,000 in income. That means you could incur a tax of more than $40,000, leaving your beneficiaries only $60,000 of the original $100,000! This is a sad but common scenario.

If you make the right decisions and create a plan for IRA distributions while you are alive, you could extend the life of your IRA to your children and even your grandchildren.

Here are several tips if you are planning to stretch out an IRA.

- ◆ Make certain the IRA stays in the decedent's name with the decedent's Social Security number.
- ◆ Make certain your IRA custodians knows what they are doing.
- ◆ Have a written succession plan in place for your IRA. You may need to go to a qualified attorney, financial or estate planner.

If the Beneficiary Is the Spouse

The spouse has many terrific strategies available to him or her for lowering the tax on a deceased spouse's IRA. The main advantage is the ability to roll the IRA into the surviving spouse's IRA and continue the tax-deferred status of the IRA. However, this is a temporary fix. Once the IRA proceeds are rolled into the surviving spouse's IRA, the account will probably continue to grow. What happens when that spouse dies? The IRS will get their money at that time—unless a plan has been set up to continue the deferral, and further stretch out the IRA.

If the beneficiary is a surviving spouse and distributions have not yet commenced, the spouse has the option of either rolling over the account to his of her own IRA, or leaving it in the deceased spouse's name and treating it as if it were his or her own. In the latter case, he or she has the following options.

- ◆ Start taking equal and periodic distributions based on the survivor's life expectancy for which payments must begin by December 31st, following the first spouse's passing. If the surviving spouse is young, the payments will be lower, thereby creating a lower tax. These payments would continue at the same rate to the subsequent beneficiaries should the surviving spouse die. This could prove quite beneficial because if the investments in the IRA do well, the account will continue to grow, allowing the income to continue to increase for the beneficiaries yet still avoiding a lump sum tax payment.

- ◆ If the deceased spouse had not started to take his or her required minimum distributions at the time of death, then the spouse will also have the option of delaying any distributions from the account until December 31st, following the year in which the deceased spouse would have turned 70½ years old. This could be a good strategy if the beneficiary/spouse is a lot older than the deceased spouse.

- ◆ If minimum distribution payments have commenced then the widowed spouse still has the option of rolling over the IRA to his or her own. If he or she chooses not to rollover the account to his or her own name, then he or she must continue to receive the distributions just as rapidly as under the method that was used prior to the owner's death. In this situation, if the spouse is younger and does not need the income payments that were required by the deceased spouse, rolling over the IRA is almost always the best option.

There are even more intricate and possibly beneficial strategies. A new hybrid method allows one spouse to use the recalculation method while the other uses the reduction method. If your spouse were to live beyond the life expectancy tables it could help to stretch out the payments for an even longer period of time. However, as with all the strategies, you need to have a written plan in place and have your IRA with a custodian who can follow your wishes.

If the Beneficiary Is not the Spouse

If the owner of the plan dies before he or she is required to take any minimum distributions and the beneficiary is not a spouse, then the beneficiary must take the proceeds by one of the following methods.

- ♦ **Lump Sum Distribution.** Depending on the size of the IRA, this method could initiate a sizable tax burden for the beneficiary. Under this method, the distribution must be made by December 31st of the year following the date of death. The entire amount of the pre-tax proceeds will be taxed as income tax in the year of the account holder's passing.

- ♦ **Distribution over five years.** Under this option, the beneficiary will have greater control over how much tax he or she will ultimately have to pay. The beneficiary can disburse as much or as little of the IRA as he or she wishes over the five years following the IRA owner's passing. Under this method of distribution, the entire account must be completely liquidated by December 31st following five years from the date of the owner's death. This is a tremendous tool. For example, if the deceased owner left an IRA worth $100,000, and you were to liquidate it IRA in the year of the owner's passing, you will incur substantial income taxes. However, if you average it over five years, the IRA will still enjoy tax-deferred growth and you will have the flexibility of withdrawing a fifth of the current value per year. This allows you to withdraw less per year and will probably place you in a lower tax bracket.

- ♦ **Distribution over the beneficiary's life expectancy.** Under this method, the beneficiary has the ability to continue the tax-deferred compounding of the IRA and would be required to take minimum distributions from the account based on the his or her life expectancy, with the first distribution taking effect no later than December 31st of the year following the IRA owner's date of death. This is a little known, yet extremely effective tax loophole. If you have a younger beneficiary on your IRA while you are alive, you have the right to combine your mortality table with this younger beneficiary in an effort to reduce your required minimum distribution. However, when you die, the succeeding payments are based on your beneficiary's mortality table. This method will allow the IRA to grow the most, pay the least taxes, and provide the beneficiary with the greatest gift over time.

Scenario

Jan and Steve each inherit an IRA worth $500,000.

Jan's IRA was established so she could withdraw the proceeds over her life expectancy (44 years). Every year for 30 years she withdrew the proper amount, paid taxes, and reinvested the proceeds in 8-percent interest paying bonds. At the end of 30 years she had saved $1.4 million outside the IRA. In the IRA, she had an additional $1.5 million.

Steve, on the other hand, was not so lucky. He immediately withdrew all of the money from the IRA, paid the taxes, and reinvested the proceeds in 8-percent interest paying bonds. At the end of 30 years, Steve had $1.5 million saved, but nothing in the IRA.

Jan's approach had earned her an additional $1.4 million.

If distributions have commenced (the IRA owner had already started to take the required minimum distributions), and the beneficiary is a non-spouse, then the beneficiary can elect to continue receiving the distributions as if the owner were still alive and his or her distribution election were still in effect. Under no circumstances, if the beneficiary is not a spouse, can the required distributions be paid out less frequently than they would have been if the IRA owner were still alive. Stretching out your IRA is critical to saving you money. Don't procrastinate on this issue.

Your IRA Custodian Could Cost You Money

Many IRA custodians do not know how to stretch out an IRA. Many banks and mutual funds will not allow an IRA to stay open in the decedent's name, which is essential to stretching out an IRA. If an IRA custodian ever takes the decedent's name and Social Security number off the account (which is automatic, when the owner of an IRA dies, at many custodial firms) you will lose any possibility of stretching out the IRA and will owe income taxes that year.

Don't assume that the forms you signed when opening an IRA will provide for all of your needs. Contact your IRA custodian. Ask if they will allow you to create five-year averaging or life-time averaging on an IRA. The majority of the custodians I have talked to at banks, mutual fund companies, and brokerage firms had no idea what to do.

The Roth IRA

Could it be that it was an election year? Or was it that the IRS was in poor standing? Whatever the case, the Roth IRA is here and it looks like it will become a permanent fixture for some time to come. The new Roth IRA is exciting and intriguing and can prove to be an extremely powerful planning tool for many taxpayers.

What Is the Roth IRA?

The Roth IRA is a new type of savings vehicle that allows a married couple (filing jointly) with income less than $150,000, or single individuals with incomes less than $95,000 to make a contribution of up to $2,000 of earned income per account to a new tax-free savings system.

There are both advantages and disadvantages to this new savings program. One disadvantage is that the contributions made to the account do not qualify for an income-tax deduction. The advantage is that once the contributions are made to the account, the account can grow and be accessed tax-free as long as certain guidelines are met.

In order to enjoy tax-free and penalty-free status, withdrawals from a Roth IRA must be considered qualified distributions. Qualified distributions are distributions that are taken for a specified reason and that meet a five-year holding requirement. Qualified reasons include: reaching age 59½, death or disability, or the first-time purchase of a home (up to a life-time limit of $10,000).

If distributions fail to meet one of these qualified reasons, they could be subject to both taxation and penalties. However, the 10-percent premature distribution penalty is waived if the distribution is used for one of the following reasons: education, medical expenses exceeding 7.5 percent of your adjusted gross income, health care insurance for an unemployed individual, or substantially equal payments over the IRA holder's lifetime.

Special Tax Loophole Using the Roth IRA

There is a little-known loophole to the Roth IRA that allows for distributions prior to age 59½. When withdrawing money from a Roth IRA, distributions are first considered to be part of your original contribution up to the extent of your original contributions. Once your contributions have been withdrawn then your earnings are withdrawn. Contributions to a Roth IRA are both tax- and penalty-free and can be withdrawn at any time—even before age 59½. Any withdrawal in excess of your contributions would be subject to both taxes and penalties unless those distributions meet the guidelines that were discussed previously.

Mandatory Distributions

Unlike the traditional IRAs, there are no mandatory distribution requirements with the Roth, which means that you do not need to begin withdrawing money at age 70½. Further, the IRA can be left to grow to an unlimited amount and all distributions to the beneficiaries will be tax-free income.

Planning Strategies

The new Roth IRA looks extremely appealing to individuals who were previously making nondeductible contributions to a traditional IRA, individuals in a lower income tax bracket today than they expect to be in the future, individuals who have the ability to make the full $2,000 contribution to the Roth and pay the taxes owed on the contributed income from a different source, and individuals who would like to keep control over how much money they need to claim as income during their retirement years.

Roth IRA Conversion

The year 1998 will be a special one for many taxpayers. This is the year that the IRS has allowed current IRA holders to convert their traditional IRAs to a Roth IRA and spread the income subject to taxation over a four-year period.

Taxpayers with an adjusted gross income (AGI) of less than $100,000 (whether single or joint) can roll assets from a traditional IRA into a Roth IRA. However, income tax will be imposed on the taxable amount that is rolled over (no premature penalty will be imposed). Although a tax will be imposed on the amount rolled over, if the amount rolled over increases your AGI to more than $100,000, it will not disqualify you from converting to a Roth IRA.

If the conversion takes place prior to December 31, 1998, the taxable amount can be spread equally over four years.

Here's How It Works

An individual who has a traditional IRA worth $100,000 can convert this IRA to a Roth IRA in 1998; however, he or she would be required to include an additional $25,000 per year for four years ($100,000/4) on his or her income tax return. This extra income will be subject to income taxes based on that individual's marginal tax bracket for all sources of income for the year.

Does the Conversion Make Sense?

If you have idle funds that can be used to pay the additional taxes as a result of the conversion and you can leave the full amount of the conversion in the Roth, chances are the conversion will work for you. In other words, if you are using the money inside the IRA to pay taxes on the Roth conversion, the sensibility of the Roth IRA is severely diminished. In most cases, the traditional IRA will be more sensible. Especially if you use the proper distribution strategies.

The following is a list of considerations that one should review prior to making a decision to convert to a Roth IRA.

- Will the result of the conversion push you into a higher tax bracket? If so, by how much?
- Will the conversion subject your current Social Security benefits to further or increased taxation?
- If you were taking itemized deductions on your tax return, how will the extra income affect your eligibility for you to continue with those itemized deductions?
- Are you expecting to be in a higher or lower tax bracket during retirement?
- What were your ultimate intentions for the account? How much income were you intending to withdraw from the account and when?
- Will your estate be subject to estate taxes?
- Do you have outside monetary sources to pay the income taxes as a result of the conversion?

The conversion to a Roth IRA will make sense for a great number of people and for others it will not. Whether or not the conversion will make sense for you will require a careful analysis of your own personal situation. Find a financial advisor who can do the calculations for you. To give you an idea as to whether or not the conversion makes sense for you, fill out the Roth IRA Conversion worksheet on pages 60 to 63.

What Is All the Hype About?

Here is the gist of why so many individuals are considering the conversion of their traditional IRAs to the Roth. Once the conversion is made, the account will continue to grow tax-deferred, but can be accessed *tax-free*. Further, one of the major advantages to the Roth is that if you are not in need of the extra income that the Roth could provide, you can simply allow the account to continue to grow; there are no forced distributions or required minimum distributions with the Roth IRA. There will be no income taxes if there are funds that are withdrawn upon the death of an IRA account holder.

The ability to spread the income tax consequences over a four-year period will no longer be available after 1998. This means that after December 31, 1998 an IRA that is converted to a Roth will be subject to 100-percent taxation on the conversion, due and payable during the tax year of the conversion. It is estimated that for tax years 1999 and beyond, the decision to convert to a Roth IRA will have limited merit.

Worksheet 3:
The Roth IRA Conversion

This worksheet assumes you are eligible for the Roth IRA conversion. See your financial advisor for more information or to verify the results.

Accumulation Period

1. Rate of return. What you expect to earn on your money, between 1 and 12 percent. _____

2. Years of accumulation. Between 5 (minimum for Roth IRA) and 30 years. _____

3. Accumulation period tax. Current federal tax rate. If you prefer to add your state income taxes in your assumption, use the following formula: [federal tax] = [(1.00 – federal tax rate) x (state tax)] = combined rate. _____

4. Accumulation period after-tax rate. Subtract tax rate (line 3) from 1.00 (1.00 – line 3). _____

5. Accumulation period after-tax rate of return. Multiply line 1 by line 4. _____

6. Rate of return during distribution. What you expect to earn, between 1 and 12 percent. _____

7. Years of distribution. Between 1 and 40 years (based on life expectancy). (See Appendix A.) _____

8. Distribution period tax rate.

9. Distribution after-tax rate. Subtract line 8 from 1.00 (1.00 – line 8). _____

10. Distribution period after-tax rate of return. Multiply line 6 by line 9 (line 6 x line 9). _____

Conversion Analysis

Step One: Calculate the Conversion Tax

11. Total value of existing IRAs. _____

12. Basis amount nondeductible contributions minus _____
any nontaxable withdrawals (IRS form 8606). If
none have been made, enter "0."

13. IRA value subject to conversion tax. Subtract _____
line 12 from line 11 (line 11 - line 12).

14. Conversion tax assessed. Multiply line 13 by _____
line 3 (line 13 x line 3).

Step Two: Calculate Account Balance at the End of Accumulation Period

15. Total value of existing IRAs (line 11). _____

16. Future value of IRAs at end of accumulation period. _____
Multiply line 15 by Divisor 1 result (see page 63).
This is the future value of your IRA.

17. Conversion tax assessed (line 14). _____

18. Future value of conversion "tax" rate of return at _____
the end of accumulation period. Multiply line 17
by Divisor 2 (see page 63)—(line 17 x Divisor 2).

Step Three: Calculate After-Tax Income from Each Option During Distribution

Nonconversion Scenario

19. Future value of IRAs at end of accumulation period. _____
Enter line 16

20. Annual pretax payment. Divide line 19 by _____
Divisor 3 (see page 63)

21. If line 12 has a greater value than 0, _____
enter it here; otherwise, enter "0."

22. Years of distribution (line 7). _____

23. Return of basis, divide line 21 by line 22. (This is _____
the approximate annual amount of each IRA
withdrawal considered a return.)

24. Annual IRA payment subject to tax.
    Subtract line 23 from line 20 _____

25. Distribution period after-tax rate (line 9). _____

26. Annual after-tax IRA payment.
    Multiply line 24 by line 25. _____

27. Return of Basis (line 23). _____

28. Annual after-tax income from IRAs. Add lines 26 and 27. _____

29. Years of distribution (line 7). _____

30. Total distribution period after-taxes. Multiply _____
    line 28 by line 9. Calculate the taxable amount that
    could be provided if you did not convert to the Roth IRA.
    Instead, you invested the value of the conversion tax in
    a taxable account.

31. Future value of conversion "tax savings" (line 18). _____

32. Enter Divisor 4 result (see page 63). _____

33. Annual after-tax payment of conversion "tax savings." _____
    Divide line 31 by line 32.

34. Years of distribution (line 7). _____

35. Total distribution period after-tax income from _____
    conversion "tax savings." Multiply line 33 by line 34. _____
    (This is the income provided during retirement.)

36. Total distribution period after-tax income. _____
    Add line 30 and line 35.

Conversion Scenario

37. Roth IRA Final Accumulation Value (line 16). _____

38. Enter Divisor 3 (see page 63). _____

39. Annual after-tax payment from Roth IRA. _____
    Multiply line 39 by line 40.

40. Years of distribution (line 7). _____

41. Total distribution period after-tax income. _____
    Multiply line 39 by line 40.

42. Compare lines 36 and 41; enter whichever is the _____
    greater amount. (This is the option, nonconversion or
    conversion, providing you with the most after-tax income.)

Divisor 1

Use Table 1 (on pages 64 and 65) to find the years of accumulation you assumed on line 2. Then find the assumed rate of return during accumulation from line 1. The corresponding number provides you with Divisor 1.

Enter Divisor 1: _____

Divisor 2

Use Table 1 (on pages 64 and 65) to find the years of accumulation you assumed on line 2. Then find the assumed accumulation period from line 5. The corresponding number provides you with Divisor 2.

Enter Divisor 2: _____

Divisor 3

Use Table 2 (on pages 66 and 67) to find the years of distribution you assumed on line 7. Then find the rate assumed rate of return during accumulation from line 6. The corresponding number provides you with Divisor 3.

Enter Divisor 3: _____

Divisor 4

Use Table 2 (on pages 66 and 67) to find the years of distribution you assumed on line 7. Then find the assumed distribution period after-tax rate of return from line 10. The corresponding number provides you with Divisor 4.

Enter Divisor 4: _____

Table 1:
Calculating Divisors 1 and 2 Interest Rate

# of Years	1.0%	2.0%	3.0%	4.0%	5.0%	6.0%	7.0%	8.0%	9.0%	10.0%	11.0%	12.0%
1	1.01	1.02	1.03	1.04	1.05	1.06	1.07	1.08	1.08	1.10	1.11	1.12
2	1.02	1.04	1.06	1.08	1.10	1.12	1.14	1.17	1.19	1.21	1.23	1.25
3	1.03	1.06	1.09	1.12	1.16	1.19	1.23	1.26	1.30	1.33	1.37	1.40
4	1.04	1.08	1.13	1.17	1.22	1.26	1.31	1.36	1.47	1.46	1.52	1.57
5	1.05	1.10	1.16	1.22	1.28	1.34	1.40	1.47	1.54	1.61	1.69	1.76
6	1.06	1.13	1.19	1.27	1.34	1.42	1.50	1.59	1.68	1.77	1.87	1.97
7	1.07	1.15	1.23	1.32	1.41	1.50	1.61	1.71	1.83	1.95	2.08	2.21
8	1.08	1.17	1.27	1.37	1.48	1.59	1.72	1.85	1.99	2.14	2.30	2.48
9	1.09	1.20	1.30	1.42	1.55	1.69	1.84	2.00	2.17	2.36	2.56	2.77
10	1.10	1.22	1.34	1.48	1.63	1.79	1.97	2.16	2.37	2.59	2.84	3.11
11	1.11	1.24	1.38	1.54	1.71	1.90	2.10	2.33	2.56	2.85	3.15	3.48
12	1.12	1.27	1.43	1.60	1.80	2.01	2.25	2.52	2.81	3.14	3.50	3.90
13	1.13	1.29	1.47	1.67	1.89	2.13	2.41	2.72	3.07	3.45	3.88	4.36
14	1.14	1.32	1.51	1.73	1.98	2.60	2.58	2.94	3.34	3.80	4.31	4.89
15	1.15	1.35	1.56	1.80	2.08	2.40	2.76	3.17	3.64	4.18	4.78	5.47
16	1.16	1.37	1.60	1.87	2.18	2.54	2.95	3.43	3.97	4.59	5.31	6.13
17	1.17	1.40	1.65	1.95	2.29	2.69	3.16	3.70	4.33	5.05	5.90	6.87
18	1.18	1.43	1.70	2.03	2.41	2.85	3.38	4.00	4.72	5.56	6.54	7.69
19	1.20	1.46	1.75	2.11	2.53	3.03	3.62	4.32	5.14	6.12	7.26	8.61
20	1.21	1.49	1.81	2.19	2.65	3.21	3.87	4.66	5.60	6.73	8.06	9.65

Table 1 continued

# of Years	1.0%	2.0%	3.0%	4.0%	5.0%	6.0%	7.0%	8.0%	9.0%	10.0%	11.0%	12.0%
21	1.23	1.52	1.86	2.28	2.79	3.40	4.14	5.03	6.11	7.40	8.95	10.80
22	1.24	1.55	1.92	2.37	2.93	3.60	4.43	5.44	6.66	8.14	9.93	12.10
23	1.26	1.56	1.97	2.46	3.07	3.62	4.74	5.67	7.26	8.95	11.03	13.55
24	1.27	1.61	2.03	2.56	3.23	4.05	5.07	6.34	7.91	9.85	12.24	15.18
25	1.28	1.64	2.09	2.67	3.39	4.29	5.43	6.85	8.62	10.83	13.59	17.00
26	1.30	1.67	2.16	2.77	3.56	4.55	5.81	7.40	9.40	11.92	15.08	19.04
27	1.31	1.71	2.22	2.88	3.73	4.62	6.21	7.99	10.25	13.11	16.74	21.32
28	1.32	1.74	2.29	3.00	3.92	5.11	6.65	8.63	11.17	14.42	18.58	23.88
29	1.33	1.78	2.36	3.12	4.12	5.42	7.11	9.32	12.17	15.86	20.62	26.75
30	1.35	1.81	2.43	3.24	4.32	5.74	7.61	10.08	13.27	17.45	22.89	29.96
35	1.42	2.00	2.81	3.95	5.52	7.69	10.68	14.79	20.41	28.10	38.57	52.80
40	1.49	2.21	3.26	4.80	7.04	1.29	14.97	21.72	31.41	45.26	65.00	93.05

Table 2:
Calculating Divisors 3 and 4 Interest Rate

# of years	1.0%	2.0%	3.0%	4.0%	5.0%	6.0%	7.0%	8.0%	9.0%	10.0%	11.0%	12.0%
1	1.00	1.00	1.00	1.00	1.03	1.00	1.03	1.00	1.00	1.00	1.00	1.00
2	1.99	1.98	1.97	1.96	1.95	1.94	1.93	1.93	1.92	1.91	1.90	1.89
3	2.97	2.94	2.91	2.89	2.86	2.83	2.81	2.78	2.76	2.74	2.71	2.69
4	3.94	3.88	3.83	3.78	3.72	3.67	3.62	3.58	3.53	3.49	3.44	3.40
5	4.90	4.81	4.72	4.63	4.55	4.47	4.39	4.31	4.24	4.17	4.10	4.04
6	5.85	5.71	5.58	5.45	5.33	5.21	5.10	4.99	4.89	4.79	4.70	4.60
7	6.80	6.60	6.42	6.24	6.08	5.92	5.77	5.62	5.49	5.36	5.23	5.11
8	7.73	7.47	7.23	7.00	6.79	6.58	6.39	6.21	6.03	5.87	5.71	5.56
9	8.66	8.33	8.02	7.73	7.46	7.21	6.97	6.75	6.53	6.33	6.15	5.97
10	9.57	9.16	8.79	8.44	8.11	7.80	7.52	7.25	7.00	6.76	6.54	6.33
11	10.47	9.98	9.53	9.11	8.72	8.36	8.02	7.71	7.42	7.14	6.89	6.65
12	11.37	10.79	10.25	9.76	9.31	8.89	8.50	8.14	7.81	7.50	7.21	6.94
13	12.26	11.58	10.95	10.39	9.86	9.38	8.94	8.54	8.16	7.81	7.49	7.19
14	13.13	12.35	11.63	10.99	10.39	9.85	9.36	8.9	8.49	8.10	7.75	7.42
15	14.00	13.11	12.30	11.56	10.90	10.29	9.75	9.24	8.79	8.37	7.98	7.63
16	14.87	13.85	12.94	12.12	11.38	10.71	10.11	9.56	9.06	8.61	8.19	7.81
17	15.72	14.58	13.56	12.65	11.84	11.11	10.45	9.85	9.31	8.82	8.38	7.97
18	16.58	15.29	14.17	13.17	12.27	11.48	10.76	10.12	9.54	9.02	8.55	8.12
19	17.40	15.99	14.75	13.66	12.69	11.83	11.06	10.37	9.76	9.20	8.70	8.25
20	18.23	16.68	15.32	14.13	13.09	12.16	11.34	10.6	9.95	9.35	8.84	8.37

Table 2 continued

# of years	1.0%	2.0%	3.0%	4.0%	5.0%	6.0%	7.0%	8.0%	9.0%	10.0%	11.0%	12.0%
21	19.05	17.35	15.88	14.59	13.46	12.47	11.59	10.82	10.13	9.51	8.96	8.47
22	19.86	18.01	16.42	15.03	13.82	12.76	11.84	11.02	10.29	9.65	9.08	8.56
23	20.66	18.66	16.94	15.45	14.16	13.04	12.06	11.2	10.44	9.77	9.18	8.64
24	21.46	19.29	17.44	15.86	14.49	13.30	12.27	11.37	10.58	9.88	9.27	8.72
25	22.24	19.91	17.94	16.25	14.80	13.55	12.47	11.53	10.71	9.98	9.35	8.78
26	23.02	20.52	18.41	16.62	15.09	13.78	12.65	11.67	10.82	10.08	9.42	8.84
27	23.80	21.12	18.88	16.98	15.38	14.00	12.83	11.81	10.93	10.16	9.49	8.90
28	24.56	21.71	19.33	17.33	15.64	14.21	12.89	11.94	11.03	10.24	9.55	8.94
29	25.32	22.28	19.76	17.66	15.90	14.41	13.14	12.05	11.12	10.31	9.60	8.98
30	26.07	22.84	20.19	17.98	16.14	14.59	13.28	12.16	11.20	10.37	9.65	9.02
35	29.70	25.50	22.13	19.41	17.19	15.37	13.85	12.59	11.52	10.61	9.83	9.16
40	33.16	27.90	23.812	18.02	15.95	14.26	12.88	11.73	10.76	9.94	9.23	

Chapter 7

Wake Up and Stop Paying All Those Taxes

Wake up is right. You are paying too much in taxes. I'll bet you did a good job preparing your tax returns; I'll bet you made the April 15th deadline. But what did you do to save on taxes?

A good tax preparer tells you how to prepare your return and a good tax plan should start now. Chances are there are numerous simple techniques to help you save on taxes. It amazes me how diligent people are at cutting coupons, waiting for sales, and negotiating good prices. Yet when it comes to taxes, they pay them without even blinking. Instead of spending the time and money to *really* save, people find someone to "prepare" their taxes inexpensively. Cutting coupons may save you a few hundred dollars per year, but cutting down your taxes could save you thousands.

As a mature American, you pay a high percentage of taxes compared to other segments of the population. Technically, the income is supposed to be lower than when you were working. But if you total your Social Security income, retirement income, and dividends, it adds up. If you are actively investing, that may further increase your taxes. Also, the deductions of the average retiree are usually few and far between. In most cases you cannot itemize your deductions, nor deduct dependents, and you have no business write-offs. Thus, your tax bracket often turns out to be higher than you expected.

When you retire, it is essential that you include potential taxes in your financial plan. The truth is that taxes, over time, are on an upward trend. Seniors have few means by which to shelter their estates from taxes, and sometimes end up in a higher tax bracket than when they were working. In addition to income taxes, you could be subject to capital gains taxes on the sale of an investment, property taxes, gift taxes, and even estate taxes or death taxes after you pass away.

All in all, mature Americans must find every legal means to reduce their tax burdens. The less you pay in taxes, the higher your true return on investments and the more conservative your portfolio can be.

Changes Under the Taxpayer Relief Act of 1997

Our government calls it the "tax simplification act." With documents weighing more than 27 pounds, with hundreds of changes, please tell me what is simple about it. Although hundreds of changes were made under the Taxpayer Relief Act, the ones we will focus on include Roth IRAs, education IRAs, gifts, capital gains taxes, and estate taxes. See Figure 9 on page 70 for an overview of these changes.

Education IRAs

An individual is allowed to create an education IRA with the purpose of paying for qualified higher education expenses.

A taxpayer is allowed to contribute $500 per person to as many persons as he or she desire. The contributions are nondeductible. However, if the beneficiary uses the proceeds for qualified higher education, the entire amount of the then accumulated IRA is withdrawn tax-free.

Exceptions do apply. If a couple's adjusted gross income (AGI) is more than $160,000, the amount of distribution may not exceed qualified higher education expenses, and the proceeds must be distributed by the time a beneficiary reaches 30 years of age.

Roth IRAs

As part of the Tax Reform Act of 1997, Senator Bill Roth created—and Congress approved—the Roth IRA. Although the Tax Reform Act was approved in 1997, the Roth IRA becomes effective for contributions made in 1998.

You can contribute as much as $2,000 to a Roth IRA (and another $2,000 for a spouse). Unlike a traditional IRA, you would not receive a tax deduction for the contribution. As a result, you will not lower your tax bill for the contribution. However, all of the money inside the Roth IRA will grow tax-free. You can buy and sell stocks, bonds, mutual funds, CDs, and myriad other investment vehicles and the earnings and growth will not be taxed. This is similar to a traditional IRA. The real benefit comes upon withdrawal of money from the IRA. When you withdraw money from the Roth IRA, the contributions are not taxed as income, capital gains, or any other tax the government can think of. The withdrawals in this case are truly tax-free. This is a major advantage over a traditional IRA, which taxes distributions as income upon withdrawal.

Figure 9:
Overview of Individual Tax Changes

Provision	1998 Phase-Out Range for Single Filers	1998 Phase-Out Range for Joint Filers	Ranges Indexed for Inflation
New Laws			
Child Tax Credit (for qualifying 2 children)	$75,000-$95,000	$110,000-$130,000	No
Educational IRA	$95,000-$110,000	$150,000-$160,000	No
Roth IRA	$95,000-$110,000	$150,000-$160,000	No
Traditional IRA	$30,000-$40,000	$50,000-$60,000	(See IRA description)
Hope Education Credit	$40,000-$50000	$80,000-$100,000	Yes, beginning in 2002
Lifetime Learning Credit	$40,000-$50,000	$80,000-$100,000	Yes, beginning in 2002
Student Loan Interest Deduction	$40,000-$55,000	$60,000-$75,000	Yes, beginning in 2003
Capital Gains Rates	No limits	No limits	N/A
Former Laws			
Personal Exemption	$121,200-$243,700	$181,800-$304,300	Yes
Itemized Deductions	$121,200	$121,200	Yes

Gifting Strategy

Most of us are familiar with how much we are allowed to gift every year before it triggers a gift tax or cuts into a unified exemption. The number is $10,000 per year per person, $20,000 per married couple. You can make as many gifts as you want to whomever you want as long as the gifts are *bona fide*.

After 1998 the $10,000 annual gift exclusion will be indexed annually for inflation. Based on the current trend, the first increase would occur either in 2001 or 2002 from $10,000 to $11,000. It's always rounded to the nearest $1,000.

Reduction and Repeal of Capital Gains Taxes

You would think that our government could just reduce the capital gains tax rate to one flat number, make it easy and be done with it. No way! There are now several capital gains rates, and a number of ways in which they apply. Use Figure 10 for help.

Figure 10:
New Capital Gains Tax Rates

Holding Period; Marginal Tax Rate; Sale Date	10%	15%	20%	28%	Ordinary Income Rates
< 12 months					X
>12 months; 15% tax bracket; sold before May 7, 1997		X			
>12 months; (and up) tax bracket sold before May 7, 1997				X	
>12 months; 15% tax bracket; sold May 7 to July 28, 1997	X				
>12 months; 28% (and up) tax bracket; sold May 7- July 28, 1997			X		
12 – 18 months; 15% tax bracket; sold after July 28, 1997		X			
12 – 18 months; 28% (and up) tax bracket; sold after July 28, 1997				X	
>18 months; 15% tax bracket; sold after July 28, 1997	X				
>18 months; 28% (and up) tax bracket; sold after July 28, 1997	X				

Capital Gains and the Sale of a Personal Residence

Qualifying homeowners will enjoy a $250,000 capital gain tax exclusion from the sale of a personal residence. A taxpayer can claim the exclusion once every two years. To qualify, a person must have owned the residence and occupied it as a principal residence for at least two of the five years before the sale or exchange.

Tax Avoidance Techniques

While tax evasion is unethical and illegal, tax avoidance is desirable. The following are some useful vehicles for reducing your tax burden.

Tax-Free Bonds

You can purchase tax-free municipal bonds as individual bonds or through a mutual fund. The income from municipal bonds issued in the state you live is completely exempt from all federal and state taxes.

Although these might be tax-free investments, you must figure out if they will pay you more money than a taxable investment (after taxes). If I were to ask you which is better, a tax-free bond paying 5 percent or a taxable bond paying 7 percent (assuming both bonds are AAA-rated and insured), what would your response be? Here's how you can figure it out.

1. Determine your federal and state tax bracket. For this exercise, let's assume it is 31 percent.

2. Subtract your tax bracket from 100 (100 − 31 = 69).

3. Divide the tax-free return by 69 (5 divided by 69 = .07246, or 7.2 percent).

With a taxable equivalent yield greater than 7.2 percent, it becomes clear that 5 percent tax-free is better than 7 percent taxable (provided our assumption of a 31 percent tax bracket is correct). In this case, it would take a taxable equivalent yield of 7.2 percent to beat a tax-free yield of 5 percent.

Let's assume that all you know is the taxable return (in this case 7 percent) and you want to determine the tax-free equivalent yield. Multiply your tax bracket reciprocal (assume it is 31 percent) by the taxable return (69 x .07 = 4.8 percent) to get the tax-free equivalent yield of 4.8 percent. This means that any tax-free yield greater than 4.8 percent is superior to a 7-percent taxable rate of return.

When analyzing tax-free bonds, be sure to take their quality into account; some are better than others. Also, be sure you know whether the bond is tax free for both state and federal purposes. Not being free of state tax means that the bond was probably issued in another state. Nothing is wrong with this, as long as the yield is higher than the double tax-free one, or the one that is fully taxable.

Problems with Tax-Free Bonds

While tax-free bonds can be the better choice at times, you must be aware of the following issues.

1. They are more difficult to analyze, because they are not all AAA-rated and insured.

2. Although the interest is tax-free, the income is still calculated in your gross income to determine whether your Social Security benefits will be taxed. Many people don't realize that this tax-free income affects the taxability of Social Security. In addition, you might be subject to the *alternative minimum tax* if your total income is grossly different from your taxable income. So if you have been creative and learned to reduce your taxable income to a level that is too low (for the IRS), this tax will apply.

3. In many cases, tax-free bonds are long-term in nature and must be held until maturity to get the principal back in periods of rising interest, because the principal value of a bond drops in an environment of rising interest rates.

Series EE and Series HH Bonds

Series EE and HH bond issues are direct obligations of the government and are free from all state tax—which makes them a more attractive investment for seniors living in states with high income taxes. For further discussion of zero-coupon bonds, see Chapter 15.

Many people have been accumulating and investing in Series EE bonds. There are two main benefits of EE bonds: They are issued at a discount, and they mature to their face value.

You may defer all the tax until you cash in the bond. The problem is that when you cash the bond, you have to pay tax on the gain all the way back to your original purchase price. Obviously this can cause you a tax problem. The only way to avoid this situation is by converting the bonds into Series HH bonds. In this instance, you have to pay taxes every year on the interest, but the interest paid is usually substantially lower.

Offset Capital Gains with Capital Losses

If you decide not to sell a stock or security because you have a taxable gain, find an investment in your portfolio on which you are willing to take a loss to offset that gain. I don't generally recommend selling the investment just because it is down. However, if you think the investment is down and is going to stay down for a long period of time, consider selling the investment for a taxable loss in order to offset capital gains from other stock. In addition, according to the 1986 Tax Reform Act you are allowed up to $3,000 per year in losses to be used to offset gains from any source of income.

Another excellent tax-reduction technique is to take year-end losses. You can sell a stock at the end of the year for a loss and buy it back 31 days later. However, be fairly sure that the price of that investment will be the same 31 days later, or you might end up missing out on the appreciation of an investment simply to avoid the taxes. And remember, if you buy a stock back within 30 days, you will be in violation of the *Wash Sale* rule and you will not be able to deduct your loss.

A similar technique is called *tax swapping*. If you own a stock that is down, and you see another stock you think would do better than the stock you currently own, you may consider a swap. You would sell the stock (and incur a capital loss), then purchase the new stock.

The benefit could allow you to upgrade your portfolio and generate tax losses at the same time. The capital losses generated from a swap would directly offset realized capital gains, which would have been taxed at the same rate as your tax bracket. In addition, you are allowed to take $3,000 of the losses and offset against any income.

Matching Passive Income to Passive Losses

Passive activity is defined as any activity that involves the conduct of any trade or business in which the taxpayer does not materially participate. It is usually referred to in regards to rental activity of either real or tangible personal property. It also could include equipment leasing and oil and gas interests, depending on how you own the asset.

If you have passive income investments, find an investment that generates a passive loss to offset the passive income. Passive income can only be offset by passive losses and vice versa. A typical investment that might generate, or "throw off," passive income (or losses) could include limited partnerships or perhaps rental real estate. For example, if you have rental real estate that generates passive income, find a type of investment that, although it might be appreciating and doing well, throws off passive losses. The result would be that income from the real estate is tax-free, to the extent of your passive income losses. You will also be able to use passive losses from another viable investment that could have gone wasted. Many tax credit programs in senior housing and low-income housing generate passive losses in addition to the credit.

Using Principal for Income

Frequently, you will hear someone say, "Never use your principal—only use income from investments." My question is, "Why not?"

If you simply take income from all your investments, you are probably not allowing yourself to make more money by dollar-cost averaging. You will be receiving many checks, some not very large, and you are paying taxes on all your dividends (unless they are from tax-free bonds).

Answer this: If you had $100,000 separated into three separate accounts, each paying 8 percent ($8,000 per year), would you simply take the income from all three accounts, or would you take the income and principal from two accounts (to equal $8,000), and allow one to compound? Consider the following scenarios.

Scenario #1

You have three accounts, each yielding about 8 percent, giving you $8,000 per year in taxable income. In five years you will still have the $100,000 principal, because you never touched it and you paid the full tax on your income. This is what most people do when in need of income—take the income from all investments. Although this scenario sounds logical, there are inherent flaws.

Scenario #2

Again, you have three accounts of $33,330 each paying 8 percent. To maintain the 8 percent per year from only two of the accounts, you take the income from the two accounts, equaling $5,330. In addition you withdraw $2,670 worth of principal every year to give you the total of $8,000. Your two accounts will be worth $53,310 in five years. Now the third account has been dollar-cost averaging every month, earning an average of 8 percent per year over the last five years. The account started with $33,300 and is now worth $50,000 as a result of successful dollar-cost averaging, as well as allowing the account to compound without withdrawing proceeds. This process is most effective using an annuity, an IRA, or other tax-advantaged investment, allowing you to avoid taxation on the compounded funds.

Now your account total is worth more than $103,000 (more than you had to start), and you paid significantly less in taxes, because you withdrew only $5,330 per year worth of income. The money you withdrew from your principal is not taxed again; only the income is taxed. I see the extra $3,000 as free income that you earned. You say you cannot afford growth? With the length of time we are living and at the high costs of living, can you afford to miss any growth?

Investing in Nonincome-Producing Investments

You are reminded throughout this book that you should not be investing until your plan is in place. One point I can't overemphasize is that, if you already have your income covered and you don't need additional income, minimize the amount you invest in income-producing assets. Income-producing vehicles include the following: CDs, income mutual funds, stocks, and stocks with dividends. All of these investments will issue you a 1099 tax statement each year showing the amount of taxable income. In fact, even if you have reinvested the income, you receive a 1099. If you have all the income you need, why not invest in vehicles that do not have income?

After you prepare your financial plan, you will know how much growth you need. Then, you can invest in stocks, mutual funds, or certain types of real estate that have no dividends, that are more oriented toward growth. These might be a wise diversification tool. Annuities defer all your income, so you can invest in guaranteed interest accounts, like CDs, but defer the income until you withdraw the funds. Similarly, if you like income-type mutual funds, invest inside the annuity to defer all the tax. That way, as long as you do not withdraw the gains built up in an annuity, you will not be taxed.

If your retirement check and Social Security benefits take care of all your living expenses and you still have extra funds, minimize any additional realized income. If you have IRAs or annuities, you could invest in all the dividend-paying, interest-bearing accounts you want and defer the tax. This would be the reverse of keeping the money liquid and receiving a 1099 tax statement every year. If you still have more money that you want to keep liquid, invest in mutual funds and stocks outside the annuity and in IRAs that do not pay dividends. I know this strategy sounds reversed, but think about it, you could constructively reduce your exposure to current taxable income without changing the amount of risk to which you are exposing your portfolio.

Tax Deferral

Tax deferral is one of the best ways to compound income and delay taxation. On any tax-deferred investments (for example, annuities and IRAs), the 1099 tax form shows no current income; hence, there is no tax to report. Social Security benefits are not affected, and reported income is thereby lowered. However, your money still continues to compound, yet at a faster rate than if taxes were taken out every year. If you invest in tax-free instruments, such as municipal bonds and bond funds, and are reinvesting the money, why not earn a higher interest rate? You can do this with a government bond fund in a tax-deferred vehicle like an annuity. You still have the advantage of investing in a conservative fund, only now you can defer all the tax. Remember that the interest from tax-free bonds and bond funds is still counted as gross income for Social Security tax purposes. If your income and age exceed the limits allowed by Social Security, you will owe taxes. In tax-deferred accounts, thousands of dollars could be appreciating for you. Until you actually withdraw the money, none of it is considered current income.

Figure 11:
Tax-Deferred Investing vs. Tax-Free Investing
(at an 8% interest rate)

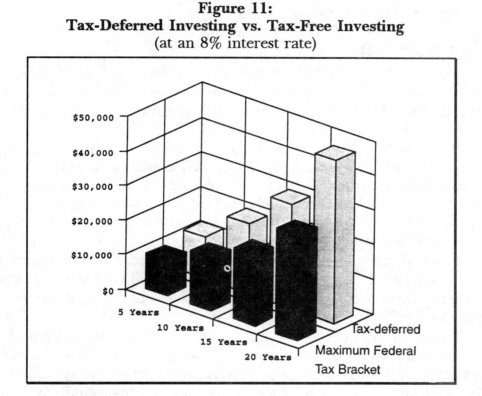

Even if you are reinvesting the money from a tax-free bond fund, you still receive a Tax Form 1099 and have to claim it as current income every year. Research this thoroughly and give serious consideration to the merits of investments such as tax-deferred annuities. A big disadvantage to annuities is the fact that the taxes will ultimately be paid when the money is withdrawn.

"Annuitize" an Annuity

If you have an annuity that is in the accumulation stage and you are ready to start taking income, but cannot bear the extra tax, consider *annuitizing the annuity*. The advantages include a higher income than that of similar investments, plus a steady income guaranteed for a set number of years with part of the income being tax-free. The biggest disadvantage would be loss of access to your principal. The principal is no longer yours; you relinquish all rights to it. If you opt for this strategy, make sure the company you choose is very conservative and enjoys the highest industry ratings. See Chapter 16 for more information about annuities.

Reducing Your Taxes

There are many techniques and strategies you can use to reduce your tax burden. Among them are the following.

Charitable Gifts

Any time you make a charitable gift (as defined by the IRS code), you are allowed to take a deduction (or credit) on your tax return. The amount you can deduct will vary, depending on the gift and type of charity. Be sure to document all gifts.

If you make gifts of personal property, such as furniture or clothing, you can deduct the fair market value of what is given to a charity. Ask the charity for a receipt showing the value of the donated items. If you cannot obtain a receipt, then keep an itemized list of the items you donated, the recipient's name and address, the date and place of the donation, and your estimated fair market value of each item.

If you are planning to gift property, it makes sense to give appreciated assets, such as stock or real estate, because you will not have to recognize the gain. However, the recipient will ultimately have to pay tax on the gain.

Those who need tax deductions and are charity-minded can consider a technique known as *deferred giving*. You can gift the "remainder interest" in your home or other asset to charity. This means the charity will inherit the home upon your death (as the owner, you have the right to live in the home until your death). The benefit is that you will get an immediate deduction on your taxes for a charitable gift. The deduction is figured using the IRS tables factoring in your income, size of the gift, and your life expectancy. (See Chapter 10 for more information on tax-reduction strategies.)

In addition to charitable gifting, many people donate time to charitable work. If you have expenses associated with this work and can prove that the services were provided to a qualified organization, you may be able to deduct certain expenses—including travel expenses. You may deduct either the actual out-of-pocket costs for gas and oil, or deduct the standard rate of 12 cents per mile. Tolls and parking may also be included.

To avoid paying capital gains tax, you can create *charitable trusts* or you can put a highly appreciated asset into an *irrevocable charitable trust*.

Once the asset is in the charitable trust, it may be sold and the entire proceeds of the sale can go into an investment to pay your income. You will receive a charitable deduction for the gift and will enjoy the income on the full proceeds, not just the proceeds less any capital gains tax that you would have otherwise paid. Plus, if structured correctly, you can show that part of the income is a return of principal and avoid paying taxes on the entire amount of income.

You can always gift property or investments to avoid paying a taxable gain (although your beneficiaries might have to pay), or you have the option of creating a life estate. (See Chapter 10 for more on this subject.)

Rental Income

If you have the tolerance, patience, and time, rental real estate can be a method of making money and reducing taxes. Just don't fool yourself into thinking that it is anything other than intensive, hands-on management. You will have to deal with vacancies, irresponsible tenants, repairs, maintenance, advertising, and inconvenience.

However, if you can purchase rental property and meet specific criteria, you can offset the rental losses against your ordinary income up to $25,000. Your income must be lower than a certain amount, you must not be in the business of rental real estate or property management, and usually you can offset losses from a rental to ordinary income only on the first rental. If you can show losses, fit the criteria, don't mind the work, and think the rental property will appreciate faster than your true losses, then consider it.

Start a Business

Nowhere is it written that once you retire you can't start a side business. Obviously, your intention will be to make a profit one day, but at the outset, the costs of starting the business may be high enough to itemize your income tax deductions. This opens the door for taking additional deductions you may now have but cannot use without itemizing.

For instance, suppose you have been a handyman for many years and have often helped friends and relatives for nominal charges. Now you decide to do this as a part-time business. You can itemize many deductions, such as part of your car payment, gasoline, an office in your home, tools, an accountant, an additional phone line, and supplies. Again, strict rules apply to taking any of these deductions, and you may be more likely to be audited. Work the numbers—if they work in your favor, try it out.

If you are self-employed and have any extra income that you don't need, you can start your own *Simplified Employee Pension (SEP)* and deduct money on your taxes that you put away in this retirement account.

Home Mortgage

People often say, "I can't wait until my mortgage is paid off." I ask, "Why?" Once again, my reasoning is not conventional. Many people find this to be extremely unorthodox, but in certain market cycles holding on to a mortgage could have merit. Let's analyze this situation.

Scenario

You obtain a 30-year, fixed-rate mortgage at 8 percent and you are confident (based on investments available, your risk posture, and portfolio track record) that your investments will earn 10 percent. If that is the case, why not borrow money at 8 percent (through a mortgage) and receive a deduction on all of the interest portion of the mortgage (which is the vast majority in the first several years), then reinvest the money at 10 percent? You can take the money you receive from the mortgage and place half into an account to pay the monthly payment, and put the other half in a mutual fund inside an annuity to grow tax-deferred. Work the numbers so that you have an account that pays the mortgage payment for you and utilizes a direct deposit system. Do not worry about using principal, because you are taking the second account and growing it. Now you are making money on borrowed money, and seeing a handsome deduction on your mortgage!

If, at a later date, you change your mind and don't want the mortgage, or if your investments aren't earning enough to justify the loan, pay it off. After all, it's not as though you don't have the funds—you just redirected them. Be careful about your choices of investments, because you cannot afford to lose this money.

Home equity loans also enjoy interest deductions. Use one if you need it. If you plan to buy a new car, use the equity line of credit to pay for the car. You will receive the interest deduction off your taxes, and a lower interest rate than you would have from a bank or dealership. However, if the interest rate on the equity line of credit is higher than what you make on your investments, consider paying for the car in cash.

Borrowing money is not so bad if you have enough money to pay off the loan and if you can make money on the borrowed money.

Reduce Your Property Taxes

So many of us pay our property taxes without a second thought. Fortunately, over the last several years real estate values have actually decreased. It is possible that you are paying taxes on what your home was appraised at before the value went down. Even if the value of your home did not decline, you may still be able to lower your property taxes. Here's how: Check to see that the dimensions of your land or improvements are documented correctly. The description may be wrong or the finished areas of your home may be listed incorrectly. Verify that all this information is in order. In most states you can go down to the county assessor's office, or the county recorder, and ask for a form requesting a reassessment of your property taxes. Even if it takes you half a day, think of the thousands of dollars you could save! The rules for property taxes vary depending on the state you live in.

Tax Credits

Despite popular opinion, viable tax credits do exist. Different sections of the tax code allow for different types of credits. If you meet the criteria and qualify, credits could exist in select areas such as: oil and gas investments, low-income housing, senior housing, and historic housing. A potential downside is that you, an individual, probably do not want to start a business in these areas to get the credit.

The most popular way to receive the credit is through some type of a limited partnership. Before any investing, especially in a limited partnership, do a lot of homework. Never invest in a limited partnership without reading the prospectus, knowing the fees (sometimes as high as 20 percent front-load), and studying in great detail the track record (usually somewhere in the back of the prospectus). See how many programs the sponsor has completed (actually returned money back to the investor) and what returns were received. How many actual credits did prior investors receive? Ask whether it is being bought for cash or through leverage. Only after you are satisfied with the answers to your questions should you consider investing in a tax credit program.

Here's how these tax credits work: The credit you receive will be deducted from the bottom line of what you would have owed as a tax liability. In other words, if you owe $5,000 in taxes, but received $2,000 in tax credits, you will owe only $3,000 in taxes.

Many people were soured on tax credits after the 1986 Tax Reform Act. Several partnerships were structured to take advantage of the tax credits being offered, without any consideration for the actual merits of a particular investment. Therefore, when Congress took away the tax credits, many of these programs went bankrupt. *Always invest in the economic benefits first. Look at the tax-credits as a bonus.* The credit being offered for low-income or senior housing shows that, even if a credit is discontinued, prior investors will be allowed to continue its use.

Maximize Your Medical Deductions

Medical expenses are deductible only to the extent they exceed 7.5 percent of your AGI. Many people think that they do not have enough in medical expenses to reach the 7.5-percent floor, and as a result don't bother to claim the deductions. Unfortunately, they are probably wasting valuable tax deductions. Many of the expenses that are deductible are things you probably would never even consider. The following is a partial list of interesting expenses that could be considered medical deductions:

♦ Acupuncture.

♦ Contact lens insurance.

♦ Dentures, hearing aides, and orthopedic shoes.

♦ Home improvements such as air conditioning, humidifiers, and heaters to benefit an ill person.

♦ Fluoridation device installed at home on a dentist's recommendation.

♦ Legal fees incurred for the commitment of a mentally ill spouse.

♦ Mattresses and boards to alleviate an arthritic condition.

♦ Special diets for medical reasons (only to the extent they exceed costs of a normal diet).

Many people do not even try to deduct medical expenses because they believe they do not have enough in expenses to equal more than the minimum. If you can plan ahead, try to "bunch" deductions. For example, if you have certain elective medical procedures that will be done, try to bunch all the procedures in the period of one year to increase medical costs. This might give you enough in medical expenses to be eligible for the deduction.

Sales Tax and State Income Tax

When mature Americans retire, one of the first questions they ask is, "Where should we retire or have our second home?"

Frequently overlooked are the state sales tax and income tax ratio of your potential new state of residence. If your estate is going to have a difficult time staying on top of taxes, you might want to seriously consider living in a state that has no sales tax or a very low sales and/or income tax. These taxes can be far more devastating than people realize. If you are paying an extra 7 percent per year in taxes in your current residential state, you might want to contemplate relocating for your retirement years.

For a more thorough discussion of retirement locations, try my book *50 Fabulous Places to Retire in America.*

Consider Filing Separate Returns

Many married Americans can actually save money by filing separate returns. Can it save you money? You won't know until you actually create two sets of tax returns, one for married filing jointly, one for married filing separately. A good example of when filing separate returns works well is if one spouse has most of the income and the other has a great deal of medical deductions.

Estate Tax

Arguably, the federal estate tax is one of the highest and most usurious tax rates. This tax ranges anywhere from 37 to 55 percent. In addition, if your state charges an estate tax as well, that will be added to your tax burden. The estate does not begin to be taxed until it reaches a value of between $625,000 and $1 million, depending on the year. For example, in 1998, an individual is allowed $625,000 in assets prior to paying a transfer or death tax.

Figure 12:
Federal Unified Credit Exemption

Year	Effective Exemption
1998	$625,000
1999	$650,000
2000	$675,000
2001	$675,000
2002	$700,000
2003	$700,000
2004	$850,000
2005	$950,000
2006 and thereafter	$1 million

In addition, if you give away large assets in your lifetime, this will count against your exclusion ($625,000 in 1998), thereby reducing the death benefit.

For example, assume that your estate is worth $900,000 in 1998, and that part of it is stock worth $200,000. Before your death, you gift the stock to your son. Usually, that $200,000 gift will be deducted from your one-time $625,000 exclusion, leaving you with a $425,000 exclusion upon your death. In this case, upon your death your estate is worth $700,000. You do not owe taxes on $425,000, but you will owe taxes on the remaining $275,000.

If your estate owes taxes, the IRS will demand payment within nine months or it will liquidate assets in order to pay the taxes. As you must know by now, the IRS is not gracious. If the estate consists mostly of real estate, the property may be liquidated at unfavorable economic times, resulting in distress or "fire sale" prices.

The IRS will value your estate after someone passes. One of the largest assets we as individuals have is our life insurance. Although life insurance may go to the beneficiary tax-free, the death benefit is still figured into your gross estate to determine the size of your estate for estate tax purposes. This means that if you have a $500,000 estate, but also have $200,000 in life insurance, when you die your estate will be valued at $700,000 and will have to pay the necessary estate taxes. Reducing estate taxes is of the utmost importance. The following is a summary of strategies.

Revocable Living Trust

If you are married, you and your spouse can create a revocable living trust with the A/B provisions (that is, successor/survivor or exemption trust). The objective is to separate the estate into two separate parts, giving each spouse his or her own exemption. In effect, in 1998 the estate would be protected up to $1.25 million before taxes would begin.

Gifting Funds

Many mature Americans gift $10,000 per person per year in order to lower their estates to below the current year's estate tax law. You are allowed to gift to as many people as you want $10,000 per year before paying estate taxes. However, gifts that pay for medical or educational expenses do *not* need to be reported. Of course, provisions apply, the main one being that the tuition must be paid directly to the educational facility. The recipient of the gift is not required to report it, but will have to report any income that is generated by the gift. Gifting can be an excellent method of reducing taxes, as long as you have time to plan and are absolutely sure you will never need the money once you have gifted it.

Other Tax Reduction Strategies

Irrevocable trusts, family partnerships, private annuities, and charitable trusts can be viable ways to lower the value of an estate and receive many benefits. However, when discussing these advanced planning techniques, or whenever you hear the word "irrevocable," you know there will be a serious price to pay for using this type of estate planning tool. Usually, the biggest price is the loss of control of your asset. Read Chapter 9 for more on this topic. And, of course, consult an investment professional prior to taking any action.

Irrevocable Insurance Trust

Basically, you can create a trust and have your beneficiary purchase life insurance through the trust. The advantage is that the proceeds from the insurance (otherwise known as a death benefit) will not be included in your estate, resulting in a tax-free gift to the beneficiary which he or she may use to pay the taxes you owe. If you simply buy life insurance, the death benefit will increase the size of your estate.

For instance, if your estate is worth $3 million and you have $1 million of life insurance, when you pass away, your estate is really worth $4 million. An estate that size falls in the 55-percent tax bracket. If this insurance was owned and paid for by a separate entity, your estate would not increase by the amount of the insurance. Although the insurance may be expensive, it very often makes sense to use that technique to avoid spending all your money on taxes. One good way to lower the insurance premium is to purchase what is often referred to as *second-to-die insurance*. In the case of a married couple, this insurance would not pay after the first death, but after the death of the second spouse, regardless of who dies first. This type of insurance is less expensive than regular insurance because the mortality tables of both husband and wife are combined, thus lowering the overall cost.

In addition, because many of these policies are placed into a trust, you cannot have access to any of the cash value built up from excess premiums. Consequently, it makes sense to buy a cheaper policy that does not increase in cash value and that has a lower premium cost.

Let's assume that you know your estate is going to owe $200,000 in estate taxes and you have exhausted all reasonable options. You can create an irrevocable insurance trust, purchasing insurance for $200,000. Let's assume it costs $4,000 per year over a 10-year period, totaling a $40,000 cash outlay. If you die after 10 years, your total cash outlay of $40,000 will result in your estate receiving $200,000. That compounds to almost a 17-percent return, not including the time value of money based on the fact you did not have to pay $40,000 all at once. In this example, you have been an excellent money manager—where else could you find a 17-percent tax-free return? (This is only an arbitrary example, and there is no way to calculate if these assumptions and rates apply to your situation. Rates vary, so seek out the appropriate counsel.)

IRS Services for Seniors

You will be glad to know that at least part of your tax dollars are going to a worthy cause. Seniors can get a special tax package, which includes the most popular tax forms used by seniors: The 1040A form, which has lines for IRA distributions, pensions, annuities, and Social Security benefits; Schedule 1, for reporting more than $400 in interest dividends; and Schedule 3, for computing the tax credit for the elderly and the disabled.

In addition, you can request a special IRS publication for mature Americans called "Tax Information for Older Americans, Form 554." This package offers many helpful hints for senior citizens and reviews recent changes in the tax laws, as well as sample tax forms printed in large type for easy reading.

Contacting the IRS

If you need tax questions answered, or you want to order tax forms or an IRS publication, you can reach the IRS at one of the following numbers.

Telephone tax assistance	(800) 829-1040
To order publications or forms	(800) 829-3676
Taped tax and refund information	(800) 829-4477
For the hearing impaired	(800) 829-4059

Part II

Estate Planning

Chapter 8

Using an Estate Plan for Wealth Transfer

One of the best ways to prepare for retirement is, obviously, to accumulate enough assets to live comfortably for the remainder of your life and to have enough money left over to leave to your beneficiaries. However, sometimes unfortunate circumstances might take away the assets you worked so hard to create. Probate costs and estate fees could take a tremendous toll on an estate. If your estate is structured incorrectly, or you use poor financial planning, your heirs can lose the assets you worked so hard to accumulate throughout your lifetime. Just look at all the costs and problems that are associated with death and a poor estate plan.

- The wrong people inherit your assets.
- Probate, death taxes, and estate settlement costs eat up the estate.
- Assets are not transferred properly; loss of control and delays ensue.

What to Accomplish with a Good Estate Plan

To ensure that your assets are transferred according to your wishes after your death and that probate costs do not devour your hard-earned savings, it is important to have a good estate plan. The following issues should be addressed in your plan.

♦ Make sure that in the event of an illness, someone such as a spouse, relative, or friend will have access to your funds to pay your bills and make medical decisions on your behalf. Many people suffer from serious illness before dying, yet most people hold their assets in ways that make the assets unavailable for their own health care or inaccessible to a loved one.

♦ While you are physically and mentally healthy, express your preference *in writing* regarding maintenance on life support systems implemented only for the purpose of prolonging your inevitable death.

♦ Make sure that in the event of your death your assets will pass to loved ones with the least amount of delay, outside intervention, and costs.

♦ Make sure your beneficiaries will pay as little as possible in taxes.

♦ These days many families are composed of multiple marriages and multiple sets of children and grandchildren. Be absolutely certain that assets will pass directly and unquestionably to your beneficiaries. Frequently, problems arise because of previous marriages.

♦ Make sure there will be no time delays.

♦ Make sure your assets are protected to include spending all your savings on nursing home care before Medicaid steps in with financial assistance.

The Probate Process

One key ingredient in any good estate plan is the reduction of the estate's exposure to *probate*. Probate is the legal method of transferring title of property from one person to another when the title holder is deceased, or survives an accident or illness that leaves him or her incompetent or disabled. Any individually titled property may qualify for probate, including stocks, CDs, savings accounts, real estate, automobiles, and personal property.

When an estate goes through the probate process, the court will make sure that all debts are paid and that the property is distributed according to the directions in your will. Probate does not happen automatically; usually, the executor of the will begins the process. Assets will be unavailable to beneficiaries until probate is satisfied and the judge frees the funds.

Although many probate avoidance techniques are used, most estates still end up going through probate if not on the death of the first spouse, then upon the death of the second spouse. State laws differ, so check with the probate division of your state's Bar Association, or research the probate code in a legal library.

Literally anyone can qualify for probate. You don't need to be rich or own other assets to be exposed to probate. Problems associated with probate include:

1. It is lengthy, averaging more than two years.
2. It is impersonal. Any stranger can learn your family affairs because courts are open to the public and anyone can listen to a probate hearing or obtain a transcript of the case.
3. It is very costly. The probate fees are set by statute and are nonnegotiable—often 6 to 8 percent of the gross value of your estate. In other words, if you have a $200,000 house with a $180,000 mortgage, the estate is computed on the $200,000 figure.
4. It is contestable, which means that anyone who disagrees with your will can contest it, so there is a very real possibility that your estate will not be disbursed exactly as you wished it to be.

Six Ways to Limit Probate

While there are situations in which probate is unavoidable, there are ways to limit the need for probate. The following are six techniques you can use to limit the need for probate in the settlement of your estate.

1. *Paid on Death (POD)* and *In Trust For* accounts. These accounts can be opened with cash and cash equivalents, such as in the case of a savings account at a bank. If you set up a POD you can designate a beneficiary to inherit that account. The benefit of this arrangement is that the asset will avoid probate. The downside is that you are limited because the beneficiary does not have access should you get sick, which could cause the account to become frozen. It limits the option on how the beneficiary receives the assets.

2. **Revocable living trusts are entities that do not die.** If a person dies, the trust lives on. A trust would stipulate what would happen to provisions in the trust and the assets in the trust in the event of the creator's (trustor) death.

3. **Joint Tenancy with Rights of Survivorship (JTWROS).** The vast majority of married couples (and even quite a few nonmarried couples) hold assets in this form. The main advantage is the avoidance of probate on the first spouse's passing. Unfortunately, JTWROS can be a probate *delay* strategy as opposed to an avoidance technique. It's true that after the first spouse's passing you will avoid probate. But when the second spouse dies a probate action will most likely be required. Further, JTWROS can pose significant tax issues and loss of control problems. For example, what happens if a prolonged or serious sickness results in one spouse's incapacitation? The other spouse cannot sell the investment, because joint tenant assets require both signatures. Just about the only way to get access without both signatures is to go to court and go through a similar process as you would for probate. In fact, the procedure is a living probate called *conservatorship*. A conservatorship action can be just as long and costly as going through probate, so this is not an ideal alternative.

4. **Designate a beneficiary for your car.** Some states allow you to name a beneficiary on an automobile. You would do this directly on the car registration form and you can name a new beneficiary by simply completing a new form. This form supersedes any designation in your will.

5. **Beneficiaries.** Life insurance policies, fixed and variable annuities, most pensions, annuities, and IRAs allow for beneficiary designations. In most cases where a beneficiary is designated, the asset will bypass probate and be inherited directly.

6. **Small estate procedures.** Sometimes your estate is virtually probate-free, except for one or two small items. It is relatively easy to have your executor use simplified estate probate procedures, which are quicker and cheaper than regular probate. The dollar limit for such procedures varies from state to state.

Using a Will Does Not Avoid Probate

The simplest definition of a *will* is that it is a letter directed to the judge of a probate court to oversee the disposition of your estate and carry out your wishes as you have outlined them. Because this matter is confusing and unpleasant, it often gets ignored. Further, many myths on the subject arise as people try to convince themselves that they will not have to go through probate.

Always remember, where there is a will there is probate. No matter how carefully a will is drafted, it will go through probate; however, as explained previously, you can limit your exposure by applying the six techniques mentioned.

Given probate costs and fees, time delays, emotional trauma, and the chance that your assets will not go to your children or designated beneficiaries, a will is usually not the best estate planning tool. However, if you don't mind the court's intervention and want a judge to oversee your affairs, a will might be the best alternative.

Another option is to not have a plan or a will. Similar to having a will, your estate will go through probate. The only difference is that the judge will have no idea how you wanted funds to be distributed and who you wanted to distribute them, so he or she will select an executor to distribute your estate according to the laws of intestate, whereby your assets will be distributed to your next of kin in accordance with the laws of your state. Obviously, having no plan results in your total loss of control and high fees and costs to your estate, so this option is not recommended.

Problems Associated with Joint Tenancy

Joint tenancy is the most common form of titling assets. It also might avoid or delay probate. However, due to all of the problems it can create, joint tenancy is often a poor way to title assets.

Joint Tenancy Could Create a Gift Tax Problem

If you gift an asset worth more than $10,000 to someone, this could be considered a taxable gift. Thus, adding someone on an account with you could be considered gifting. You may be able to avoid immediate tax by using your once-in-a-lifetime $625,000 (in 1998) exclusion, but this will reduce the amount that can be applied to your estate after your death. Giving a gift while you are living, instead of after you die, may result in much higher capital gains taxes, and you will lose your step-up in cost basis for tax purposes. Every person you put on title with you now has to approve anything you might do with the property.

Joint Tenancy Can Increase Your Capital Gains Tax

Another problem with owning investments as joint tenants deals with taxes and the cost basis of the asset (the original cost). The difference between the current market value and the cost basis is called the taxable gain. When a person dies, his or her assets will receive a step-up in tax basis (IRS Code 1014b). This means your cost basis will be increased and will incur less taxes. However, the amount of the step-up in basis for tax purposes depends upon how you hold title to the asset. Consider the following scenario.

Scenario

A married couple purchased a mutual fund for $50,000. The mutual fund is now worth $150,000. The husband dies. Half of the mutual fund will enjoy a step-up in basis to their fair market value of $75,000. Then the surviving spouse sells the mutual fund for $150,000. She has a $50,000 taxable gain, because her half of the mutual fund did not step-up in basis.

Now assume the mutual fund had been placed in a living trust. The whole enjoys a step-up in basis, resulting in no taxable gain when the survivor either sells the mutual fund for $150,000, or when the survivor dies and the mutual fund get sold.

You must research your state laws before executing this technique because different states have different criteria. However, my point is that you should research what is best for your situation. In most circumstances, holding property as joint tenants is very detrimental. A more sensible technique used to transfer assets to avoid probate is utilizing various types of trusts. See Figure 13 for to see how joint tenancy affects your step-up in basis.

Children as Joint Tenants: A Big No-No

Be very careful before adding children as joint tenants with you on your assets. Although you may be doing this with the best of intentions, the repercussions could be disastrous.

For example, should your child be sued or file for bankruptcy, you could lose your assets. If your child gets a divorce, his or her spouse may have a legal interest in your investment. Or, your child may think of you as incompetent and try to control your assets.

Figure 13:
Step-Up in Basis: Joint Tenancy vs. Living Trusts

Basis is the original cost of the investment involved. The difference between the current market value and the basis is a taxable gain. IRS code 1014(b) permits a step-up (increase) in basis when a person dies. How much the step-up is depends on how that person held title.

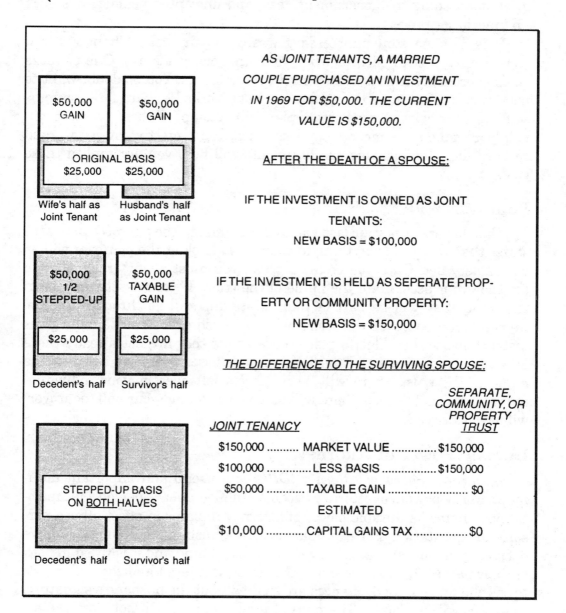

AS JOINT TENANTS, A MARRIED COUPLE PURCHASED AN INVESTMENT IN 1969 FOR $50,000. THE CURRENT VALUE IS $150,000.

AFTER THE DEATH OF A SPOUSE:

IF THE INVESTMENT IS OWNED AS JOINT TENANTS:
NEW BASIS = $100,000

IF THE INVESTMENT IS HELD AS SEPERATE PROPERTY OR COMMUNITY PROPERTY:
NEW BASIS = $150,000

THE DIFFERENCE TO THE SURVIVING SPOUSE:

JOINT TENANCY		SEPARATE, COMMUNITY, OR PROPERTY TRUST
$150,000	MARKET VALUE	$150,000
$100,000	LESS BASIS	$150,000
$50,000	TAXABLE GAIN	$0
	ESTIMATED	
$10,000	CAPITAL GAINS TAX	$0

(Diagram labels)

$50,000 GAIN $50,000 GAIN

ORIGINAL BASIS
$25,000 $25,000

Wife's half as Joint Tenant   Husband's half as Joint Tenant

$50,000 1/2 STEPPED-UP $50,000 TAXABLE GAIN

$25,000 $25,000

Decedent's half   Survivor's half

STEPPED-UP BASIS ON BOTH HALVES

Decedent's half   Survivor's half

6 Essential Documents

Go to a job interview unprepared, and you will probably not get the job. Buy a stock without doing research, chances are you will not be a successful investor over the long-term. Plan you tax saving strategies on April 10, and there is little doubt you will be paying extra taxes. Die without a plan, and your heirs will suffer more than just your loss, but the financial grief of watching the government, fees, and unwanted beneficiaries suck up their inheritance.

It is time to stop unnecessary waste. Having read Chapter 1 you should have a clear idea of what your financial goals are. One of those goals is probably to maintain control of your assets. You no doubt want to maximize and preserve the money you have worked so hard for—for yourself and your heirs. A good estate plan will accomplish these tasks. It will help you make more money, pay less taxes, and protect what you worked so hard for. The following six documents will help you accomplish these goals.

Pourover Will

This document is your last will and testament. The *pourover provision* states that you give everything to your trust. Look at the pourover will as your safety net. Once you create a trust, you must always remember to transfer your assets into the name of the trust. If your assets are not in the trust, they will be part of your estate and will go through probate. Remember, a pourover will won't help you avoid probate—it simply gives instructions to the judge to place those assets that are not already there into your trust. But if you have all of your assets properly titled in the name of the trust, there will be no assets left over in your individual name. If this is the case, there will be no probate and your will (pourover) will never be read.

Durable Power of Attorney

A *Durable Power of Attorney (DPA)* is a useful and important document. Many powers of attorney become nullified upon a person's incapacitation, whereas a durable power of attorney remains in effect after a person's incapacitation. For example, picture a husband and wife who have been married for 30 years. They own a mutual fund and it is titled in both of their names. If the husband becomes incapacitated and the wife needs to sell the mutual fund, chances are that without the husband's signature, the asset will be frozen. The mutual fund company will not close the account and send the wife money without both signatures. The same would happen with any other asset the wife tries to liquidate.

Assets are frozen far too often. If you were to end up in a situation where your assets were frozen, you would need to appear in a conservatorship court and ask the conservatorship judge for a court order appointing you conservator and allowing you the right to make financial transactions without your incapacitated spouse's signature.

A durable power of attorney is a useful and important document because it can give someone the right to make decisions on another's behalf. Unlike a regular power of attorney, which usually becomes null and void when the creator becomes incapacitated, a durable power of attorney remains in effect.

The durable power of attorney can be broad or specific. You can grant the person you choose to represent you (attorney-in-fact) control over a specific asset only or over all of your affairs.

A *DPA for property and financial issues* will allow the person you appoint as attorney-in-fact to carry on with important property and financial decisions such as buying and selling assets or paying creditors.

A *DPA for health purposes* will give power to the person you appoint to make medical decision on your behalf. This might include certain medical treatments or autopsy. You should appoint someone whom you know well and whom you feel will responsibly perform these tasks. If you do not appoint someone, you will be dependent on a state-appointed administrator.

Although a DPA is conceptually a great document, they often don't work well. Banks or brokerages, for example, would probably not want the liability of simply giving a person—even with power of attorney—access to another person's accounts without a court order. As a result, try while you are healthy and in control to ensure that these institutions will honor the wishes of your DPA.

To accomplish this, contact your bank manager, broker, mutual fund company, and any other institution where you hold assets. Show them your power of attorney and ask for a letter in writing that this will be accepted should you become incapacitated. You might need to sign one of their forms, or have the agent you appoint to act as your attorney-in-fact sign a form, but take care of it now to avoid problems later.

Living Will

A *living will* is a critical estate planning document for individuals who do not wish to be connected to life support systems in the event of a terminal illness or accident. The document certifies that, at the time of signing, you are competent and understand your decision.

Usually, a living will states that if two physicians certify that you are terminally ill and life support will only prolong an inevitable death within a short period of time, it should not be used. I would recommend having a professional create this document, having it witnessed, and then making copies to be kept by someone in your home, in your safe deposit box, and in your medical file.

Some living wills are incorporated into a durable power of attorney for health care. However, I recommend making these two separate documents; combining them often results in misinterpretation and confusion.

Anatomical Gift Declaration

Organ donations should be included in your gift declaration. Many people like to specify which, if any, organs or body parts they wish to donate. You can draft a form stating your anatomical gift or acquire a form from your hospital or Area for the Aging.

Document Locator

This often-neglected document organizes your estate and helps your beneficiaries account for all of your assets. It lists your assets, who holds title to them (the trust), where they are located, property deeds, the location of safe deposit box keys, passbook savings accounts, and insurance policies. You would be surprised how many millions of dollars are never claimed from banks and insurance companies every year because the heirs are not aware the assets exist.

Letter of Instruction

Letters of instruction are used to inform heirs, or trustees, what must be done immediately following an individual's death. In preparing a letter of instruction, list your key advisors and provide advice regarding your assets, including instructions for the sale of your home.

In addition to outlining general guidelines, the letter of instruction can list specific wishes and provisions, such as instructions for your funeral, including the color of the flowers, the use of personal effects, and any expressions you wish to convey.

Unlike a will and testament, a letter of instruction is not usually considered a legal document; however, it does carry moral persuasion and help executors settle disputes, especially over tangible property such as jewelry or paintings.

You should prepare a letter of instruction and review it periodically. Many times you can write this document in the privacy of your own home at little or no cost. As always, it is a good idea to have the document reviewed by legal counsel to ensure that it coordinates with your other legal documents. When preparing your letter of instruction, keep the following guidelines in mind.

♦ Tell the intended recipient where the original letter is, so after your passing he or she will know of its existence and where to find it.

♦ Send a copy to your attorney and have him or her check for conflicts between your will and the letter.

♦ Send another copy to your executor.

♦ Write the letter so that a third party can understand it.

♦ Be specific.

Reviewing and Changing Your Estate Plan

Your estate plan should be reviewed at least once a year, to make sure everything is as you wish it to be. You do not need to change your estate plan documents every time you buy or sell assets; most living trusts allocate assets using percentages, never stating specific assets. As long as you always remember to buy assets in the name of the trust, that is sufficient, though it is recommended that you track all your assets using a document locator.

Your estate plan should be changed if you have material changes, such as a change of beneficiary or change of trustee (for example, your children may be better able to handle financial responsibilities that you would not have entrusted to them at an earlier age), or if the laws and regulations that affect the estate plan change.

Chapter 9

Creating and Using Trusts

A popular option for wealth transfer is the creation of a trust. Trusts not only allow you to avoid probate, but can also reduce many other problems associated with transfers of assets. These are the two major types:

1. *Testamentary Trust*—becomes effective upon your death and is created as a result of a will. For example, if you create a will and, upon your death, you want your assets to be held in trust for an heir, that would constitute a testamentary trust.

2. *Living Trust*—becomes effective at the time it is created and finalized. Many times the trust will continue to last after your death. The living trust is an effective tool to use for estate planning purposes and has many advantages.

A living trust is a legal document that handles your estate in a manner that differs from a will. There is no probate if your assets are held in a living trust. Consequently, you will eliminate the court costs, time delays, and loss of privacy. Unlike wills, trusts are difficult to contest.

Think of a living trust as a private corporation. When you create a trust, you automatically become the *trustor* (creator). Usually, you nominate yourself as the trustee, or both you and your spouse as co-trustees, which is equivalent to being the president(s). You set forth any provisions you wish to implement, such as placing no restrictions on what you do with the assets during your lifetime. You also nominate the *successor trustee* whom you want to be president if you die or become incapacitated.

By means of this trust, you designate to the successor trustee exactly how you want the assets handled in the event of your death, whom you wish to receive the assets, when, and under what conditions. You can change direction as often as you wish with absolutely no problem. In fact, most of the changes are anticipated and you can make them yourself.

Advantages of a Living Trust

Although it is not a cure-all for estate planning problems, a living trust has many advantages.

Avoidance of Probate

Properly structured, the assets in a living trust will avoid probate. If you create a trust, you must place all the assets (that you don't want to go through probate) into the name of the trust, taking them out of an individual or joint tenancy title and transferring them into the name of the trust. By doing so, your trust technically owns everything and you (and your spouse) technically own nothing—so you will have no need for probate. The probate court becomes necessary when someone dies; when you set up a trust, nominate yourself trustee and subsequently die, the trust doesn't die, and you have already nominated a new successor trustee.

Control

Nowadays, especially with so many divorces, second marriages, step-children, and divorced children, any time an estate becomes public and goes to probate, the estate becomes vulnerable to argument and may be contested. Because a trust is a private document, it is much more difficult to contest; therefore your assets are more likely to go to the people you have chosen. In addition, you can manage your finances normally, opening or closing bank accounts, buying and selling real estate and stocks—whatever you want. As long as you place assets in the name of your trust, everything will be fine—you do not have to change the trust. I encourage you to keep a document locator to make it easy for your heirs to locate your assets.

Another advantage to a living trust is that you can be absolutely sure who is going to receive your inheritance. For example, if you willed money to your daughter, but she passed away, you might have chosen the inheritance to go to your grandchild. If your will goes through probate, a chance exists that your daughter's husband will manage the money for your grandchild. If you do not trust your son-in-law or do not want him to have this responsibility, your wishes would count for very little. If, however, you had a living trust, you would make provisions stating something to the effect that, in the event your daughter dies, you want the money to go to your grandchild at the age of 25. (Most wills designate age 18; with a trust you can extend the age.) Furthermore, you would want the successor trustee to manage the money, instead of your daughter's husband. This trustee would probably be another one of your children or a professional trust institution.

Certain Trusts Help Reduce Estate Taxes

As previously discussed, estate taxes could be the largest tax burden your family will ever face. The tax rate is between 37 and 55 percent. For example, if a person dies in 1998 with an estate worth $1 million, the transfer (death) tax could be more than $200,000. And the IRS demands this money within nine months after a person's death. Would your beneficiaries be able to write a check for that amount? In all likelihood, they would have to sell your property at "fire sale" prices to come up with the money to pay the taxes.

Figure 15:
Gift and Estate Taxes (Unified Transfer Tax)

Amount Subject to Tax		Tax on Amount in Column 1	Tax Rate on Excess over Amount in Column 1
Exceeding	**But not exceeding**		
$10,000	$20,000	$1,800	20%
$20,000	$40,000	$3,800	22%
$40,000	$60,000	$8,200	24%
$60,000	$80,000	$13,00	26%
$80,000	$100,000	$18,200	28%
$100,000	$150,000	$23,800	30%
$150,000	$250,000	$38,800	32%
$250,000	$500,000	$70,800	34%
$500,000	$750,000	$155,800	37%
$750,000	$1,000,000	$248,300	39%
$1,000,000	$1,250,000	$345,800	41%
$1,250,000	$1,500,000	$448,300	43%
$1,500,000	$2,000,000	$555,800	45%
$2,000,000	$2,500,000	$780,800	49%
$2,500,000	$3,000,000	$1,025,800	53%
$3,000,000	$10,000,000	$1,290,800	55%

(For capital gains taxation, see Figure 10 in Chapter 7.)

When creating a trust, you could arrange for an *A/B Provision*. Technically, you will be forming two trusts: *an exemption trust* and a *survivor trust*. Most couples use what is called a *marital deduction*. This means that when one spouse passes away, that spouse gifts all of his or her property to the surviving *spouse free of taxes*. Marital deduction is a nice benefit. However, you just wasted a $625,000 exemption (in 1998) that the deceased spouse was entitled to give. If both spouses fully use such an exemption, you can receive a total benefit equal to $1.25 million in 1998. Or, if you live until 2006, the personal exemption is $1 million per person, allowing a couple an estate worth $2 million. This is obtained by creating your living trust with a provision that automatically separates the trust upon the death of the first spouse, thus the A/B provision. Each trust will now be able to claim its own personal exemption.

Everyone is allowed a one-time exclusion of $625,000 (in 1998, growing every year until it reaches $1 million in 2006) on the estate before the estate taxes are levied. As long as your estate is worth less than $625,000, you don't have to pay estate taxes. If you are married, usually assets are commingled, which permits both of you only one gift of $625,000. However, by separating the two trusts, you will each receive a $625,000 exclusion, allowing the estate to be as large as $1.25 million before taxes are levied.

For couples who have children from previous marriages, creating an A/B trust can help solve other problems. Once the A/B trust is established, neither spouse can change the other's beneficiaries once that spouse has passed away. This means that if the surviving spouse has remarried, he or she can't change the deceased spouse's beneficiaries to include the new husband or wife, or to give the money to his or her children.

A Living Trust Prevents Conservatorship

As mentioned previously, joint tenancy can be a terrible way to hold title. One of the worst problems is that if one spouse becomes incapacitated, the other joint tenant will lose his or her ability to sell or refinance the property. The healthy spouse would have to go through conservatorship action, which is another court proceeding that is almost as long and costly as probate.

The living trust, properly implemented, has provisions stating that if one spouse gets sick, the other can make medical and financial decisions.

A Living Trust Is Completely Revocable

A revocable living trust can be established, changed, or canceled at any time, as long as both trustors (or creators) of the trust are living. In fact, if you do not need the trust or do not wish to retain it at any point, transfer assets back into your own name and then tear up the trust. If you want to make a change, all it takes is a simple amendment.

Who Needs a Living Trust?

The living trust part of an estate plan is no longer just for the wealthy. In many states, if you own a home and have assets worth more than $60,000, your estate will go through probate. If you prefer a private process, have loyal successor trustees, and want to avoid probate, you should learn more about trusts.

Use Percentages When Giving Away Assets

In disbursing the assets in a trust, you usually gift assets in percentages rather than dollar amounts, actual accounts, or pieces of real estate. With this method, if you sell an asset before your death, less confusion will arise after your death. If your trust states that you want your two children to split your estate 50/50, it will be much easier for all concerned.

Obligations of the Surviving Spouse

This subject should be seriously considered and extensively reviewed while both spouses are living and healthy. If you have a revocable living trust (with an A/B provision), the survivor will have the responsibility of becoming sole trustee, and thus the sole decision-maker.

After the first death, there will be a great deal of administrative work. The surviving spouse will have to keep accurate records about assets, cash flow, acquisitions, and sales. Assets may continually have to be appraised as well. Further, extra tax forms may be required for the trust and a final tax form must be completed for the deceased, and a tax return for the "B" trust will need to be completed every subsequent year.

When the first spouse dies, it is wise to appraise all assets and create two logs: one for the "A" trust and one for the "B" trust. Principal assets in each trust and income received from them should be listed along with all sales and purchases of assets.

Upon the first death in an A/B trust, assets will normally be split equally in terms of dollar amounts, up to $1 million (depending on the year of death) for the "B" trust. However, be sure to place the assets in the correct trusts. Some assets are better in the "A" trust rather than the "B" trust. For example, it may be better for your home to remain in the "A" trust because you might want to sell it at a later date. If you held a home in a "B" trust, which is different than individual ownership, you may have to pay capital gains taxes if the home is sold.

Usually, the services of an experienced estate planning accountant must be retained. Nevertheless, all of this work is often simpler than the probate process in many states. Make sure you understand in advance what will be expected of you as trustee, after the death of your spouse. One major negative aspect may be the strain it puts on your relationship with the beneficiaries. Unlike with the probate process, a trustee cannot blame his or her decisions on the judicial system. If you are concerned, you may choose to opt for an institutional trustee, such as a trust department at a bank.

Provisions to Include in Your Trust

The more you know about what should be included in your trust, the more you can be certain that your wishes will be carried out and that your assets will be distributed according to your wishes.

♦ Be sure to stipulate that children and grandchildren do not receive assets until a specific age—one that you feel is appropriate—for example, age 25. The stipulation might state: "Assets will be held in trust until my grandchild reaches the age of 25, with the exception of education, medical, and living expenses."

♦ Specifically name your beneficiaries. For example, don't give a gift to your daughter's family, but name your daughter explicitly. Also, encourage her to hold the assets as separate property once she receives them (in case of a divorce).

♦ Include provisions that make the beneficiaries of the first deceased irrevocable after his or her death. This will prevent a spouse from changing the beneficiaries to the new spouse.

♦ Specify whether, in the unfortunate case of your child's death, the beneficiary will be your grandchild or whether you prefer it to be another one of your children.

♦ Indicate specifically if you do *not want* someone to get something. This way, a judge will know that you *intended* to prevent someone from getting certain assets.

Questions to Ask When Establishing a Living Trust

It is very important to have all the facts and a clear understanding of how the trust will affect your estate before you enter into a trust agreement.

What Will It Cost?

When speaking to your financial advisor, ask what the total fee will be, including all the necessary documents, the funding of the trust, notarization, and quit-claiming the properties.

Will This Be an A/B Trust?

If the estate is growing and worth $625,000 or above (or you think it will be upon death), ask the attorney if this will be an A/B trust. Also, make sure you will have full and complete control over the assets while you (and your spouse) are living. After the first spouse's death, the other spouse will not be able to change that spouse's beneficiaries. This is partly what the A/B trust would accomplish. The other task it will accomplish is to protect up to $2 million (in 2006 or later) of your estate from estate taxes.

You should ask what will happen to the assets after both spouses die, and how they will be disbursed to the beneficiaries. Obviously, through a properly structured trust, the trustee would be in charge of that process.

What About Taxes?

After the Omnibus Reconciliation Act was amended in 1993, trusts were taxed differently. In fact, if the trust earns as little as $7,500 you will be taxed at the highest individual rate of 39.6 percent! This tax usually only applies to irrevocable trusts. However, when one spouse passes on, the trust usually becomes irrevocable. Make sure this higher tax is not paid. The best way to avoid this is to not keep any of the earnings in the trust; rather, assign it out—usually to the living spouse. But review your trust. Some trusts restrict how much income can come out of the "B" trust and this could get you in trouble. You could also put non-income-producing assets or tax-free investments in the "B" trust to help minimize this.

What Happens in Case of an Illness?

As you may know, most people have an illness before passing away. This is a hardship, especially for single individuals and widows or widowers. Should you have an illness, what will happen to your affairs if you cannot make decisions? Usually, the courts will decide who will make medical decisions and who can have access to your bank accounts. This is obviously not a position you want to be in. You should decide who can make medical decisions concerning you and who can have access to your finances. A properly structured trust will address these issues. Along with the trust, the durable power of attorney and living will accomplish these tasks.

Who Should My Trustee(s) Be?

Consider a provision in your trust that will name one of the beneficiaries as acting trustee after you and your spouse are no longer living. The trustee should be a person (or persons) in whom you have confidence and faith. Although the trustee is required to follow certain laws, codes, and ethics, trustees are not strictly governed. Therefore, choose a trustee who is honest, good with financial matters, and who will represent your wishes accurately.

If you feel that the beneficiaries are not competent to act as trustees, you can hire another relative or friend, or even an institutional or corporate trustee. There are companies that are in business to act as trustees. One possible solution is to have joint trustees, one being a beneficiary and the other an institutional trustee. If there have been previous marriages and children, possibly one child from each side of the family should be represented as a trustee. As you well know, money can turn friends into enemies, so try not to select more than two trustees.

If you feel that you have a child who is incompetent, give discretion to the trustee as to how that child must receive funds. You have the prerogative of giving your trustee either a great deal of control or very little control.

How Should I Designate My Beneficiaries?

Make sure that your gift is directed to a specific person—for instance, your son John, not John's family. That way it is not family property. Technically, an inheritance is to be kept as separate property by the recipient. If your beneficiary keeps the inheritance as separate property, should a divorce ensue, the funds will maintain their separateness.

How Is Property Transferred to a Trust?

Until the property is placed into the name of the trust, the trust is like a vase without water. You must change all of your assets into the name of the trust, so that each one of your statements, deeds, and bank accounts reads your name as trustee for your trust. You must make copies of your trust, send them to the various places where you hold assets, and make sure that each establishment transfers the name into your trust, exactly as it is shown.

Chapter 10

Advanced Asset Protection Techniques

You pay taxes all your life, then, when you die, if you were fortunate enough to have assets, your survivors could have to pay taxes on your estate. These taxes could be known either as a transfer tax, death tax, or estate tax. Uncle Sam will get you in death, too—unless you have a plan.

The good news is that with proper planning, documentation, and advice, you can minimize or even avoid these taxes. This chapter will provide you with an overview of a few important asset protection strategies.

Gifting Assets

If handled correctly, gifting can help you avoid capital gains, reduce values of an estate, get funds out of an estate for Medicaid purposes, assist with a grandchild's education, and much more. However, the repercussions can be severe if you are not careful.

Anyone, at any time, is allowed to give a yearly gift of up to $10,000 before a gift tax is imposed. If you have two children and want to give a maximum yearly gift, with a husband and wife, a total gift of $40,000 per year ($10,000 to each child per spouse) is permissible.

How do you decide which assets to gift? If you gift cash, then you do not pay taxes and the recipient of the gift does not pay a tax on the gift. Of course, if the recipient invests the money, he or she will pay a tax on any earnings. If you have an appreciated asset (stock or real estate), should you sell it and then give the gift? Think hard. If you sell it, you pay the capital gains tax. If you gift it, you avoid paying the tax; the recipient of the gift will have to pay the tax upon selling it.

Say you purchased stock for $5,000 and it is now worth $10,000. If you sell the stock, the capital gain will be paid by you. If you gift the stock worth $10,000, the capital gain is transferred to the recipient of the gift. The basis of the original purchase ($5,000) stays the same. However, if you die, the entire basis of the stock (your original $5,000) is stepped up in value to the fair market value upon your death. In this case, we are assuming the fair market value is $10,000, meaning the recipient of the gift would pay no capital gains tax if the stock was sold at $10,000!

When a person inherits property, the capital gains tax is treated differently. Upon a person's demise, the new tax base for the new owner will be whatever the fair market value of the property is. This effectively eliminates a capital gains tax on property that is inherited.

Advantages of Gifting Assets

Gifting after death, unlike simply willing an asset to a beneficiary, avoids paying a capital gain on an appreciated asset. Obviously the benefactor of the gift may eventually pay, but his or her tax rate could be different from yours.

If you gift assets 36 months prior to entering a nursing home, you might be eligible for Medicaid, provided you qualify in all other areas.

Estates worth more than $625,000 (in 1998) could owe high estate taxes. If you gift $10,000 per year per person (to as many recipients as you choose) to keep below the $625,000 limit (this will increase to $1 million by 2006), it may save enormous amounts of money in estate taxes once you pass away. Unless you state that you want to use the $625,000 exclusion (or part of it) on a particular gift while you are alive, it is reserved for use after your death. This allows you the $10,000 yearly gift per person without affecting the $625,000 exemption.

Disadvantages of Gifting Assets

The biggest disadvantage of gifting is the loss of the step-up in basis. If you gift assets while you are alive, someone may eventually have to pay the capital gains tax. If your assets are inherited, the step-up in basis will avoid the capital gains tax on most assets.

Another major problem with gifting assets is your loss of control. Many people put a son or a daughter on the title of their accounts as joint tenants. This is a form of gifting. But in doing this, you can lose control of your property, because you cannot sell or refinance without the signatures of all parties involved. This may be a well-intentioned option, but think of the implications. What happens if the person you put on your property title is sued, goes bankrupt, or gets a divorce? Any of these situations could result in the loss of your property.

Generation Skipping—A Terrific Gifting Strategy

One of the least understood and greatest estate planning tools is that of the generation skip. Look at the scenario as it might typically play out: You leave all of your assets to your children, your estate pays a transfer tax (death tax), your children then use the money (or what's left) to invest, gift to their children (your grandchildren), or for their education or anything else. Typically, the money will grow and then your children will die and leave the money to their children, at which time the estate will be reduced again as it will have to pay its own transfer or estate taxes.

A logical solution is to bypass one generation by giving part of the inheritance to the next generation. You will eliminate the potential double taxation. Further, if this is done through a trust, you could have your children manage it, stipulate when the grandchildren receive it, or a myriad of other possibilities.

The generation skip rules do have limitations. The total of the gifts cannot exceed $1 million. However, gifts made for medical or educational purposes where the gift is paid directly to the medical or educational facility directly are excluded from the $1-million gift. Thus, if you have grandchildren, a terrific gifting technique is the generation skipping rule, because gifts for health or educational purposes can be given to grandchildren, in unlimited amounts, free of gift taxes.

Use a Survivor/Bypass Trust (a.k.a. A/B Trust)

Consider carefully whether you truly need all the assets in your estate. Each asset will increase the value of your estate, and as you know, assets more than the $625,000 exclusion (in 1998) will be taxed as high as 55 percent. This means that if you are earning a 10-percent interest rate on your investments, you can count on giving 5 percent to Uncle Sam.

Consider the life insurance you have. What do you need it for? Most likely, if your and your spouse's estate exceeds $1.25 million (in 1998), after the first death the survivor will not need a large insurance proceed.

And the death benefit from a life insurance policy will increase the value of your estate. Whenever you calculate your estate's worth for estate tax purposes, remember to include the value of your life insurance. If you have old policies that you do not really need, cash them out and enjoy yourself—or take the cash value and buy long-term care insurance.

As mentioned earlier, if your estate is growing rapidly, start slowing down. Enjoy yourself and take more trips. I know plenty of people who have estates valued at more than $625,000 who continue to make high-risk investments, going for higher returns and increasing the value of the estate. Would you take that kind of risk for half the return? After a certain amount, the estate taxes will be more than 50 percent anyway. Why not take the low-risk 8 percent, rather than risking more for 16 percent and then having to give half to the government anyway. The other solution is to use the techniques and loopholes available to protect the assets and allow your estate to grow with minimal estate tax burden.

Irrevocable Trusts

As previously discussed, irrevocable trusts are a powerful estate planning tool. An irrevocable trust can be used to get assets out of the estate and thereby reduce its value, and can be created in such a way as to have the assets go to the heirs that you have selected. Many mature Americans create an irrevocable trust and place a sum of money in the trust. The trustee might purchase a government bond, then stipulate that all income is to be received by the creators of the trust. Upon death, the trust is instructed to give the money to whoever has been previously named.

The advantage to this is that it reduces the size of the estate by the value of the gift and that the money is protected from creditors and assured to go to the beneficiaries. Also, in many cases the irrevocable trust has its own income tax rate and tax-ID number. This could be beneficial if, for example, you instructed the trust to retain the income it generated, and you, the creator, receive none. Now the asset is out of your estate and you are not taxed on what it earns.

However, potential disadvantages do exist. Unlike a revocable trust, the creator cannot be the trustee or the beneficiary. You cannot change or revoke this type of trust in any way, and you might have to pay gift taxes. Be careful of the amounts and potential gift-tax traps, in addition to how the trust is worded. Don't do anything until you seek professional investment assistance for your particular situation.

Irrevocable Charitable Remainder Trusts

The irrevocable charitable remainder trust is one of the more popular irrevocable trusts, for many good reasons. For example, say you have a highly appreciated piece of property that you no longer wish to own. Your estate is large, and any possible way of reducing the amount you would pay for estate taxes would help. However, you have children whom you feel deserve to have what you worked so hard to earn. The property was bought many years ago for $20,000, and it is now worth $200,000. If you sold the property, the capital gains taxes would be tremendously high. Although the property appreciates, it provides no income, which is something you would like to increase.

The solution: You and a qualified charity get together and draft a charitable remainder trust. You place the property inside the trust and immediately sell it for $200,000. The trust is then instructed to put the proceeds of the sale into a AAA-rated annuity that will guarantee a 9-percent interest rate for both your lifetime and your spouse's. By selling the property *inside* the trust, you accomplished these goals:

1. Avoiding capital gains tax. The full $200,000 went into the annuity paying 9 percent, instead of the net amount you would have received had you sold it and paid the taxes on your own.

2. Reducing income taxes. Because you made a charitable donation, the deductions on your taxes will be sizable.

3. Increasing income. Your income is now augmented by more than $1,500 per month.

4. Contributing to charity. Upon your death (or your spouse's death) the charity will get the principal of the trust. You received the income while you were alive, but they own the asset once you die. You did a good deed.

Of course, the downside is that you just gave away a $200,000 asset that your beneficiaries could have used. What you could do to compensate for that is have the trust contribute to an insurance policy in the amount of $200,000 to be paid directly to your children after you die. There are several benefits to this: Although your estate made the gift of the property, your beneficiaries will still receive $200,000. What's more, because the irrevocable insurance trust is the owner of the policy, it is not included in the total value of your estate; therefore, it will not be taxed or increase the size of your estate by the amount of the insurance proceeds. It bypasses your estate and goes directly to your children. Now your estate is not reduced as a result of the gift, it did not cost you anything, and you paid no taxes. In fact, you received tax deductions by giving a generous donation to charity and also received additional income.

Why would the charity spend a few thousand dollars a year on an insurance trust to pay if both trustees die? It is because you gave them a $200,000 gift, and this is one of the best investments it could make.

The biggest downside to this technique is that you lose control of the money. Be certain that this is what you want to do before doing it.

Two Common Types of Charitable Trusts

When creating a charitable trust, you must choose between a Charitable Remainder Annuity Trust (CRAT) or a Charitable Remainder Unit Trust (CRUT). Regardless of whether you create a CRAT or a CRUT, the obligation to pay the preset amount begins the day the trust is created and funded. Let's take a look at the difference between the two forms.

CRATs pay income to you in one of the following ways:

1. A fixed amount of dollars out of income and, if income is insufficient, out of principal.

2. A fixed percentage out of the initial fair market value of assets transferred to the trust and, if income is insufficient, out of principal.

Once the dollar payout is set, it is fixed for the trust term and no subsequent reevaluations are made. Any excess income is retained in the trust and added to the principal.

CRUTs will pay in one of the following ways:

1. A fixed percentage of net fair market value of trust assets, revalued annually, out of income, and if income is insufficient, out of principal.

2. The lesser of either option 1 or the actual trust income, with deficiencies in distributions made up in any later year when trust income exceeds the payout for the year.

3. The lesser of either option 1 or the actual trust income, with deficiencies in distributions *not* made up in later years.

For any of the these examples, excess income is retained in the trust and added to the principal. This area of planning and law is rapidly changing, so be sure and consult the proper counsel before making any decisions.

Tax Bypass Insurance Trusts

I know what you're thinking: "I don't want anything with the word *insurance* in the name." In many cases, I might agree. But if you have estate tax problems, and you want to keep what you've worked so hard to earn, read on!

Keep in mind that once the value of your estate exceeds $625,000 (in 1998), the estate tax must be paid within nine months of your death or the IRS will gladly sell your assets for you.

When you create an insurance trust, you set up an irrevocable trust. The only thing you place in this trust is a life insurance policy. The irrevocable trust consists of you (the insured), the trustee, and the beneficiaries. A life insurance trust keeps your insurance policies from being included in your taxable estate and is one of the least expensive ways to pay estate taxes.

Figure 15:
Irrevocable Life Insurance Trust Flow Chart

Grantor	Irrevocable Life Insurance Trust	Beneficiaries
You gift cash to the irrevocable life insurance trust.	Trustee notifies beneficiaries of gift. Trustee uses gift to pay insurance premium. Trust is owner and usually beneficiaries of policy. When you die, trustee distributes proceeds to beneficiaries according to you trust instructions.	Beneficiaries refuse gift.

For married couples, the type of insurance purchased through the trust is usually called *Second-to-Die Insurance*. This means that the proceeds (death benefit) would be paid after the death of the *second* spouse. As a result, the mortality tables are combined and the policy is less expensive.

Because the irrevocable trust, not the estate, is the owner of the insurance, the insurance is not figured into your estate upon the second death. Rather, it will immediately be paid to your beneficiaries, avoiding your estate. While it is a good idea to get rid of unnecessary insurance policies, a policy that does not increase the value of your estate could help you avoid taxes. If your insurance is owned by a trust, it will not increase your net worth. (See Chapter 1 for help with determining your net worth.) For example, let's say both you and your spouse are 65 years of age, your estate is worth $900,000 and is growing at 7 percent per year. In 20 years, your estate would be worth $3.48 million. You have created a revocable A/B trust providing protection from estate taxes up to $2 million (if death occurs after 2006). Your estate is vulnerable to taxation on more than $1.4 million. You'd much prefer to give the assets to your children instead of Uncle Sam.

Based on $1.4 million, you can owe more than $600,000 in estate taxes (depending on deductions). To avoid paying $600,000 in taxes, consider creating an insurance trust with your children as the trustees and you and your spouse as the insured. If you and your spouse pass away in 20 years and the insurance on $600,000 will cost $6,000 per year for the next 20 years, the total cost will be $120,000. The insurance benefit bypasses your estate and is paid directly to your children free of taxes and expenses. The $600,000 in estate taxes (on the $1.4 million) is then given to Uncle Sam; however, your insurance trust paid the $600,000 in taxes for you, and it only cost you $120,000. (Of course, the insurance premium will vary depending on your age and health status.)

There are numerous arguments against this option, and I have heard them all: "Let the kids pay the taxes." "Insurance is a bad investment." "I can do better in other investments." "I will spend down the estate." Nevertheless, seriously consider this approach. In the above example, it cost $120,000 over 20 years to receive $600,000. Not counting the value of money over time, you received a return on your investment of approximately 8 percent—*tax-free!* Shop around and make certain that this is a good investment for you, but don't reject the idea out of hand.

Although there are many complex reasons to use a life insurance trust, you can put everything else aside and look at this very simply: If you are single and have an estate worth more than $625,000 or married with $1.25 million (in 1988), you will pay estate taxes. An insurance trust may be a good money-saving investment. In addition, life insurance proceeds are available soon after death, whereas if your estate is not liquid, your beneficiaries might not receive its full value.

Figure 16:
Two Estates Worth $1.2 Million in 1998, With and Without
Life Insurance Trusts

$1,200,000	Net worth (assets less debts)	$1,200,000
+ 400,000	Life insurance you own	+ 0
$1,600,000	Net estate	$1,200,000
– 140,000*	Federal estate taxes	– 0**
$1,460,000	Balance	$1,200,000
+ 0	Proceeds from insurance trust	+ 400,000
$1,460,000	Amount of assets for beneficiaries	$1,600,000

*Note that both scenarios used an A/B trust to preserve both spouse's exemption if both spouse's exemption were not utilized (as in the case most often when a will is used) a great deal more in estate taxes would have been owed.
Also note that the $140,000 in federal estate taxes is an estimate.

**If both spouses' exemptions were not utilized (in this case by an A/B trust) an additional amount of estate taxes would be owed. The taxes would probably exceed $200,000.

Remember to be sure that the proceeds from the insurance (death benefit) are not included in the gross value of your estate. Do not name your estate the trustee of your insurance trust. Perhaps the same person who is the trustee of your living trust can be the trustee of your irrevocable living trust. There are also institutional trust companies or banks that will administrate the trust for a fee. Be sure that, as a result of not being the trustee and because this is an irrevocable trust, you do not lose control. For these reasons, be certain to set forth strict provisions in the trust to ensure that the trustee administers your wishes exactly as you desire.

In addition, you might want to make the irrevocable insurance trust the beneficiary of the insurance policy instead of your children. If you have a separate trustee and the trust is also the beneficiary, these proceeds can be used to first pay any taxes owed upon your death.

Finally, be sure that neither you nor your spouse pay a single penny of the insurance premium. If you do, the policy may be considered a part of the total value of your estate. As discussed previously, you are allowed to gift up to $10,000 per year per person ($20,000 per married couple). Therefore, gift $10,000 per beneficiary of the trust, but give the money to the trustee. The beneficiaries must sign a special provision call a *Crummey*

Provision. In layman's terms, this states that the beneficiary *willingly forfeited* the gift to be used for the purposes of the insurance premium inside the trust.

Consider Figure 17, showing the difference in estate taxes on a $3-million estate using three strategies. When the Marital Deduction is used, no estate taxes are due upon the death of the first spouse; after the death of the second spouse, $1,098,000 (or 37 percent) of the estate, would be consumed by estate taxes. An A/B living trust protects $1.2 million, which still incurs $784,000 in estate taxes. An A/B living trust with a life insurance trust reduces the cost of paying the $784,000 in estate taxes to $122,000—only 4 percent of the estate's value. That's approximately how much it costs to purchase $784,000 in life insurance, which is a 1 to 6.5 ratio: Every dollar spent on insurance premiums pays $6.50 in estate taxes!

Figure 17:
Effects of Estate Taxes on a $3-Million Estate Using Different Estate Planning Techniques

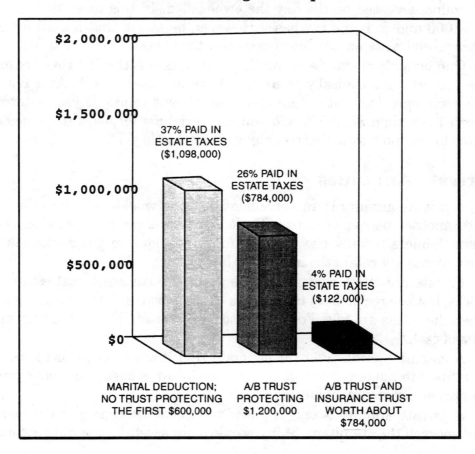

Life Estate

A *life estate* gives its holder the right to use, possess, or enjoy property and the income it produces for as long as he or she lives. The key here is that the holder of the life estate has the right to use the property but does not own it. The person holding title to the remainder interest owns the balance of the interest in the property not held by the life tenant. A life estate is appropriate when someone wishes to gift a home to someone else, but wants to retain all rights and access to the home. Upon the death of the life tenant, the ownership of the property reverts to the holder of the remainder interest. Benefits include the fact that you may be able to protect your assets from creditors such as Medicaid (but watch out for the 36-month *look-back rule;* see Chapter 14 for a complete discussion of this rule). The house will also pass probate-free.

Another advantage of a life estate is that the property could receive a step-up in basis for tax purposes. For example, say the owner of the life estate bought the property for $50,000, but when he or she dies, the property is worth $150,000. The tax basis for the property is the new fair market value, assessed on the day the owner died. In this case the value is $150,000 and so is the tax basis. However, be aware that not all life estates receive a step-up; it depends on how the life estate is structured.

One possible downside to creating a life estate is the fact that because the property is technically yours, you have not made a gift. As a result, this technique does not reduce the value of your estate. If your estate is worth more than $625,000 and you are searching for ways to reduce its value for tax purposes, this technique may not help you.

Private Annuities

A private annuity is an agreement that you would enter into directly with another person or entity. There is no insurance company involvement. Seniors usually use this planning technique to get assets out of their names but retain the income for life.

Private annuities work for assets such as businesses, real estate, or stocks, but the recipient of these types of assets will still pay capital gains when the assets are sold. For this reason, private annuities work best with gifts of cash.

A potential problem for the donors is that if the recipient is unable to or refuses to make payments, or if the recipient is sued, the donor could lose his or her stream of income.

A private annuity is only a gift if you make someone else the owner and yourself the annuitant. Many people place assets in a private account, making their child (or children) the owner and beneficiary. However, the parents remain the annuitants, whereby they receive all income. The child receives all benefits related to the principal and will acquire the asset, probate free, upon the parents' death.

The advantage is almost the same as the life estate: The asset is out of the estate, and no creditors can touch the principal, including the parents. All the other obstacles discussed under life estate also apply to private annuities.

Family Limited Partnerships

A *Family Limited Partnership (FLP)*, when used as part of a properly designed overall strategy, can be an outstanding device for providing asset protection, and can also be a very effective estate planning tool.

A typical FLP is set up so that husband and wife are each general partners and other family members are limited partners. After setting up the FLP, assets are transferred into the partnership. Ideally, through a gifting program, husband and wife will each own a 1-percent general partnership interest and the other 98 percent will be owned by the limited partners. As general partners, husband and wife have full control over the FLP assets, even though most of the assets are owned by other family members as limited partners.

The FLP must be set up for a valid business purpose and cannot be used to avoid a debt (if you set one up after a judgment is entered against you, the IRS will likely term it a "fraudulent transfer"). The purpose of the FLP should be outlined within the agreement itself.

Asset Protection Benefits of Family Limited Partnerships

Under the provisions of the Uniform Limited Partnership Act, a creditor of a partner cannot reach into the partnership and take specific partnership assets. The creditor may not possess, own, or vote the interest of the debtor. The creditor cannot compel a dissolution of the partnership to gain access to or ownership of its assets, nor does the creditor have a vote to remove the general partner.

The only remedy available to a creditor is a *charging order,* which simply directs the general partner to pay over to the creditor any distributions from the partnership that would otherwise go to the debtor partner, until the judgment is paid in full. Thus, to protect itself, the partnership would not make any distributions when a charging order has been placed against a partner.

Estate Planning Benefits of Family Limited Partnerships

What is the value of an asset if it cannot be sold or liquidated for cash? This is the key to understanding the estate planning benefits of the FLP. For example, if I own 50 percent of an FLP worth $1 million, but there is no guarantee of distributions and I cannot liquidate that interest for 35 years, what would someone pay for that interest? It would probably be far less than $500,000. This is called the *lack of marketability discount.*

Ownership of the FLP is controlled through ownership units. If the total worth of the partnership is $1 million, the value of the FLP may be entitled to discounts ranging from 15 percent all the way up to 87 percent, depending on how creatively you have stretched IRS guidelines. The discounts for lack of marketability are controlled by the FLP agreement, which will have restrictions that allow discounts. There are also discounts for *minority* or *noncontrolling* shares. If a partner cannot unilaterally withdraw his interest or force a liquidation, then the partnership is entitled to a discount for minority or noncontrolling shares. What does all this discounting mean in real life situations? Let's take a look.

Scenario

John and Jane have assets of $1.7 million that they hold in FLP units as general and limited partners. Other family members have $300,000 worth of limited partnership units. Upon death, the FLP is worth $2 million. If there were no FLP in place, estate taxes would be assessed on $500,000. However, if an FLP is set up properly, it will claim discounts for minority-owned shares and lack of marketability. This would reduce John and Jane's $1.7-million interest of and potentially eliminate all estate taxes.

It must be remembered that discounting varies from case to case, and no final determination can be made without having the FLP professionally evaluated.

Setting Up a Family Limited Partnership

A Family Limited Partnership is merely a business entity similar to a limited partnership. It is similar to setting up a corporation. Once set up, the family members transfer assets into the partnership. In return, the transferees receive partnership units.

The usual FLP is set up in the following manner: Husband and wife set up the FLP, then transfer their assets into it, in return for partnership units. They arrange the partnership so that they each own a 1-percent interest as general partners and the remaining interest as limited partners. The next step is to have the FLP valued.

At this point, an appraiser would value the FLP, taking discounts into consideration. Once the discounts are figured, the appraiser will give the FLP a value. Each unit can then have a certain value (for example, 100 partnership units and an FLP appraised at $1 million would result in each unit being valued at $10,000). At this point, each spouse can gift $10,000 (one unit) to any family member, tax-free. The family members are then designated as limited partners. Each year this gifting program would take place to minimize the estate taxes having to be paid. This could potentially reduce income taxes by placing the units into a lower tax bracket.

The practical effect of the above example would be to increase the gifting allowance from $10,000 per person to $20,000 per person. This allows a quicker gifting program. Plus, the assets remain within the FLP and you and your spouse retain control over those assets as general partners.

Upon the parents' death, a final tax return is filed giving the appraised value of the FLP. After the gifting program, they will own fewer units, and the final tax return would be based upon their units. If everything goes smoothly and the appraised value is accepted, then ideally *no estate taxes are paid.* After a determination is made by the IRS, the FLP can be dissolved, and the units owned by the parents can be distributed according to their trust.

Qualified Personal Residence Trusts

For many taxpayers, their residence is the single most valuable asset they own. By putting the residence into a *Qualified Personal Residence Trust (QPRT)* during their lifetime, the taxpayers can transfer the residence to their children at a significantly lower transfer tax cost than if the residence was left to them through a will.

An individual creates a QPRT by transferring the personal residence to a trust and retaining the right to use the residence without the payment of rent for a specified period of time. The asset in a QPRT can only be the personal, principal residence of the donor. To place a second residence, such as a vacation home, in trust, use a second QPRT.

When the residence is transferred to the trust, the donor is treated as having made a gift to the family members who will receive the residence at the end of the specified period of time. The value of the gift is the fair market value of the residence, reduced by the present value of the right to live in the residence rent-free for that specified period. This reduction amount is determined by using IRS valuation tables and the IRS code section interest rate for the month of the transfer. The result of the transfer is an unrealistically high discount for gift tax purposes, but one that the IRS cannot challenge.

Under very strict guidelines, additional assets may be placed into the trust. Examples of such assets could include a replacement residence, enough cash held in a separate account to pay six months of expenses (including mortgage payments and improvements), insurance on the residence, and any proceeds from the sale of the residence.

The property is held and administered by a trustee. In a properly drafted QPRT, the trustee may be the donor. The trustee is held to the standards set out in the trust document. The residence can be sold, and a new residence can be purchased. The trust can be converted to an annuity trust under certain circumstances, and would then have the same characteristics of an annuity trust, such as the payment of a minimum annuity amount. The donor retains the right to occupy and use the property for a specified term of years and may continue to occupy the residence after the term expires; however, at that time, fair market value rent must be paid. All income from the trust asset is paid to the term holder, who is specified in the trust and is not necessarily the donor.

During the term of the trust, the donor may still use the following: the $125,000 exclusion of gain by a taxpayer who has reached age 55; the deduction for qualified residence interest payments; any deductions applicable for state and local real property taxes; and the nonrecognition of gain on the sale of a principal residence that is replaced within two years.

At the end of the specified time period, title to the residence passes to the next generation free of any additional gift tax, even if the property has appreciated in value since the trust was created. This means that the transfer tax savings that can be achieved are especially high if the trust is created at a time when real estate market values are low.

If the donor is still living at the end of the term, the residence will not be included in the gross estate for estate tax purposes. Further, near the end of the term, the donor may choose to repurchase the residence from the trust, or enter into an agreement to lease the property. A properly executed repurchase of the property will allow a step-up in basis of the property, and avoid capital gains tax.

Scenario

A 60-year-old homeowner transfers his $800,000 residence into a QPRT with a term of seven years. This first step is the calculation of the right to receive income for the seven-year period. Using the IRS tables, the required income factor is 0.410108.

Next, the value of the right of return to the residence is the event of death prior to the end of the seven-year term is calculated. For this example, the reversion factor, based on the IRS tables, is 0.088403.

Third, the remainder interest factor is calculated by subtracting the income factor and the reversion factor from 1. This results in a remainder interest factor of 0.501489.

Finally, the remainder interest factor is multiplied by the value of the residence to determine the value allocated to the remainder interest. $800,000 multiplied by 0.501489 equals $401,191. This is the value of the gift that will determine the amount of gift tax due.

From this example, it becomes apparent that a properly structured QPRT can allow an individual to gift an asset valued at half of its current value. This is an extremely effective tool for reducing the value of assets for estate tax purposes.

Chapter 11

What to Do When a Spouse Dies

The period immediately after a spouse's death should not be a time to worry about financial problems. Hopefully, you will have planned ahead and will be well-prepared financially. First and foremost, make sure you are clear about your loved one's funeral wishes; a good funeral director can handle most of the arrangements.

When you are ready to take care of financial matters, review the appropriate document locator. This paper should have been prepared by your spouse and should provide the names and numbers of attorneys, accountants, and financial planner and should also list all assets and where original documents can be found (for example, a stock certificate held at the company or a bond certificate in the safe deposit box). Assets listed on the document locator should also note how title is held, such as Joint Tenancy with Rights of Survivorship (JTWROS), or in the name of the family trust. The document locator should also show all sources of income and what will happen to the income after death (for example, whether it will be reduced or eliminated).

Steps to Follow after the Death of a Spouse

Once you have reviewed the contents of the document locator, follow these steps to make sure everything is handled in a timely fashion.

1. **Obtain several certified copies of the death certificate.**
    The funeral director or county clerk's office can provide
    these. Whatever number you think you will need, double it—
    make at least 15 copies. If you have to go through probate,
    your marriage certificate and your and your spouse's birth
    certificates may be required as well.

2. **Request any insurance proceeds.** Call the companies with
    which you hold insurance. Tell them the circumstances, and
    ask how to proceed. If you are the beneficiary, you will have
    to provide a copy of the death certificate before any of the
    proceeds will be released to you.

3. **Go through all retirement income sources.** These may
    include a military pension, work pension, Social Security, and
    others. Call the various entities paying this income and ask
    them to tell you the procedure following a death. Compare
    your own records to the information you are given. Your spouse
    might have elected full *retirement benefits to spouse* after his
    or her death. Always save the paper stating this, because
    even big companies make mistakes. As for Social Security
    benefits, first decide whose income is greater, and select that
    one—you cannot take both.

4. **Have all of your assets appraised.** There are two reasons
    for doing this. First, you need to establish a tax basis on your
    assets so that when your assets are sold, you have a tax basis
    figure for capital gains purposes. Second, you need to know
    the size of the estate in order to determine the estate taxes
    that may be owed. Have your assets appraised more than
    once, and use the lowest appraisals in order to decrease the
    amount of estate taxes owed. Your assets can be appraised
    from one of two dates: either the date of death or six months
    later (this is known as the *alternate evaluation date*). You
    must use the same date for all assets.

5. **Change the name on all your assets.** Change the name
    on all assets from your spouse's to yours, or to the title of
    your trust.

6. **Contact an attorney.** If assets are in separate names, or a
    valid will exists and it is necessary to obtain assets, contact
    an attorney. Your attorney will file the will in court and then
    try to get on the docket as soon as possible. This could be a
    long, tedious process, so be patient.

7. **Contact your accountant to provide a final tax return.**
If you did not go through probate, and an audit or appraisals were not performed to this point, the IRS may do a final audit. Your accountant might suggest that you appraise certain assets as well. Remember, if you own a piece of real estate, for tax purposes you will need to know the appraised value at the time of death. If the estate owes taxes, they must be paid within nine months after death. The deceased's income taxes must be filed by April 15th.

8. **While you wait for insurance money or probate to finish, adjust your financial plan.** Calculate your new monthly income and see whether it is higher or lower. Review your expenses and decide whether you are spending more money or less. Then readjust your plan accordingly. If your estate is now substantially larger, review gifting techniques and ways to shelter it from estate taxes. If you will need more income, determine how much principal you can use each year and still be fairly certain you will not run out of money. Should a large insurance sum be forthcoming, carefully plan how to invest the money. If you cannot immediately make a decision, simply place the funds temporarily in a money market and take your time reviewing options.

9. **Be certain that the last expenses of your spouse are *bona fide*.** Sometimes you may receive bills that are simply schemes. A bill may look like a medical bill or something official, but don't believe it until you thoroughly research it. Along the same lines, many hospital and doctor bills are incorrect. (I have heard that they are incorrect more than 60 percent of the time—and most often in their favor.) Check every bill, and dispute it if it's wrong. If your spouse did all the work on your estate, and money matters are new to you, enlist a professional to help you. Many attorneys, financial planners, and estate planners are very competent and will be able to assist you, and most professionals will grant you a free initial consultation. Don't settle on the first person; interview at least three, take copious notes, and write down all your questions to ask each candidate.

Assets in a Revocable Trust

If your and your spouse's assets are in the name of a trust, do not change the name. Remember that the trust is like a corporation, and the death of one of the trustees does not mean you have to change the name of the corporation. If you have a trust, you might want to notify all the places where you have assets by sending a certified letter. In the letter, state that the other trustee has died and you would like his or her name removed as co-trustee of the trust. Have the letter *signature-guaranteed* (a brokerage firm or bank can provide this service), and enclose a certified copy of the death certificate with it. Make an appointment with your accountant. It is very important to understand what type of trust you have (revocable, A/B, or irrevocable) and how to proceed if you are the trustee. Make sure a visit to your estate planning accountant is one of the first steps you take.

If you have an A/B trust, it is necessary to place some assets in the deceased spouse's trust (that is, the "B" or bypass trust). Once you decide which assets will go into the "B" trust (with the aid of your estate planner, accountant, or attorney), you will need to transfer assets to it. The asset should reflect that you are the trustee of the "B" trust.

Assets in JTWROS

If your and your spouse's assets are in JTWROS, they will not go through probate and you will not owe an immediate tax. (Taxes will be owed after *your* death.) Accounts will not be frozen, and you should be able to change the assets into your name with little resistance.

The assets should be transferred to your name only. This is done by sending the signature-guaranteed letter requesting removal of the joint tenant with a certified copy of the death certificate, to any entity holding an asset (brokerage firms, banks, mortgage companies, etc.).

Assets as Community Property

Assets held in this manner are very similar to those held in JTWROS. The major difference is that, after the second death, taxes are not owed on most assets as a result of the automatic step-up in tax basis.

Warning: Be careful about putting someone else's name on your property, including your children. After one spouse dies, the survivor will often put children and other beneficiaries on title with them. This is not recommended. First of all, you may be giving a gift greater than the $10,000 allowed yearly, which will then be subject to gift taxes. Second, you will lose control of the assets. If, for example, you put your son on the property title with you, should your son go through bankruptcy or be sued, your property is jeopardized. Furthermore, in addition to your son's signature, if your son is married, that of his wife may also be required when you decide to sell or refinance the property.

Chapter 12

Agencies, Advisors, and Other Information

As Francis Bacon said, knowledge is power. In this chapter, you will gain more useful knowledge that will help you in your retirement planning. Further, you will become familiar with key resources that will be of use to you in your planning.

Some Useful Agencies and Services

Although we all resent the amount of money we spend on taxes, there are actually many worthwhile federal and state services available for mature Americans that are funded by our tax dollars. In Chapter 7, all the IRS telephone numbers were listed and special assistance designed for seniors was enumerated. Here you will find other agencies that can be of assistance to you—some are government agencies funded by our tax dollars, others are nonprofit organizations.

Among the many services and agencies available for seniors, your local Agency for the Aging (see Appendix B) is an excellent source of advice and knowledge. Chances are, if they do not have the answer to a question, they will know where to find it. The services provided are all-encompassing and you should become familiar with them.

For assistance with Medicare-related issues, such as a disagreement you might have with Medicare, assistance with choosing a good Medicare supplement, or if you fail to understand what an insurance agent said, call your State Insurance Commissioner and ask what help is available in your area. Sometimes a volunteer counselor will even come to your home. Numerous states have organizations that will help you dispute Medicare claims and choose a Medicare supplement. These services are provided at very little or no cost. Also, many states have legal services for senior citizens, which may provide assistance with matters such as a will, power of attorney, quit claim deed (the form used to transfer title for real property), homesteading, conservatorship actions, or Medicaid counseling. To find out about these services, call your State Bar Association or the local Area Agency for the Aging. Other wonderful services include the hospice program, active lobbyists, caregiver associations, and many more. Your local Area Agency for the Aging can help you locate these services, or you can look in your local telephone book.

In addition, many retirees now face the problem of caring for their elderly parents. The following agencies may be of assistance.

National Association of Professional
Geriatric Care Managers   (602) 881-8008
(Provide names of private care managers in all parts of the country.)

National Academy of Elder
Law Attorneys   (602) 881-4005
(Provide referrals for attorneys in estate and Medicaid planning.)

Health Information Center   (800) 336-4797
(They help in a wide variety of medical problems and are an
excellent source for referrals.)

Alzheimer's Disease and Related   (800) 621-0379
Disorders Association   (800) 527-6037
                                               (Illinois)

The Dependent Care Connection   (203) 226-2680

Where Should You Live During Your Retirement?

Although you might not be thinking about finances when you decide to pick the location where you will live during your retirement, you should be. One of the biggest costs in retirement could be the taxes associated

rea where you live. State and local taxes vary widely. As a sen-
ı, most states will give you a break, but the amounts can differ
ɪsly. In my book *50 Fabulous Places to Retire in America* is a list of
locations rated on state and local taxes (and a great many other
factors).

You really have to calculate all the taxes and then weigh your options.
Some states have no state income tax, and some have no sales tax. However, several states tax Social Security benefits. The most generous states
exclude all pension income from taxation, but other states tax *all* of
your pension income. The next important tax to consider is the property
tax. Most states (and the District of Columbia) grant property tax relief to
elderly homeowners and renters. This is accomplished through state-
financed "circuit-breakers," or homestead exemptions. By means of a
circuit-breaker, property taxes (or rent equivalents) are reduced through
a state-financed credit or rebate when they exceed specified percentages
of household income. With a homestead exemption, a specific dollar
amount is subtracted from the assessed property value, thus lowering the
mature homeowner's taxes. See below for a list of states that offer no property relief on taxes. Further, in addition to federal estate taxes, several
states impose estate taxes of their own.

The following is a listing of important state tax guidelines to consider
as you choose a retirement location.

States with no sales tax:
- Alaska
- Delaware
- Montana
- New Hampshire
- Oregon

States with no state income tax:
- Alaska
- Florida
- Nevada
- South Dakota
- Texas
- Washington
- Wyoming

States with no property tax relief for seniors:
- Florida
- Louisiana
- Minnesota
- Oregon
- Vermont
- Wisconsin

States that tax only interest and dividends:
- New Hampshire
- Tennessee

States that tax Social Security benefits:

- Colorado
- Connecticut
- Iowa
- Kansas
- Minnesota
- Missouri
- Montana
- Nebraska
- New Mexico
- North Dakota
- Utah
- Rhode Island
- West Virginia
- Vermont
- Wisconsin

States with estate taxes:

- Indiana
- Kentucky
- Louisiana
- Maryland
- Massachusetts
- New York
- Ohio
- Pennsylvania
- South Dakota

States that exclude all pension income from taxation:

- Alabama
- Hawaii
- Illinois
- Pennsylvania

States that tax all of your pension income:

- Connecticut
- Rhode Island
- Vermont

States that tax pension income of nonresidents:

- Arizona
- California
- Colorado
- Connecticut
- Kansas
- Louisiana
- Massachusetts
- Michigan
- Minnesota
- Mississippi
- Montana
- New York
- North Dakota
- Oregon
- Utah
- Vermont
- Wisconsin

Choosing Advisors

Regardless of the complexity of your situation, the size of your estate, and the amount of your own involvement, it is prudent to have qualified advisors working for you on your behalf. I call this your Board of Advisors. You should enlist the services of three different professionals to create your board: an accountant, a financial planner, and an attorney.

The Accountant

An accountant will serve several purposes during your retirement. You must find an accountant who understands the special needs of senior citizens, understands trusts, and is very proficient in preparing final tax and trust tax returns.

The first step in finding a good accountant is to ask your friends for references. Perhaps the best suggestions might come from the others on your board—your attorney or financial planner, interview at least three potential candidates before making a selection. If you feel pressure or too much eagerness from a candidate, consider that a warning signal.

Be sure to check credentials. Obviously, the most widely known designation is the *Certified Public Accountant (CPA),* although the *Enrolled Agent (EA)* designation is gaining popularity.

Have a list of prepared questions ready for your interview. If the candidate does not answer them to your satisfaction, scratch him or her off your list. Questions you should ask an accountant include:

1. How many final tax returns have you completed?
2. How long have you been in practice?
3. What is your area of specialization?
4. What is your fee schedule? (Be careful if he or she charges by the hour without having a cap on fees.)
5. What is the cost of a phone call?
6. What is the cost of a consultation?
7. What is the cost for the yearly returns and booking?

Also, ask his or her opinion regarding some general subjects. If the accountant knows the rules, he or she will give you a definitive response rather than vague answers. Perhaps a good general question would be, "What is involved in completing a tax return for the 'B' side of a trust after the first death?"

Finally, get references. In order to avoid a "good buddy" reference, I specifically ask the attorney for clients who share your zip code, or ask for three references with last names beginning with the letters A, B, and C. If the accountant cannot produce a reference for each, perhaps the practice is not very extensive. Also be sure and ask for one or two professional references.

The Financial Planner

The financial planner is an essential member of your board. A good planner will know many of the general guidelines regarding arrangements made by your attorney and your accountant and be available to explain them to you. This person will advise you and suggest what your attorney and accountant should be doing on your behalf.

Unfortunately, it is harder to determine who is a good financial planner, because almost anyone can use that title. An important credential to look for is the *Certified Financial Planner (CFP)*. This is the industry's certification, requiring a broad understanding of true financial planning and involving lengthy training followed by a difficult exam.

Many times a financial planner will be licensed to transact security business. This is a plus, because such a planner can transfer your assets, suggest various components of your plan, and help with your investment choices. If the financial planner is registered to transact security business, you will see "member NASD/SIPC" on his or her business card. The National Association of Security Dealers (NASD) is the self-regulatory body of securities dealers. The NASD polices members in order to detect and prevent unscrupulous or unfair practices (very much like the bar association does for attorneys). SIPC is the Securities Investors Protection Corporation. Ask the planner for his or her CRD number, which is his or her identification number with the NASD. You can call NASD at (800) 289-9999, give them the ID number, and ask how long the candidate has been licensed, whether there are any pending or past lawsuits against this planner, and what the outcome was. Be very careful if you discover that your candidate is not a member of the NASD.

Before engaging any services, you should ask the candidate to prepare a letter with goals envisioned for your financial plan and how his or her expertise will help. Ask for specific details. Many planners will do this for no charge. Some may be leery that you will use this information to forward to another planner, and may charge a nominal fee, but most are willing to do the preliminary work for little or no fee to "show you what they've got." You make the decision. A good financial planner is well-worth the money.

After you feel comfortable with your planner's qualifications, you need to know about compensation. Some charge an hourly fee, others charge annual rates, still others charge a commission. If a fee is charged, check to be sure that a commission is not received as well. Ask for a letter stating that all investments and insurance recommended and used in your plan are purchased on a *no load, no commission* basis. Be certain to get this in writing. Also, ask whether there is a cap (maximum) on the planner's fees, and whether there is a fee reduction after a certain number of hours.

One advantage to fee-paid planners is that the planner is not making decisions based on sales. It is more difficult for you to discern and regulate the costs of commission-paid planners.

If a planner charges a commission, your questions should be directed in the following manner: "Show me two choices for every investment or strategy you suggest. What is the commission for each? What is the performance of the investment or insurance after the commission is deducted?"

Some investors argue that it is actually better to use financial planners who earn commissions rather than charge fees. This rationale is based on the fact that many commissioned investment products enjoy the same performance as noncommissioned products, net of commission. Therefore, if you do not have to pay a fee out of pocket, your investments will perform the same as noncommissioned products, and you are actually receiving the services more cheaply. Some might ask, "What incentive does the planner have to continue doing actual planning work if no commissions are to be earned?" Some planners feel that the commission justifies the ongoing planning work, and if the client does not stay pleased, the planner may lose the client's business, which is incentive for financial planners to do their best for their clients rather than be motivated by potential commission earnings. Ultimately, you must decide which arrangement is right for you.

The Attorney

The selection of an attorney is an extremely important decision. Follow the same steps used for the other two advisors, including calling client and professional references. If you are looking for an estate planning attorney, it is wise to peruse sample trust documents. Questions to ask would include how long this has been the attorney's area of expertise, and what the results of prior similar cases were.

Call the Bar Association in your state to check on the attorney. Ask the length of time the attorney has been licensed, whether any complaints have been registered, and whether any lawsuits are pending against him or her.

During the interview, ask the attorney what part of the law is his or her specialty. In this day and age, seniors need advisors who specialize. How could a lawyer be an expert at worker's compensation and estate planning at the same time? The amount of experience, knowledge, and continuous education required for estate planning is enormous. Also, ask whether he or she is a member of the Estate Planning Section of the Bar Association. Perhaps you might even call the attorney's office anonymously to ascertain whether a different kind of case would be handled there or referred elsewhere.

You must create a competent board of advisors. You can always make alterations, but don't procrastinate. Taking no action at all to establish your board could cause your estate much harm.

Are Second, Late-in-Life Marriages Practical?

Many people choose to marry later in life, often for a second time with each spouse having grown children already. No doubt finances are not the only consideration to take into account when deciding to wed, but it is worthwhile to weigh all the pros and cons from a financial perspective to determine if a later-in-life marriage is prudent. The following are a few points to consider when doing this exercise. Keep in mind that both pros and cons exist; I am not trying to discourage later-in-life marriages, but there are some important ramifications to keep in mind.

Income Taxes

It usually works out that your joint income taxes will be lower if you file as married and filing jointly than if you are single and file as a single person. I highly recommend you get together with your tax planner and have the numbers run both ways to see which is more advantageous to you.

Long-Term Care Planning

Most people are worried about spending all of their money in a long-term care facility. Rarely do Medicare, Medicare supplements, or HMO providers pay for any substantial time in a care facility. Even if you keep your assets separate from your spouse's, and even if the assets were yours prior to getting married, your personal assets are still considered part of the "community" and are deemed available for costs associated with long-term care. You would receive no support from Medicaid until you have spent your money down to the allowable Medicaid limits.

Scenario

At the time of one senior couple's wedding, the wife had $300,000 and the husband had nothing. Two years after their marriage, the husband had a stroke and needed to recover in a care facility. Most *of the wife's $300,000 had to be spent before Medicaid began to cover any of the costs. If they were not married, the husband would have qualified for Medicaid immediately.*

Estate Taxes

As discussed in detail in Chapter 8, each individual is allowed an estate valued at $625,000 (in 1998) prior to estate taxes being owed. If one individual has a large estate (more than $625,000), and the other spouse does not have much in assets, if they are married they can each use the $625,000 (in 1998) exclusion to give the estate a value of $1.25 million prior to any estate taxes being owed.

Social Security Benefits

It is very rare for Social Security to accept common-law marriages. If you are not legally married to someone, it will be difficult to be "insured" by Social Security under your significant other's insured status.

Pension and Military Benefits

If you are married and your spouse is eligible for pension or military benefits, you might receive certain benefits when your spouse dies. For example, there could be clauses in the monthly pension income that the monthly income (or a portion of it) will continue for a surviving spouse.

How Should You Own Your Safe Deposit Box?

Safe deposit boxes are kept for myriad reasons: to hide valuables, to protect important papers, to make sure someone knows where to go to find important documents. If you use a safe deposit box simply to hold important papers (such as trusts and power of attorney) that people would need should you become incapacitated or at the time of your death, you might consider placing the box in the name of the trust and making your successor trustee a signor on the trust. Notify your successor trustee of this and communicate to him or her where the key is located.

If you are using the safe deposit box to safeguard assets, you should probably consider a different strategy. It is incredibly easy for someone to find out that you have a safe deposit box if it is registered in your name. Many people will set up the safe deposit box in another name, or corporation. You could even have your attorney as the signor on the safe deposit box.

Answers to 15 Common Questions

Here are some questions you might have and answers you must know as you plan your retirement.

1. I go to the accountant every year, but it stills seems like I am paying a great deal in taxes, any suggestions?

First, study your taxes. Do you take all possible deductions, such as medical deductions, tax credits, etc.? Did you pay taxes on income that you didn't need? Often, stocks, certificates of deposit (CDs), and mutual funds pay dividends or interest. Although you may reinvest, you will still receive a 1099 tax statement and pay taxes. Consider deferring this income until you need it, use stocks that don't pay dividends, and consider tax-free investments.

2. Are bond mutual funds a good idea?

Many people have bond mutual funds. Government bond funds, high yield, and income funds are usually bond funds of some sort. Bond mutual funds, including government bond funds, enjoy no guarantees. In periods of rising interest rates, bonds often underperform and even lose money. Bond mutual funds have no set maturity and you still have to pay management fees. This means that bond mutual funds have unique and inherent risk. If interest rates rise, the value of the bonds inside of the fund could go down. The fund has expenses and no set maturity. The positive aspect of bond mutual funds is that the fund has a professional manager who is experienced and diversifying your money in a wide range of bonds.

Research the wisdom of investing in bonds directly to complement or in lieu of bond mutual funds. Be sure you stagger the maturities, find out what the yield to maturity is before investing, and know the credit rating of the bonds.

3. I've heard that there are pros and cons to junk bonds. Can you explain the meaning of "junk" and do you think they are appropriate investment vehicles?

Junk bonds (also called high yield) do not have a high rating (a BB or better). Standard & Poors, Moody's, and Dulph and Phelps are the three main rating agencies. Usually, new companies or companies with weak balance sheets have lower ratings. To attract investors, most junk bonds pay a much higher interest rate. Sometimes the higher interest rate is worth the risk of a lower rated bond. Research the company thoroughly before investing.

4. My home is valued at $210,000 with a mortgage of $50,000. Should I pay off the mortgage now or invest those funds in the market?

To answer this question, you must conduct two tests. The first is the pillow test: If by paying off the mortgage you feel more comfortable when your head hits the pillow at night, then pay it off. The second test is the financial test: If you are earning more money investing the money, then borrow money all day long—especially if you receive a tax deduction, as in the case of a home mortgage. If it ever comes to the point where the investment is not earning more than the mortgage, then pay the mortgage off. Obviously, you must be careful not to make risky investments and lose the money.

5. How can I find out if I am receiving the right amount from my pension plan?

You would be surprised how many people receive the wrong amount on their pension checks. Perhaps your employer figured the interest incorrectly or perhaps the error is more sinister. Either way, remedies are available if you feel you are not collecting all the benefits to which you are entitled. For more information, an Internet directory has been set up. The address is http://www.dol.gov. Or you can call toll-free at (800) 400-5678.

6. How do I avoid paying a great deal of taxes on my IRA at the time of my or my spouse's death?

You have several options. One option is to convert the IRA to a Roth IRA (see Chapter 6). Although you should always check the numbers to see if converting to a Roth makes sense for you, a good rule of thumb is that if you have a long time to compound the money in the IRA and your current tax bracket isn't excessively high, converting probably makes sense. But regardless of whether the Roth IRA makes sense for you or not, consider stretching your IRA after you die. This involves setting up a plan whereby your IRA will pay a smaller amount out over many years. Thus, you will have to pay a smaller amount in taxes because your annual income will increase as greatly as if you were to receive a lump sum from your IRA.

7. What are the biggest reasons people fail during retirement?

Failure always reverts back to poor planning, whether it's financial failure or emotional failure due to a lack of sense of purpose. Without a sense of worth and drive, it is easy to get depressed and feel like a failure. Even the most successful person can begin to feel like a failure without a plan and focus during retirement. Regardless of whether you are striving to improve your golf game or to see the world, purpose is of the utmost of importance.

Once you know your purpose, inadequate planning can still result in failure. If you didn't budget properly, didn't maximize your investments, didn't realize how much risk you were taking until it was too late, you can still be subject to not achieving your purpose.

8. Once and for all, who qualifies for probate?

Just about anyone can qualify for probate. The biggest myth is that a will avoids probate. It does not. The second biggest myth is that you only qualify for probate if you are rich. Not so. Literally any asset such as a home or a bank account could qualify you for a probate action. Finally, most people think that joint tenancy avoids probate. The problem is that while this may avoid probate after the first tenant dies, upon the death of the second tenant, probate will be necessary.

9. How long should I hold on to my "important papers"?

It is a good idea to keep tax returns for a minimum of five years, statements of accounts also for a minimum of five years (but just the last one of the year). Deeds to real estate should be kept for five years after the property is sold. In general, five years is a good rule of thumb for the length of time you should hold on to important papers.

10. Where should I store stock and bond certificates?

Original certificates are best kept at a brokerage house that is insured and bonded. If you must keep your own, keep the certificates in a fail safe, fire-proof box or, best of all, in a safe deposit box.

11. What's the difference between tax-deferred, tax-deductible, and tax-free?

Tax-deferred will allow the investment to grow every year free of tax, thereby earning income on money that would otherwise have been taken out as tax. The account holder receives no 1099 tax statement and will not have to pay taxes until the money is withdrawn. Once the money is withdrawn it is taxed as ordinary income for the year in which it is withdrawn.

Tax-deductible is something that will help reduce your gross income, which should result in a tax savings. For example, if you had income of $30,000 and contributed $2,000 to a tax-deductible IRA, you will have an adjusted gross income (AGI) of $28,000. This will reduce the amount of taxes you will owe.

Tax-free would be interest that you receive tax-free. Municipal bonds purchased in the state in which you live enjoy both federal and state tax-free income on interest they earn. The trade-off here is that the interest is usually lower.

12. How will my loved ones know what to do if I get sick or die?

Be sure and prepare a document locator and letter of instruction (see Chapter 8). Following your written instructions should make the whole process much easier.

13. This is my second marriage. My spouse and I have agreed to keep our assets separate and give them to our respective children. But we don't want to have to sell the home when one of us dies. What do you suggest?

In your situation, consider using a life estate (see Chapter 10). A life estate will allow either spouse to continue living in your home or a comparable home until the second spouse's passing. At that point, the proceeds are divided according to both spouses' instructions.

14. How are my Social Security increases determined?

Social Security increases are determined based on what inflation is averaging. Inflation is calculated based on the Consumer Price Index, but as discussed in Chapter 3, the Consumer Price Index does not always accurately reflect the living expenses of seniors.

15. Should I be investing in stocks this late in the game?

It is impossible to answer that question without knowing more information, for example, your age, what your investment and income needs are, how much you are investing, etc. Therefore, prepare your financial plan and meet with your financial advisor to find out what approach is right for you.

Part III

Health Care Planning

Chapter 13

Health Care During Retirement

The good news is that we are living longer than ever before; the bad news is we are living at a higher cost. A large portion of that cost can be directly attributed to health care.

Medical science has done a terrific job in helping sustain life. However, this means that people need all sorts of health care services in order to live longer. Much of these services are paid for by (you guessed it) you. You think Medicare or your health maintenance organization (HMO) will pay? Doubtful! Medicare spends money poorly and has too many people to care for and HMOs are predominately for-profit institutions unwilling to spend money on procedures they deem unnecessary or useless.

In order to avoid going broke because of medical costs, you have several options. The following are a few ideas:

♦ **Maximize Medicare Benefits.** If Medicare denies a claim, resend the claim. If they still refuse to pay, petition Medicare. You can call Medicare and ask for a hearing or a petition form. You may want to contact your local Agency for the Aging and ask if they know of any attorneys who will help you with your case. Many attorneys will do *pro bono* work is this field.

Be well-informed about what Medicare will and will not pay for. If Medicare does not pay for routine physicals, visit the doctor when you are having a problem. The doctor might recommend a physical, which may then be covered under Medicare. Further, Medicare only approves home health care if it is intermittent care, and under a doctor's prescription. So, make certain you get a doctor to prescribe the care.

◆ **Consider insurance.** Medicare supplements, long-term care, and home health care insurance are viable forms of insurance. Make sure you don't get too much coverage, though, and that you get the coverage that is most applicable to you. Don't overpay; only buy insurance through qualified companies that enjoy a high rating (at least "A+" by AM BEST). This chapter will give you more information on this subject.

◆ **Squeeze all you can from your HMO.** If you get sick, get all you can from your HMO. If your doctor refuses to allow you to see a specialist, create a stink. If you are denied a procedure that you feel you need, be vocal. Unfortunately, it is the squeaky wheel that gets the grease.

HMOs are very sensitive to bad publicity, almost as sensitive as they are about profits. If you send certified letters to the doctor, to the customer complaint department, and the president of the company, your situation will get noticed. In your letter, clearly explain your situation: that you are on limited income and have limited assets. Create a list of every TV and radio station in your area and enclose the list with your letter, explaining that you will be sending the stations a copy of your letter, telling them your story. I bet you'll get a speedy response.

◆ **Qualify for Medicaid.** Medicaid pays certain medical bills if you are considered impoverished under Medicaid guidelines (note that Medicaid guidelines differ from regular poverty rules). With proper planning, you can preserve your assets and income and still be eligible for Medicaid. (See Chapter 14 for a complete explanation of Medicaid benefits and guidelines.)

Medicare

Medicare, the current federal health care insurance system used by most people over the age of 65, will pay for certain medical claims of qualified recipients. Usually, any person age 65 or older who is eligible for Social Security benefits is eligible for Medicare benefits.

How Do I Get My Medicare Card?

Medicare is administered by the Health Care Financing Administration (HCFA), which is an arm of the Department of Health and Human Services.

Three months prior to reaching age 65, you should go to your local Social Security Administration office and complete an application for Medicare and get some basic information. Within two or three months, you will be sent your Medicare card. Keep the card with you at all times and make a copy to put in your safe deposit box.

What Medical Expenses Does Medicare Cover?

Medicare is divided into two parts: Part A and Part B. Part A is free to everyone who is eligible for Medicare benefits. Part B is voluntary insurance coverage that you may decide to purchase. Normally, when you enroll in Medicare, you are automatically signed up for Part B. If you do not want Part B, you must instruct the office in writing to omit you from enrollment; otherwise, your Social Security check will automatically include a deduction to pay for Part B. This cost is currently $46.10 per month, and it rises every year.

Medicare Part A

Part A covers hospital-related claims. Although there are numerous deductibles, it will pay most costs of the first 60 days in a hospital (after the deductible). For the 61st to 90th days in a hospital, you pay $184 per day and they pay the rest. There is no coverage after the 90th day.

Nursing Home Care

Medicare may also pay for a portion of a skilled-care facility. Most people do not use such facilities, which only handle patients with the most severe ailments. Skilled-care is defined as round-the-clock supervision for persons requiring aid in handling routine daily activities such as eating, using bathroom facilities, or administering medication. Medicare will pay the amount over the first $89.50 per day, if you meet certain criteria: First of all, your stay must be followed by a minimum hospital stay of three days, and beginning within 30 days of leaving the hospital. Second, you must have been hospitalized for at least three days prior to entering the nursing home. Medicare pays 100 percent of the first 20 days. Then, for the next 80 days, you pay up to $92 per day and Medicare pays the remaining allowable charges. No benefits are available after 100 days.

Hospice Care

This service includes medical social services, home health care, counseling, and therapy. The bad news is that in order to qualify you must be terminally ill with a maximum life expectancy of six months. However, continuing services are provided to a survivor of the deceased. If your doctor or hospital does not offer you enough information about these services, I encourage you to call your local hospice and ask them to send you some information.

Home Health Care

This is another fairly good service offered by Medicare. If a doctor prescribes treatment for intermittent home health care, costs will be covered. However, the care must be part-time, which is defined as care up to six days per week for up to three consecutive weeks. Treatment cannot exceed a total of 35 hours per week.

Figure 18 on page 147 provides a breakdown of medical expenses covered by Medicare.

Medicare Part B

Part B is the optional portion of Medicare. In all fairness, it is a good plan for the price. Unless you have a supplement provided by your previous employer that costs you very little, do not hesitate to pay for Part B. Figure 19 on page 148 provides a breakdown of expenses covered under Part B.

Visits to a Doctor's Office

Although many services are excluded, Medicare Part B covers the following: surgery, consultation, diagnostic procedures that are part of your treatment, some medical supplies, medications, physical therapy, speech therapy, and speech pathology. Sometimes certain dental, psychiatric, and other medical specialties are also included.

Hospital Outpatient Services

Usually covered are costs billed to a hospital for outpatient X-rays, laboratory work, or emergency services.

Figure 18:
Medicare Part A

Service	Medicare Benefits	Your Cost
Hospitalization	Full cost after deductible is met (1st-60th day).	$764 per benefit period in 1998.
	Full cost after coinsurance (61st-90th day).	$190 per day coinsurance in 1997.
	$0 after 90th day.	$380 per day coinsurance in 1997.
	Or	
	$0 after 60 reserve days are used.	Full cost.
Post-hospital care in a certified skilled-nursing care facility (SNF)	100% of approved amounts for the first 20 days of care each benefit period after 3-day hospital stay.	$0
	Full cost after coinsurance (21st-100th day).	$95 per day coinsurance in 1998.
	$0 after 100th day.	Full cost.
Immediate and custodial nursing care	$0	Full cost.
Home health care	100% of approved amounts for Medicare-approved services.	$0
	80% of approved amount for durable medical equipment.	20% of approved amount in 1998.
Hospice	All but limited costs for outpatient drugs and inpatient respite care.	Limited cost-sharing for outpatient drugs and inpatient respite care.
Blood	Full cost after first 3 pints.	First 3 pints plus 20% of approved amount for additional pints (2).

Figure 19:
Medicare Part B

Service	Medicare Benefits	Your Cost
Physician and surgical services, medical supplies, diagnostic tests, durable medical equipment	80% of approved amounts exceeding the annual deductible of $100.	$100 each year; 20% of approved additional amounts charged by doctors who do not accept assignment; 100% non-Medicare approved charges.
Laboratory services: blood tests, biopsies, etc.	100% of approved amounts.	$0
Home health care	100% of approved amounts for Medicare-approved services (no deductible). 80% of approved amount for durable medical equipment (after deductible).	$0 20% of approved amount.
Outpatient hospital care	80% of approved amount (after deductible).	20% of approved amount.
Blood	80% of approved amount after first 3 pints.	First 3 pints plus 20% of approved amount for additional pints (2).

Approved Charges

It is extremely important to understand what is meant by *approved charges*. If a doctor charges you $200 for a service, but the Medicare-approved fee for that service is only $100, you must pay $20 for the first 20 percent deductible of the $100 that Medicare covers (assuming you've already met your $100 deductible), plus 100 percent of the $100 beyond the approved charge. Your total cost will be $120 for the $200 service.

To regulate approved charges, the HCFA recently initiated a five-year phase-in system. Prior to every January, the HCFA establishes fee schedules to which physicians must adhere for all services covered under Medicare. However, there is much room for individual interpretation because the formula for a "reasonable" fee schedule is complicated.

Although the new system supposedly addresses all questions regarding fees, inevitably there will be disputes and discrepancies regarding what is covered and the amount of coverage. You must learn how to properly contest a ruling when you feel you have been charged incorrectly. The rule of thumb is that a doctor who does not accept Medicare assistance cannot charge more than 15 percent of the approved charge.

How to File a Medicare Claim

To file a Medicare claim, submit a Medicare Payment Form, 1490S, which most authorized medical facilities, approved carriers, and Social Security offices provide. The instructions on the back of the form are fairly clear, but assistance is available for completing the form. For Part B claims, all bills must be submitted by your doctor or Medicare carrier without charge to you. The Medicare carrier will withhold the $100 deductible and pay 80 percent of the amount determined to be reasonable. It will be your responsibility to pay the difference, which will include 100 percent of the amount that was charged to you in excess of the "reasonable charge" that Medicare specifies. Usually, you reimburse your doctor only for the 20 percent deductible that Medicare does not pay (and the $100 annual deductible). Physicians are not permitted to charge a Medicare patient more than this 20 percent. However, as with any other business, some dishonest people will try to get away with charging you more money than they should, so be careful, know and demand your rights, and question everything!

Disputing a Medicare Payment Decision

In the event that Medicare refuses to pay for a particular medical expense, you are entitled to an itemized bill from Medicare that lists the services rendered, the health insurance claim number, a description of and charge for each service, and the name of the doctor who performed a particular service. You may always appeal a Medicare decision by contacting the carrier in your state or the local Social Security office. However, remember that you are dealing with a bureaucracy, so disputing a claim is usually a long and difficult process—but persistence will be rewarded. In addition, many states have peer review organizations that may be of service in these situations.

You are entitled to a review of a claim that is handled by a Medicare carrier if you request it in writing. Send your letter to the Social Security Administration and the Health Care Financial Administration to initiate the process. If you are not satisfied with the answer you receive to your written request, you can ask for a hearing with the Medicare carrier. You must submit the request for this hearing with the same agencies with which you filed your request for a review. Requests for reviews or hearings must be made within six months after receiving the initial determination or the review determination.

If you are also covered by an HMO or Medicare supplement group, you can legally appeal a decision. When you sign up to become a member of an HMO, you should be provided with a full packet of information explaining exactly how to initiate an appeal. Hang on to those papers, you may need them.

Medicare Supplements

If you are concerned about the cost of all the expenses that Medicare does not cover, you might consider purchasing a Medicare supplement insurance policy. These policies are designed to pay for medical expenses that Medicare does not cover.

Under the new rules of the National Association of Insurance Commissioners (NAIC), there are now 10 standard Medicare supplemental policies, identified by the letters A through J. While all states might not have every option available, the basic policy, Plan A, must be offered to Medicare recipients nationwide. When shopping for a supplement, you should look for the following.

1. **Coverage.** Know exactly what you are buying. A good policy will pay all the coinsurance amounts. For example, if Medicare covers 80 percent and you owe 20 percent, the supplement should pay the 20 percent. When a doctor bills you for more than the Medicare approved charge, the supplement should cover that amount. If Medicare will pay for home health care only on a part-time, intermittent basis up to three weeks, the supplement should provide coverage for six weeks. Another point before purchasing the supplement is to ask about any "preexisting condition" clauses. For example, if you had an operation on your back before signing up, will the policy you are planning to buy exclude any coverage for your back? If so, for how long?

2. **Quality of Carrier.** The quality of the carrier is one of the most important considerations in choosing a Medicare supplement. An A+ rating by AM Best is among the highest. Since you are paying the premiums, you want assurance that the company is going to be around for some years. You

also need a company that has a good name in the Medicare supplement arena. This does not necessarily mean a *big* name, but one that has proven to be excellent in paying most claims very promptly. A good question to ask an agent of your prospective insurance company is what percentage of claims are paid. While 100 percent is unrealistic, the higher the statistic, the better. I suggest visiting a library to research all the articles written about the carrier that you are contemplating using. This will give you an accurate, unbiased perspective of the pros and cons about that company, and what others said about it.

3. **Type of Filing.** Despite the fact that Social Security officials are attempting to simplify the filing of Medicare claims, the procedure is often cumbersome. However, some insurance companies that offer Medicare supplements now use an electronic filing system, which means you do not have to submit claims or send anything to anyone. Electronic filing offers expedience and convenience.

4. **Accessibility.** It is important to ascertain whether the carrier has good customer service. If a toll-free number is available, call the home office to ask a question before you buy the insurance. If you are transferred on the phone to more than three people or put on hold for more than three minutes, think carefully about whether you want that company handling your claims. You should also check to be sure that your doctor(s) is comfortable working with the company; if your doctor(s) has trouble dealing with the company, think twice.

5. **Cost.** You have probably heard the saying, "If you buy a diamond for a dime, it is probably worth a dime." I believe that the same is true about Medicare supplements. Two different policies that seem to offer identical coverage can have an almost 50-percent difference in price. But if you look closely you will surely find that the coverage really is very different. When purchasing insurance, first determine whether the premiums will rise as you get older, and by how much. Second, inquire whether your cost will increase if you have a claim as a result of an illness or accident, and by how much. Another good exercise is to confine your search to three carriers without looking at the price. Phone all three and request a "specimen policy." Be sure to read

each word-for-word and don't take seemingly irrelevant phrases for granted. This way, you will have a better idea of the best policy and how much it should cost.

Although supplements are wonderful, they can be expensive and confusing. Do the research in advance of reaching age 65 so as to avoid being forced into a rushed decision.

Standard Medicare Supplement Plans

Here are the 10 standard Medicare supplement plans and the benefits provided by each.

Plan A (the basic policy) consists of these core benefits:

- ♦ Coverage for the Part A coinsurance amount ($190 per day in 1997) for the 61st day through the 90th day of hospitalization in each Medicare benefit period.

- ♦ Coverage for the Part A coinsurance amount ($380 per day in 1997) for each of Medicare's 60 nonrenewable lifetime hospital inpatient reserve days used.

- ♦ After all Medicare hospital benefits are exhausted, coverage for 100 percent of the Medicare Part A eligible hospital expenses. Coverage is limited to a maximum of 365 days of additional inpatient hospital care during the policyholder's lifetime. This benefit is paid either at the rate Medicare pays hospitals under its prospective payment system or another appropriate standard of payment.

- ♦ Coverage under Medicare Parts A and B for the reasonable cost of the first three pints of blood or equivalent quantities of packed red blood cells per calendar year unless replaced in accordance with federal regulations.

- ♦ Coverage for the coinsurance amount for Part B series (generally 20 percent of approved amount) after $100 annual deductible is met.

Plan B includes core benefits plus:

- ♦ Coverage for the Medicare Part A inpatient hospital deductible ($760 per benefit period in 1997).

Plan C includes core benefits plus:

- ♦ Coverage for the Medicare Part A deductible.
- ♦ Coverage for the Medicare Part B deductible.

- Coverage for skilled-nursing facility care coinsurance amount ($95 per day for days 21 through 100 per benefit period in 1997).
- Coverage for medically necessary emergency care in a foreign country.

Plan D includes core benefits plus:

- Coverage for the Medicare Part A deductible.
- Coverage for the skilled-nursing facility care daily coinsurance amount.
- Coverage for medically necessary emergency care in a foreign country.
- Coverage for at-home recovery. This benefit pays up to $1,600 per year for short-term, at-home assistance with activities of daily living for those recovering from an illness, injury or surgery. There are various benefit requirements and limitations.

Plan E includes core benefits plus:

- Coverage for the Medicare Part A deductible.
- Coverage for the skilled-nursing facility care daily coinsurance amount.
- Coverage for medically necessary emergency care in a foreign country.
- Coverage for preventive medical care. This benefit pays up to $120 per year for preventive services, such as a physical examination, flu shot, serum cholesterol screening, hearing test, diabetes screenings, and thyroid function test.

Plan F includes core benefits plus:

- Coverage for the Medicare Part A deductible.
- Coverage for the Medicare Part B deductible.
- Coverage for the skilled-nursing facility care daily coinsurance amount.
- Coverage for medically necessary emergency care in a foreign country.
- Coverage for 100 percent of Medicare Part B excess charges.*

Plan G includes core benefits plus:

- Coverage for the Medicare Part A deductible.
- Coverage for the skilled-nursing facility care daily coinsurance amount.
- Coverage for 80 percent of Medicare Part B excess charges.*
- Coverage for medically necessary emergency care in a foreign country.
- Coverage for at-home recovery (see Plan D).

Plan H includes core benefits plus:

- Coverage for the Medicare Part A deductible.
- Coverage for the skilled-nursing facility care daily coinsurance amount.
- Coverage for medically necessary emergency care in a foreign country.
- Coverage for 50 percent of the cost of prescription drugs up to a maximum annual benefit of $1,250 after the policyholder meets a $250 annual deductible. (This is called the "basic" prescription drug benefit.)

Plan I includes core benefits plus:

- Coverage for the Medicare Part A deductible.
- Coverage for the skilled-nursing facility care daily coinsurance amount.
- Coverage for 100 percent of Medicare Part B excess charges.*
- Basic prescription drug coverage (see Plan H for description).
- Coverage for medically necessary emergency care in a foreign country.
- Coverage for medically necessary emergency care in a foreign country.
- Coverage for at-home recovery (see Plan D).

Plan J includes core benefits plus coverage for:

- The Medicare Part A deductible.
- The skilled-nursing facility care daily coinsurance amount.

- Medicare Part B deductible.
- 100 percent Medicare Part B excess charges.*
- Coverage for medically necessary emergency care in a foreign country.
- Preventive medical care (see Plan E).
- At-home recovery (see Plan D).
- 50 percent of the cost of prescription drugs up to a maximum annual benefit of $3,000 after the policyholder meets a $250 per year deductible. (This is called the "extended" prescription drug benefit.)

*Plan pays a specified percentage of the difference between Medicare's approved amount or Part B services and the actual charges (up to the amount of charge limitations set by either Medicare or state law).

Health Maintenance Organizations (HMOs)

As stated previously, supplements can be very costly. For this reason, many people elect to join health maintenance organizations (HMOs). HMOs provide an excellent alternative to the high costs of private supplements. The downside is that you have a limited number of doctors to choose from. If you don't mind this, you should consider HMOs as a viable option. When reviewing the various HMOs available, ask the same questions you would when examining Medicare supplements. Find out such information as costs and how they rise, coverage, the relationship to Medicare, and whether or not they pay for prescriptions. Further, determine the locations of their various physicians, urgent care, and emergency centers. Make sure specialists you might one day need to see are nearby.

Ask about their policy on second opinions. If you are going to have a major operation, it is simply prudent to have a second opinion. This particular policy could affect your decision to use that HMO.

Some of the best research is obtained by asking friends what their experience has been. When asking friends if they had a good experience with an HMO, be sure to ask friends who have already been ill. Questions you should ask include, Did you have to wait long? Were the doctors friendly? Was the receptionist helpful? and Are the costs reasonable?

One area of concern regarding HMOs involves provisions that limit the quality of care that many HMOs provide. One limitation is a gag order on doctors that prevents them from recommending procedures not covered by the HMO—even if the doctor feels it would benefit the patient.

How doctors are compensated is also important. Many HMOs will actually compensate doctors *more* for referring fewer patients to specialists.

Keep these things in mind, and read the HMO agreement carefully before signing it. Pay particularly close attention to what is covered and what is not. A tricky provision might be that there is no coverage for experimental medicine. At first, this might sound acceptable, but be aware that bone marrow treatment for cancer patients is still considered experimental by most HMOs. As with everything discussed in this book, I urge you to be cautious and do your homework.

Whether you decide to utilize a private Medicare supplement or a HMO, you will not be covered for every contingency. One of the biggest costs facing mature Americans is the enormous expense of long-term and home health care.

Nursing Homes

You may feel that you will never go into a nursing home, but you must still consider it a possibility. What if you have a stroke or get Alzheimer's and cannot make decisions? What if your spouse passes away? The number of people using some type of assisted living is astronomical, and a stay in a nursing home could turn a wealthy person into a pauper.

Usually even the best of Medicare supplements or HMOs do not pay for more than 100 days in a nursing home, and because so many coverage restrictions apply, many people are forced to pay nursing home care out of their own pockets.

When we speak of nursing homes, it is important to remember that several kinds exist. The three most common are skilled care, intermediate care, and custodial care.

Skilled Care

This provides 24-hour supervision; a registered nurse is always on duty to administer prescription drugs and help with everything. Ironically, this type of care has the best Medicare coverage but is the least used (by only 5 percent of seniors), as it is primarily for seniors with major incapacitating ailments, such as severe strokes.

Intermediate Care

This type of care is not for patients who require 24-hour supervision. However, these patients demand more care than someone needing postoperative assistance. About 4 to 5 percent of seniors use this service.

Custodial Care

This care is commonly used by seniors recovering from surgery or experiencing the early stages of Alzheimer's. In this case, help is provided for routine, daily activities. This is the service that is most used, but almost never covered by Medicare.

The costs of nursing home care are astounding: sometimes more than $150 per day, not including prescriptions or incidentals. It is estimated that half of the people who enter a nursing home face impoverishment within 13 weeks. If you need nursing home care, what will you do? It's a tough question.

A special Senate Committee on Aging report showed that the average person's health care costs break down as follows: 19 cents per dollar on Medicare-eligible claims and 81 cents per dollar on long-term care. Statistics confirm that the population is growing older, but they are not showing that it is growing healthier with age. Women tend to be the longest users of nursing home care.

Out of all the ingenious tricks that people have attempted in order to avoid the expense of a stay in a nursing home, three methods seem to make the most sense: Using a nursing home insurance plan, converting current life insurance into a special policy that will cover a nursing home stay, or finding a way to persuade Medicaid to pay.

Using a Long-Term Care Insurance Policy

I have no objection to someone using insurance to pay for a nursing home stay, if it is done properly. Too many consumers misunderstand the coverage, and by the time they need it, it is too late to correct the mistakes. Another problem is that the coverage can become quite expensive. It is not typically too costly until you reach your mid-60s or early 70s, but then, watch out! If you plan to purchase this coverage, I urge you to purchase it while you are as young as possible and still eligible.

To analyze long-term care insurance properly, call at least three companies and ask for sample policies. After receiving these, accurately research the points outlined below. Don't talk to an agent until you have narrowed down your options and assessed the coverage; otherwise, it is likely you will merely become confused.

The following items should be included in long-term health care insurance policy benefits:

- ♦ The policy pays the costs of an average stay in a nursing home.
- ♦ The coverage carries an inflation rider.
- ♦ The policy permits payments to any type of care facility, including skilled, intermediate, and custodial.

- Restrictions are minimal. You do not need to go directly from a hospital or to have a doctor's prescription for entering a nursing home. Also, be sure that you can use this facility for physical and mental conditions, such as senility and Alzheimer's disease.

- Provisions for home health care insurance are available.

- The insurance starts paying on the first day of entering a nursing home. In addition, know whether your coverage pays for a set number of years or for your lifetime.

- The cost of the premium stops within a certain amount of time after entering the care facility.

- It covers preexisting conditions. If, for example, you had a back operation two years prior to buying this insurance, will coverage be provided for going into a nursing home because you are recovering from a back operation? A good policy would not increase your premium just because you become older and entered a nursing home.

Once you have these facts, compare costs. Phone the companies that interest you to discover how easy it is to get through and whether employees are courteous and helpful. Ask some pertinent questions, such as, What percentage of claims do you actually pay? and What is your insurance company rating? The latter is especially relevant as you may be relying upon payments many years in the future. You want assurance that the carrier will be around. Also, request a history showing premium increases. This will give you an idea of what premium increases to expect in the future.

Converting a Current Life Insurance Policy

As previously mentioned, the number of people using care is growing dramatically, and the costs are growing just as dramatically. Many creative insurance companies have come up with a possible solution: Convert an existing life insurance policy to a special one that will cover the cost of nursing home care when you need it. This makes sense. You currently have an old insurance policy (or policies), with a certain amount of cash value. You are at the point where you (or your spouse or beneficiaries) do not need the death benefit. Certain companies will transfer your cash value through a tax-free exchange into a new insurance policy that is designed to pay a certain amount of the death benefit to a nursing home, should you need the care. If not, the death benefit would go to your spouse or beneficiaries as planned.

Obviously, this conversion could be tricky and may or may not be practical in your case. It is possible that the restrictions on actual coverage for a nursing home claim would be too numerous, or that the death benefit might be diminished too significantly. However, the benefits with an appropriate policy could be very rewarding.

Have Medicaid Foot the Bill

The last option that might pay for a nursing home stay is Medicaid. The good news is that Medicaid will pay for a nursing home stay if you qualify. The bad news is that you may have to be broke to qualify. Chapter 14 will explain this massive government health plan.

Chapter 14

Getting the Most from Medicaid

Medicaid is a federal- and state-funded health insurance program for people who need financial assistance for medical purposes. Although requirements and names vary from state to state (for example, in California, Medicaid is called Medi-Cal), they are still part of the Medicaid system, controlled by the Health Care Financing Administration (HCFA).

Scenario

Mrs. Smith, a widow, was sick and needed care in a nursing home. Mrs. Smith's estate consisted of a home worth about $80,000 and a savings account with $15,000 in it. She gave her son power of attorney to manage her affairs.

The goal was to admit Mrs. Smith into a nursing home as a private pay resident, and then subsequently divest her of her assets in order to have Medicaid cover the nursing home costs. To do so, the son transferred the $15,000 and his mother's home to himself. After nine months in the nursing home as a private payor, the son applied for Medicaid on his mother's behalf. In the application, it asked if any gifts were made within three years. The son forgot to mention the gift (as it properly was, because the asset was not transferred for fair market value). However, Medicaid discovered that gifts were made and the Medicaid application was denied. Having no assets in her name, the mother faced discharge from the nursing home due to nonpayment.

This, unfortunately, is not an unusual occurrence. In fact, similar cases have actually gone to hearings and appeals and the people were still denied Medicaid. People try to plan without proper knowledge or any expert advice. What follows is a cursory overview of the Medicaid system and some planning ideas. The planning tools and techniques are changing daily with new opinions, court cases, and legislation, so use the following as a generic guideline, not as your only resource. If you have a specific problem, consult a specialist in your area.

In discussing the costs of long-term care, Medicaid is an extremely important part of the discussion. As you may know, most people age 65 or older, regardless of their financial situation, will receive Medicare benefits. Medicaid is not Medicare; it is a public benefit program supported by federal and state taxes designed to pay for certain medical costs when an individual does not have the financial resources.

Nursing home costs range from an average of $40,000 to more than $100,000 per year. How many people do you know who can afford $100,000 per year for long-term care for a sick spouse, and still afford to maintain the standard of living for the well spouse? Probably not many. Medicaid pays for about half the people in nursing homes today. That may sound reassuring, except for one thing: *Most people on Medicaid are broke.* You will have to spend most of your money before you can receive any assistance from Medicaid.

Should you plan to receive Medicaid benefits or not? This is a decision you must make when creating your "elder-care" plan. Many people do not *want* to qualify for Medicaid. They view it as being on welfare, and most people do not want to accept this. In addition, there are concerns about whether the quality of care is different if you are a private payor or a Medicaid recipient.

While, the vast majority of middle-class retirees have a good amount of money saved, should any unexpected expenses arise, such as long-term care, even middle-class retirees may well be broke within a year.

Before figuring out how to protect your assets, you must have a fairly strong knowledge of the Medicaid system. This chapter is simply an overview; specific questions should be directed to Medicaid specialists (probably Medicaid or elder-care attorneys) in your area. All states (and most counties) have different rules pertaining to Medicaid. You must know these rules as well as how your state interprets the federal laws.

The Omnibus Reconciliation Act of 1993

The *Omnibus Reconciliation Act of 1993 (OBRA 93)* severely changed rules for Medicaid and how people plan for Medicaid. Four main areas of the law were affected:

1. The look-back rule.
2. Exempt assets.
3. Qualifying trusts.
4. Joint tenancy.

The Look-Back Rule

You just can't give away all your assets the day before applying for Medicaid. There are time restraints within which you can give away money. This is what is known as the *look-back rule.*

Prior to OBRA 93, the look-back period was 30 months; any gift transfer of resources—be it cash, securities, real estate, etc.—by an applicant (or his or her spouse) during the 30 month period preceding application incuffed a period of ineligibility for nursing home benefits. Now this look-back period is 36 months (three years) for assets transferred from an individual to another individual. If you are transferring assets from or to a trust (including revocable living trusts), the look-back period could be 60 months (five years). As under prior law, the period runs back from the date the applicant is both institutionalized and has applied for Medicaid. If the applicant is not institutionalized when applying, the look-back period runs back from the date of the Medicaid application.

Exempt Assets and Qualifying Trusts

An exempt asset is one that Medicaid does not include into the amount of assets allowed, and which you can keep even after applying for and receiving Medicaid. OBRA 93 clarified that exempt assets do exist in determining Medicaid eligibility; however, the exempt assets are not exempt for estate recovery purposes. This means that after someone dies, formerly exempt assets (such as homes) can be liened in order to collect reimbursement for benefits that the agency had provided to a recipient during a recipient's lifetime. In fact, states have now been instructed to aggressively recover and lien property that was considered an exempt asset (such as a personal residence) after a Medicaid recipient dies. Here are some examples of exempt assets:

- ♦ **Your personal residence.** A married couple owning a home will not have to include their residence in the Medicaid asset limitations, and most states do not stipulate the size or dollar value of the home. However, usually one spouse must still be living in the house to use it as an exempt asset. In addition, home furnishings, home improvements, and collectibles are usually exempt.

- **One car, usually of any dollar value.**

- **Jewelry in certain amounts.** Usually this includes a wedding or engagement ring, etc.

- **$1,500 cash value of a permanent insurance policy.** (However, you can have any amount of term insurance.)

- **Burial plot, usually at a $1,500 maximum value.**

- **Certain types of irrevocable trusts.** If structured correctly and in the proper time frame, the principal could be exempt in certain types of irrevocable trust. A simple rule of thumb is, if you have no access to or control of the money, you have an argument that Medicaid should not be able to access your money either. (See the section "Trusts for Medicaid Planning" in this chapter for further explanation.) Most trusts would probably have to be set up prior to applying for Medicaid and the duties of the trustee must already be predetermined and remain unchanged. In creating trusts, I urge you to be familiar with all the new law changes, and how your state has determined certain rulings.

- **Assets given away in the proper time frame.** If you gave away assets prior to the beginning of the look-back period, Medicaid cannot recapture the assets.

- **Properly structured annuities and private pension plans.** In the past, annuities have been a widely accepted planning tool for protecting assets. OBRA 93 severely restricted the use of annuities, as well as many other planning options. OBRA 93 has closed certain techniques, paving the way for new planning strategies. The passing of the Kennedy-Kassenbaum bill restricted planning for Medicaid even further. The bill attempted to make it a crime for an individual to try and protect assets from Medicaid. It was so ludicrous in its nature that the bill was renamed "Grandmother goes to Jail." After public outcry, the bill was amended. It now has made it a crime for an advisor to recommend planning in an effort to protect assets from Medicaid.

  In any event, the use of annuities has been restricted. An annuity is just a general name for a huge category of options. There are good and bad ones, safe and risky ones. If you wish, you can even create your own. The fact is, properly structured, an annuity may still be a prudent way to protect your assets.

Now that you know the general areas of protected assets, you can determine how to use these exemptions to your benefit.

Joint Tenancy

Congress went overboard in an attempt to foil abuses of joint tenancies. The new rules provide that any assets held in joint tenancy or "similar arrangement" will be treated as having been transferred if either the applicant or any other person takes any action that reduces or eliminates such individual's ownership or control. In other words, if a daughter removes money from a joint bank account she holds with her mother, a disqualifying transfer seems likely to arise for the mother—even if the funds clearly belong to the daughter. This rule is likely to trap many more applicants than intended and its constitutionality will probably be disputed.

Qualifying for Medicaid

The two factors determining qualification are *household income* and *assets*. Technically, to qualify for Medicaid, individuals must be impoverished. In 1989, the Spousal Impoverishment Act was passed. This federal act set the guidelines that limit the total income and assets of Medicaid recipients in care facilities and the assets and income of their spouses. The act allowed for spouses of Medicaid recipients to retain or exempt certain assets in Medicaid's determination of eligibility.

The act set forth a range of assets and each state has subsequently chosen an amount in that range for its guidelines.

Is My State an Income or Benefit State?

For Medicaid purposes, you are either in an *income state* or a *benefit state*. More and more states are becoming income states, which do not allow residents to receive Medicaid for any reason if their income is over the set limit. A benefit state (also known as a "medically needy" state) usually follows the same guidelines, with one major exception: If your income is over the limit amount, but less than the average cost of nursing homes in your area, they will still consider you for Medicaid eligibility. Also, in benefit states you can "spend down" your money for medical needs, and thereby lower your available income—which will help bring you closer to allowable limits for Medicaid.

To get a current list of income states and benefit states, contact your local Agency for the Aging, Social Security office, welfare office, or an eldercare attorney.

Income Test

As of 1998, most states capped the well spouse's income to be eligible for Medicaid. Although the numbers vary from state to state, California's cap is just over $2,000 per month. There will be an index for inflation on a yearly basis for these income levels. For single individuals, the income allowed for the Medicaid beneficiary is almost nothing—basically enough for a few incidentals.

Remember, if you live in a benefit state you can usually petition to be allowed income over the set limit for viable reasons, and if you plan ahead, you might be able to get your income low enough—and keep it low enough—to qualify for Medicaid.

The following are some suggestions to help you get the assistance you need from Medicaid.

1. Take Social Security at 62 years of age to get the lower amount.
2. When you retire, take a lump sum instead of a guaranteed income option.
3. Use investment vehicles in which you can control income or that do not have any income.
4. Move to a benefit state where the cost of nursing homes is higher than your income.
5. Look into special trusts that limit your income (see pages 172 to 176 for more on this topic).
6. If you have caregivers who are family members and are not being paid, pay them. It is not a gift if your caregivers are charging you fair wages for the services they are providing, such as running errands, and preparing meals for you.
7. Petition Medicaid to request more income than what the "monthly maintenance allowance" or "spousal allowance" is. Sometimes it is possible to show that the monthly maintenance allowance is insufficient to maintain one's basic needs.
8. If you are married, make an effort to have all of your income paid to the well spouse, because in certain counties, if the income is in the well spouse's name, the well spouse can refuse the community spouse resource allowance (CSRA), and keep his or her own income.

Asset Test

The second test you must pass to qualify for Medicaid is the *asset test*. The Spousal Impoverishment Act of 1989 changed most of the guidelines regarding assets and Medicaid eligibility. The numbers vary from state to state, but a certain amount of assets can be maintained by married couples. You are allowed certain exempt assets and a specific amount of nonexempt assets. The CSRA—the nonexempt asset that is allowed to be kept by the well spouse—starts at a minimum of roughly $15,000 for a married couple, with a maximum of $80,000 for married couples in some states. These amounts increase each year. Although the rules vary, a good rule of thumb for figuring out how much you can have is to take all of your nonexempt assets (cash stocks, real estate, bank accounts, etc.) and divide the assets by two (one spouse's half of the assets). Either you get whatever the number turns out to be or the maximum of allowed by your state.

How to Increase Your Eligibility for Medicaid

You can increase your eligibility for Medicaid by reducing your exposure to nonexempt assets. To accomplish this, follow these guidelines.

- ♦ **Give away money three years before applying for Medicaid.** If you are worried that you may one day have problems and need nursing home services, give away your money. Instead of staggering out the gifts, however, consider just making a one-time gift. The longer you drag it out, the greater your chances of not beating the look-back period. If you are worried about giving outright gifts, make the gift into special entities, such as trusts or other planning vehicles. Be careful though—if you have access and have *discretion*, or any incidence of ownership of the funds after you make a gift, then there is a good chance that Medicaid can deem the proceeds available to you. The point is, if you do use a trust, do it right, so the transaction does not haunt you later.

- ♦ **Pay off your home if you still have a mortgage on it.** If the house is protected, why have unprotected cash in areas outside the house? If you pay off the mortgage, the money will be sheltered.

  For that matter, some experts actually recommend purchasing a newer, bigger house. Remember, regardless of the size of the house, it is a protected asset. If you need to make home improvements, or need to buy new furnishings or jewelry (within limitations), these assets would also be exempt from Medicaid. Be careful of the liens that are put on property after death.

◆ **Buy a new car.** If you are allowed one car, make sure you have a valuable new car, that can also be used for medical purposes (such as driving to the hospital and carrying a wheelchair).

◆ **Pay off debt.**

◆ **If your income is too high and you live in a benefit state, petition Medicaid.** If your income is over the limit set by your state, and you live in a benefit state, petition Medicaid and ask for a higher income allowance. Of course, you will have to prove that you need the extra income and anything less will cause you undue hardship.

◆ **Transfer ownership of insurance.** Even if there is no immediate Medicaid threat, there might be many reasons why someone should not own the policy by which they are insured. Of course, this should be done prior to the beginning of the look-back period. One caveat is that there could be gifting problems and gift taxes on the amount of cash value that is transferred. Study this option to do it right should you decide to do it.

◆ **Make sure your caregivers are being paid.** As mentioned previously, consider paying your caregiver for work he or she does for you (even if it is a son or daughter who expects no compensation). However, it is important to pay a caregiver long before you need to apply for Medicaid. If you never paid your caregiver before applying for Medicaid, starting payment after you apply may be looked upon as an attempt to defraud Medicaid and the payments may be disallowed in determining your eligibility.

◆ **Protect your liquid cash and investments.** If annuities such as private pension plans, private annuities, personal annuities, and tax-deferred savings plans are still a viable planning option in your state, consider this tool.

◆ **Utilize the proper trusts for your situation, in the proper time frame, to protect your assets.**

Is Divorce an Option?

You have heard tragedies about couples divorcing to become eligible for Medicaid. Sadly, these couples may actually be divorcing so as not to go broke. Unfortunately, it doesn't always work.

Scenario

Thelma and Harry have been married for 40 years. Harry develops Alzheimer's. Thelma figures the cost of care is going to be in the hundreds of thousands of dollars over the next several years. She knows she will go broke. In an attempt to avoid this, she files for divorce.

Do you think a judge will award Thelma 100 percent of the estate? Harry is incapacitated and the judge does not know exactly what Harry wants.

If divorce is an option, consider the ramifications in advance and plan carefully. Follow these guidelines.

1. Try and initiate the divorce before the sick spouse is incapacitated.

2. Have a good reason for divorce other than to protect from Medicaid restrictions.

3. The sick spouse should transfer all the assets—or possibly all the "nonexempt" assets—to the well spouse's name and explain that he or she wants the other spouse to have all the assets if there is a divorce. Obviously, you should not say to the judge, "Hey, give her the stocks, but I'll to keep the car because it's an exempt asset."

Even using those straightforward guidelines (among others), the judge still might not give all the assets to one spouse. So, although divorce may be an option, it is not always a viable one.

Using Annuities to Protect Your Assets

The way annuities have worked historically was that you put a sum of money into the annuity, then, at a later date, the annuity would "annuitize,"—pay you a guaranteed income for a set number of years or a lifetime. The good news was that the income was guaranteed. The bad news was that you no longer had access to your principal. This is how many pension plans work: You choose to take either the lump sum or take the income.

The benefit of an annuity in regards to Medicaid is that, properly structured, it turns an asset into income. If you deposited $100,000 into an annuity, and annuitized it, it will pay you income in your retirement. Technically, it is not an asset, which means that Medicaid cannot include it in your net worth. However, Medicaid can figure it as income, and if it is more than the Medicaid limit, it could be the Achilles' heal of this strategy.

A properly structured annuity has intrinsic advantages, including:

1. **All assets inside the annuity grow tax-deferred.** This is a big consideration for people who switch mutual funds often and pay capital gains, for people who continually roll-over certificates of deposit (CDs) and pay the tax on income every year, and for people who invest in tax-free bonds and bond funds but do not need the income.

2. **All income deferred inside the annuity is not figured into your gross income at the end of the year, and your 1099 tax statement will show no income.** The benefit is that your taxable income will not be increased by the amount made inside the annuity, thus helping you stay below the income limitation on the taxation of your Social Security. Remember that although municipal bond interest is tax-free, it is still included in gross income for Social Security purposes.

3. **You do not have to give up access to your income or principal while you are healthy.**

4. **You can create these annuities in a favorable way to choose where you want the investments directed.** You can select mutual funds, government bond pools, or CD-type insured accounts (insured usually by the company, or assets the company has in, not the FDIC).

5. **You can use the annuity to create an exempt asset for Medicaid purposes**—in certain situations, in certain areas, if it is implemented correctly, and if the law is not changed. This means that it is possible that you could keep your money, yet qualify for Medicaid. Remember that creating an annuity and transferring your assets into it will not make the assets exempt. How annuities are structured determines whether the assets are exempt.

Certain rules and guidelines for exempting assets and protecting assets must be followed. If you are using an annuity, you must create one containing all the proper provisions and wording. If you use a prototype annuity, be sure the company issuing the contract allows you to put in the provisions needed to help with Medicaid protection.

Say you create an annuity with your and your spouse's names on the contract, and make one of your children the beneficiary. You then choose mutual funds, or fixed interest rate bonds to invest inside the annuity. You carry on as usual, switching funds, taking income, reinvesting. If one spouse dies, the funds will not go through probate, so the surviving spouse can keep the account active or liquidate it and take the funds. Note that once an annuity is created, it is very similar to an IRA. If you make withdrawals prior to reaching 59½ years of age, you will have to pay IRS penalties. In addition, some annuities have other penalties.

Again, let's assume you have this annuity, and one spouse gets sick and you are considering applying for Medicaid. It is at this point that you invoke the provisions already established when you created your personal annuity. The first of these would be the *spousal transfer,* under which you can transfer assets without disqualification under the three-year look-back rule. So, immediately make sure the annuity is in the healthy spouse's name, preferably as the owner and annuitant. In addition, the beneficiary must not be the sick spouse.

Next, you must invoke certain provisions that should have already been established when you created your annuity. You must begin a periodic payment stream of both principal and interest for a set number of years. This is known as "annuitizing." Compute what the least amount of income and principal is that you can take to remain below the income limitations for Medicaid. The HCFA has mandated that annuities must be actuarially sound (based on the owner's mortality table), so the provisions might be tough. Basically, you do not have to pay yourself all that your annuity earns, because you want to lower your income when applying for Medicaid. This is where the loophole is. I don't think Medicaid anticipated that seniors would create their own personal annuities with the ability of implementing these provisions.

Some annuity companies will not allow you to pay yourself whatever interest or principal you want. Many will base the payoff on mortality tables depending on your age and how long you want to receive the income. The longer the payout period, the lower the income, which is helpful when you're trying to meet Medicaid eligibility requirements.

Even if you choose the longest payout option and get the lowest interest rate, many companies will allow you to change your mind (called the *bailout provision)* after a certain number of years. You can then withdraw whatever is left of your account. In many income cap states, an annuity payout will boost you up over the income cap, thereby disqualifying you for Medicaid.

While on Medicaid, your annuity is making minimal payments to you of principal and interest, you have no access to principal, and it has a set number of years for payments. The major difference is that when you created the annuity you implemented provisions so that after a specified period (say five years), the income and principal payments stop, the cash becomes available again and is paid to either the healthy spouse or the beneficiaries, or the income simply continues for your beneficiaries to enjoy.

Remember, not all custodians allow you to break an annuity, so make sure the custodian you use to create your annuity allows you to stop the annuity once you have begun the periodic principal and income stream.

When creating an annuity, consider not making either spouse the beneficiary to prevent Medicaid from making a claim on the asset should one spouse receive the money after the other spouse's passing. Further, consider placing someone else's name on the annuity as annuitant. The best strategy is to do this well before the look-back period so that it won't be considered a gift subject to the look-back rule. There are advantages to using someone else as annuitant. First, it is an excellent way to transfer income to the annuitant. Second, you might be able to reduce the amount of income by combining your mortality with that of the annuitant. If the annuitant is younger than you, the income will be lower, helping once again to reduce your income for Medicaid eligibility purposes.

It is also possible to make the owner of the annuity your living trust. Most living trusts have provisions that state that if someone is going to apply for Medicaid benefits, that person is no longer trustee of the trust and loses all access to the assets in the trust, including the annuity. Although this loophole might still exist in many Medicaid areas, based on OBRA 93, this is something that will be carefully scrutinized, because if there is an asset, even in a trust, it is deemed available for Medicaid purposes and the trustee at the time has to pay it off. Thus, it probably would not help to make the trust the owner of the annuity; in the case of a married couple, it would probably be better to make a well spouse the owner.

Note: This strategy is very complex and should be thoroughly discussed with an expert in this area before taking action.

What Are the Costs of Annuities?

If you understand investments, you can implement an annuity without a broker commission or load fee. Some annuities have maintenance charges or early-withdrawal fees. Some have no fees and work very much like a CD.

To save money on setup fees, you should consult an expert either in elder-care law or Medicaid planning. Ask for the expert's credentials and references. I have heard of experts charging more than $1,000 for this service, though some will include it as part of a complete estate plan or living trust package.

Watch out for *surrender* and *mortality and expense* charges. It may be a good idea to compare these among various annuities. Make sure you understand all the good and bad points. Also, understand that laws can change at any time, causing loopholes to close. Whoever creates this plan for you should use the highest quality custodians, making sure that some type of insurance from a very reputable carrier backs up the deposit.

Trusts for Medicaid Planning

Planning for Medicaid eligibility by using trusts is incredibly tricky and confusing. However, there are viable trusts that might make sense in the right circumstances, in the right time frame, for the right person, and in the right state. (Is it starting to become clear that there are many restrictions?) As with any specific question about a particular situation, see a specialist who is familiar with the laws of your region.

After OBRA 93, many of the more popular types of trusts became invalid, such as the *Medicaid qualifying trust*. The new rules created a great deal of confusion, and there is not a great deal of case law to help clarify the issues. Even elder-care attorneys might disagree about which types of trusts will work. These changes, and lack of court precedence, make it too new of an area to deem any one device, tool, or technique a surefire way to protect assets. The bottom line is that elder-care planning is not an exact science. Consult a specialist in your area.

Trusts that Will Not Protect Your Assets from Medicaid

The following are a few examples of trusts that people have used under various circumstances to help shelter assets in order to apply for Medicaid. But just because a creative attorney engineered an innovative trust, it does not mean the trust will be deemed valid by a court of law.

Revocable Living Trusts

Some individuals tout revocable living trusts as a Medicaid protecting strategy. These are trusts that can be amended, and over which the trustor has full discretion. These trusts serve numerous purposes, from probate planning to estate-tax planning. What they do *not* do is protect your assets from Medicaid. If someone recommends the use of a revocable living trust for Medicaid planning, be very skeptical.

Medicaid Qualifying Trusts

OBRA 93 rendered these trusts invalid. Now, Medicaid qualifying trusts actually *disqualify* you from Medicaid eligibility. This is because if you nominate yourself as beneficiary of a trust that you create, the proceeds will be deemed available to you if the trustee (regardless of who it is) has the authority to distribute assets from the trust, whether or not such assets are actually distributed.

The goal of these trusts was to create an irrevocable entity and transfer assets to it. The creators of the trust would also make themselves the beneficiaries. The trustee would usually be one of the children. The creators of the trust would tell the trustee to give them money (either income or principal) whenever they chose. If one of the trust creators gets sick, the trustee would use the trustee powers to give the creators nothing. This was a way to show Medicaid that the creators or persons applying for Medicaid had no money because it was transferred to an irrevocable trust of which they were not trustee, and to which they did not have access to principal or income.

Although this kind of trust can no longer be used, it is still important to be aware of it. Many people created these trusts in the past, and some so-called elder-care planners are still creating them. If you have one of these trusts, be aware that they were not *grandfathered*—meaning this kind of trust will not enable you to qualify for Medicaid regardless of when you established it.

Income-Only Trusts

After Medicaid came up with the law banning Medicaid qualifying trusts, attorneys began drafting new trusts to get around this. They created trusts similar to a Medicaid qualifying trust; however, they would limit the trustee's powers. For example, the trust would not give the trustee the discretion to distribute principal-only income. This was a way to make sure the principal would be sheltered and only have the income attachable to Medicaid. These types of trusts were commonly named income-only trusts. Instead of this strategy, consider looking into the Miller Trusts (discussed on page 175).

Special (or Supplemental) Needs Trusts and Support Trusts

Prior to OBRA 93, many types of trusts were used in Medicaid planning, in particular *special needs trusts* and *support trusts*. A special needs trust was designed to give the beneficiary of the trust (usually also the Medicaid recipient), certain benefits for select items. This might include dental work, grooming, etc.

These trusts are also instrumental in creating a trust for a disabled child and to hold assets for a child (or any loved one) who is on public benefits and does not want to be disqualified from these benefits.

Support trusts are designed to actually support an individual by paying for housing and other necessities. Prior to OBRA 93 these trusts were most widely used. After OBRA 93, use of these trusts has become much more restrictive. Medicaid has stipulated how and which trusts can be used. The interpretation of Medicaid's guidelines is still vague and there is not a great deal of case law that exists yet, but it seems that it is easier to establish a special needs trust than a support trust.

Although OBRA 93 has made Medicaid planning restrictive, it did outline three exceptions that allow specific trusts to work so as not to disqualify individuals from Medicaid eligibility. These trusts are *(d)-4A, (d)-4B, and (d)-4C Trusts.*

OBRA (d)-4A Exemption Trusts

If you use this trust properly, it could be a viable planning tool. In general, to create a (d)-4A trust the following requirements must be met.

1. You must be under age 65.
2. You must be disabled—as outlined in the Social Security Administration's definition of disability.
3. The trust must be created by a child, parent/guardian, or court. You could literally create one of these trusts the day before applying for Medicaid.

In terms of who creates the trust, often the parents are deceased so this is not a viable option. Many times, you should actually go to court and ask the court to create the trust for you.

Once everyone agrees that the trust can be created, assets are funneled into it (remember the look-back period does not apply). Now, more confusion sets in. Let's assume your son is the trustee. What is your son allowed to do? Is this a support trust or supplemental needs trust? Again, as this is so new, that is a hard question to answer. Basically, what we are asking is: What is the standard of distribution; how can the trustee distribute assets? Many Medicaid experts feel supplemental needs are too restrictive. However, if it is a true support trust, you will probably have too much income for Medicaid eligibility.

This type of trust is probably what is know as a *discretionary trust,* meaning the trustee has the discretion of when and how assets are distributed. If too much money is distributed in any one month, then you may lose public benefits for that month, but that's all. The catch to this trust is that your state has a claim on your trust and will recapture money they spent on your care after you die.

My question is, what exactly can the trustee do? Can the trustee try and constructively spend the trust down to nothing? Will the court have a claim at that point? Be very careful when creating these trusts. Look at the state rules. I have heard that some states are limiting what you can put into these trusts. Some states have outlined that you can only put proceeds from personal injury lawsuits under this trust.

OBRA (d)-4B Exemption Trust (also known as Miller Trusts and Utah Gap)

This trust is designed for those who are domiciled in income cap states—states that have established an income cap on the amount that a well spouse in a community could receive and still be eligible for Medicaid.

Many people have no assets, but do have income. The concept of this trust is that it is wrong to deny individuals Medicaid if they have no assets but have an amount of income over the Medicaid eligibility. A case went to court over this issue and the court agreed that Medicaid applicants who do have income in excess of the state income cap should qualify for benefits as long as they meet certain criteria

The first two criteria are relatively simple: First, the beneficiary (of the income) must be the Medicaid applicant. Second, all of income from the individual's income, from all sources, must be paid to the trust.

The next criteria involve the *standard of distribution*—or how the assets can be distributed. First, the trustee of the trust is allowed to distribute income to the beneficiary (the Medicaid applicant) a monthly income that is at least one dollar less than the state cap (thus qualifying for Medicaid under the income guidelines). The second rule states that after the Medicaid recipient dies, the remaining assets in the trust are to be paid to the state. So, although the trust states income is to be paid to the Medicaid recipient, can the trust do anything else with it? Can the trust give away money to other individuals or hire workers or family members for work related to the Medicaid recipient? Can excess income be used to pay for grooming, gifts, etc.? Most states don't allow it to be used for anything; the state gets it. Other states allow its use for supplemental needs.

OBRA (d)-4C Exemption Trusts: Irrevocable Trusts

This trust is much different from the (d)-4B, and (d)-4A trust. The general guidelines for creating this trust include:

1. You can be any age.
2. You do not need to be disabled.
3. Assets have to be given to a "pooled income trust."
4. Must be established by parents, grandparents, guardian, or court.

Think of a pooled income trust as a mutual fund that is set up by a nonprofit agency as a "master trust." You put your assets into this *pooled income fund* sponsored by a nonprofit agency. Your money is then commingled with other individuals' money, and assets are purchased. It's likely that the reason Medicaid allows this is that the assets left over after a person dies go back into programs to help other people, or benefits Medicaid in some way.

The key in determining whether an exemption trust will protect your assets from Medicaid is the discretion that you as creator of the trust and the trustee have. If you create a trust prior to the five-year look-back rule for trusts and give away assets to the trust, the assets could be sheltered from Medicaid. If the trust is worded in such a way that you have no access to the money, the trustee cannot have the *discretion* to give you money, you cannot influence the trustee, and you have no ties to the assets or the trust, then the assets would probably be protected. The tricky part, as I am sure you are beginning to realize, is to set up trusts that still allow you some benefit.

Medicaid Planning for an Unmarried Person

Medicaid planning for a single individual is even harder than it is for a married couple. The primary reason is that married couples have the community spouse resource allowance (CSRA), by which the well spouse can be given a certain amount of assets that are exempt from Medicaid. The other difficulties in planning for Medicaid as a single person include:

1. You cannot take advantage of spousal transfers.
2. A home might have a lien placed on it after the Medicaid recipient dies.
3. The income and asset allowance for a single people is almost nonexistent.

The reason a home is a protected asset is because one spouse (or tenant) is living in the home. However, if there is not another tenant in the home, the house would usually not be a protected asset and might be liened upon the single tenant's death.

To get around this problem, these popular tactics are often used:

♦ **If a home is liened, fight the lien.** An interesting series of events transpired in California when the state liened several homes. Upon the death of the surviving spouses the state sought to collect money it had spent on Medicaid benefits. A class action lawsuit was subsequently filed charging that the State of California did not follow the proper channels of a lien process.

   The court ruled for the homeowners (or their survivors) mostly because the State of California had not followed proper procedure. The moral of this story is that if a home is liened, fight it on a technicality.

- ◆ **Give away money three years before applying for Medicaid.** Medicaid has no business asking you what you did with your money as long as it was transferred prior to the look-back period, so give some away. There are wonderful ways to give money. For example, you could create a trust for your personal residence that could allow you to continue living in the home but not own it, you could get charities involved in certain trusts, or own trusts in another country.

- ◆ **Get a letter of intent.** You can still protect your home with a doctor's help. If you can get your doctor to sign a Letter of Intent stating that your stay in a nursing home is temporary and that you should be able to move back home in a short time (usually within six months), then the house would be protected.

- ◆ **Create a life estate.** In a life estate, you sign the deed over to your children (or other beneficiaries), and as long as you are living, the children have no right or access to the home. Upon your death, the home would go to the children. Then, if you were to apply for Medicaid, your home is protected because, technically, it is not yours; and upon your death, Medicaid cannot place a lien on the property because the home is not owned by you. Seek counsel before employing this option, and be aware of disadvantages. (See Chapter 10 for more on this subject.)

- ◆ **Create a trust.** Research the trusts that are allowed for Medicaid under OBRA 93. The rules, although still subject to interpretation, offer some relief by using trusts. The biggest concern would be whether Medicaid may capture the assets inside the trust after the Medicaid beneficiary dies. (See Chapter 9 for more on trusts.)

- ◆ **Create an annuity.** Research annuities. The income limitation is very low for single individuals. But a properly structured annuity might work. Invoke all the provisions discussed earlier but make someone else the annuitant. By nominating someone else the annuitant, you are allowing them to be the recipient of all the income, thus ensuring that your income will not be increased. In addition, you might be able to lower the income by combining your mortality, as the owner, with that of the annuitant. One concern with this strategy is that by placing someone else's name on as annuitant, although you are still owner, it might be viewed by Medicaid as a gift and subject to the look-back rule. You might consider creating an annuity and placing someone else's name as annuitant long before you foresee a need for Medicaid.

You will also have to nominate someone else as the beneficiary. If you are the beneficiary, upon your death Medicaid might have a claim to the assets. You lose control of the principal while you are on Medicaid for a set number of years, but it is better to keep your money and lose a bit of control than to waste all your hard-earned money on health care. If you "annuitize" an annuity and do it prior to the 36-month look-back period, Medicaid is unlikely to try to seize the asset.

Sometimes you cannot transfer the income. If this is the case, still consider making another person the annuitant—usually someone very young. What many annuity contractual provisions allow you to do is combine the owner's mortality rate with the annuitants to start an annuitization payout schedule of a very low amount. This will help to not catapult you over the income limitation of Medicaid. This is currently under discussion and may result in income having to be paid based on the owner's mortality—thereby disqualifying the owner for Medicaid.

- ◆ **Look into a reverse mortgage.** It may surprise you to know the number of people who are "equity-rich and cash-poor." An example of such a person is someone who owns a home worth a large sum of money, but has very little income or other assets. Such a person might be able to tap into the equity in the home for increased income by employing a *reverse mortgage*—giving up some portion of the equity or future appreciation for guaranteed income.

  You might also be able to create a reverse mortgage in such a way that you still own the property (to avoid transfer restrictions) but establish a very low income stream, irrevocable over many years. You might be able to make the income lower and last longer by having a combined owner who is much younger, possibly a child. The reason for doing it this way is to establish an irrevocable reverse mortgage that cannot be changed to possibly avoid the Medicaid lien after you die, but still give your family income instead of an asset. This strategy is new, but your state might already have imposed restrictions against it.

As reverse mortgages are still relatively new, many reverse mortgage plans have been terrible deals—schemes and ways for the mortgage company to make a great deal of money and the homeowner to receive very little. Many times there are hidden costs, so be very careful before actually signing any reverse mortgage papers.

Getting into a Quality Facility and Protecting Assets

While you're healthy, check out care facilities. Look for facilities that have Medicaid beds. Be sure that if you go in as a private payor, and then go broke and subsequently apply for Medicaid, you cannot be moved to a different facility.

If you can afford it, try to find quality long-term care insurance for three years. If you can afford three years of coverage, that should give you ample time to either give away your money or create an alternative plan. If you can afford the insurance coverage, you will be considered a private payor and should be able to get into the facility of your choice.

The Medicaid application is long and tedious, and there are tricks to completing it. If you have access to Medicaid specialist or elder-care attorneys, solicit their help and guidance. You can apply for Medicaid as often as you want. Medicaid officers who review your application are often not as familiar with the Medicaid laws as they should be; therefore, if you are turned down, appeal the decision. This should also be done with the help of a counselor who has a thorough understanding of Medicaid. Often, people who appeal a Medicaid decision are pleasantly surprised when the decision is overturned.

For more on Medicaid, refer to my book *Safeguard Your Hard-Earned Savings*.

Where to Invest Your Money

Chapter 15

Types of
Investments

There are probably more places to invest money than you can fathom. When investing, it is important to understand what is best for *you*, based on your unique situation.

You won't be able to decide *where* to invest until you are comfortable with *how* to invest. It is possible to spend your whole life learning about investments, reading books, and educating yourself, and still be unsure about your selections.

The two chapters in Part IV are specifically designed to give you a handle on making financial decisions for yourself, or at least give you enough knowledge to know what questions to ask. Always remember the first rule of investing: If you are thinking about your investments when your head hits the pillow at night, you are probably involved in the wrong investments. In determining where to invest, you can separate your decision into two categories of thought: *technical* and *emotional.*

Keep It Technical

If you can remove your emotions from your investment decisions and invest based only on fundamental and technical reasons (logic, numbers, historical data, economy, industry, and your financial plan), then you have a much greater chance of success. If you cannot remove your emotions when making an investment decision, just don't invest. If investing makes you nervous, again, don't invest. If this means you lose purchasing power by placing your money in a checking account at the bank, that's okay. If this is what makes you feel better, then do exactly that. But remember, you can lose money not only in an investment, but also to inflation. Both are hazardous; inflation is one of the major destroyers of a happy retirement. And investing smartly can help you beat inflation. With that in mind, let's look at the major categories of investment options available to mature Americans.

The Bank

Banks insure your deposits up to $100,000. The insurance is provided by a corporation called the Federal Deposit Insurance Corporation (FDIC), which is backed by the government. Although the FDIC is not actually part of the government, the government has pledged 100-percent backing. This means that, should your bank fail, the FDIC will pay you lost principal up to the amount of $100,000.

The FDIC

It is important to understand the role of the FDIC. The first thing to realize is that you are insured for only a total of $100,000 of all the accounts in your name at any one bank. In addition, if you open up similar accounts at two different branches of the same bank, you are insured only for the $100,000 total. Therefore, if you have a $100,000 balance in the branch "A" checking account, and $100,000 at branch "B," you are only insured for a total of $100,000.

Having several joint accounts will not get you around this law. Some investors try to get additional coverage by changing the order of the names or the Social Security numbers on the accounts. This will not work; the FDIC deems these to be all the same account.

In addition, any account held in trust for someone else is still an account considered to be in your name. (This does not refer to a living trust, but a trust account.) Instead, you must open an account for someone whom the FDIC defines as "a natural object of your bounty," which is a child, grandchild, or spouse. These accounts are judged to be separate from each other and are each insured for up to $100,000.

What Banks Offer

Once you have selected a bank, you can usually choose a passbook savings account, checking account, or a common certificate of deposit (CD). Usually the owner of a CD will enjoy a better interest rate for allowing the bank to tie up the money for a specified period of time.

Many banks offer brokerage services that sell government and growth mutual funds, stocks, bonds, and annuities. Although these services are not bad, make no mistake about how they work. In-house bank "investment counselors" usually work for a separate department within the bank or a separate corporation affiliated with the bank. Normally, your investments are *not* guaranteed by the FDIC and are not deposited in your bank. The counselors customarily earn a separate commission for your investments. In advance, understand how that commission works. Know all the risks, fees, and caveats. Read the prospectus as though you are investing in a company outside the bank.

The strongest feature of a bank is the insurance from potential loss of your principal. Additional advantages of the bank might include the ease of depositing and withdrawing money, using ATMs, and the convenience of transmitting funds.

The downside of using a bank is that you pay an enormous price for those conveniences. In today's economic environment, the bank's interest rates are so low that, after inflation and taxes, you might be actually *losing* purchasing power. This is a critical fact for mature Americans to know.

Bonds

Historically, bonds have been a terrific source for higher income with relative security of principal. Bonds are usually considered safer than a stock or an equity position, because you are lending money to a company, government, or municipality (risk is determined by the type of bond). If a bond issue goes broke and declares bankruptcy, the bondholder will usually be paid before an equity investor.

Simply stated, a *bond* means that you, the investor, are lending money to an entity at a specified interest rate for a specified time. Bonds are usually offered in denominations of $100 or $1,000. A typical bond would work like this: You lend $1,000 to an entity (for example, the U.S. Government). In return, the borrower promises to pay you 8-percent interest (or $80) per year until the bond matures. If the bond is stated to mature in 10 years, at the end of that time you are returned your $1,000, plus the interest income.

The guarantee in any bond is represented by the entity or the insurance company backing it. The bond in the previous case is guaranteed by the government, which most investors would agree is very safe.

Remember, it is not the bond itself that is safe or risky. A bond is just a type of security. The risk of the bond depends upon the type of bond you buy. You might read a headline in the paper stating, "Bond prices are going down." Don't let a statement like that influence your decision. There are so many bonds and so many differences between bonds, not to mention how people use them, such a headline might not even pertain to your situation at all.

It is relatively easy to track a bond to determine its safety. Because this should be a major criterion when choosing a bond, it is worth doing some investigative work. First, go to the library and research the bond rating. The primary rating services are Standard and Poors (S&P) or Moody's, which use a scale from AAA for the best to C (Moody's) and D (S&P) for the worst, provide information about the bond offering, and present their opinion of it. To arrive at a rating, many factors are considered, including the debt structure, financial statements, and solvency. The following chart explains how bonds are rated.

Moody's		S&P
AAA	Highest quality	AAA
AA	High quality	AA
A	Good quality	A
BAA	Medium quality with some speculative qualities	BBB
BA	Speculative but with some defensive qualities	BBB
B	Highly speculative	CCC
CAA	Bonds that stated interest is not being paid or those in default	CC
C	Lowest rating	D

In addition, within each category, these rating companies might add a (+) or (–) in order to be more precise.

Bond Insurance

Many times you see advertisements for AAA-rated insured bonds. It is extremely important to know who is insuring any bond. Is the bond issued by the government or one of its direct agencies (such as a Ginnie Mae)? This implied backing is the full faith and credit of the government and is considered AAA-rated and insured by the government.

Issuers of municipal or corporate bonds will often "insure" their bonds in order to receive a better rating. Be sure to ask who is insuring the bond. Usually a bond is insured in the same way you buy life insurance. Bond issuers go to an insurance company that specializes in insuring bonds and pay for the insurance. If the bond defaults, typically the insurance on the bond will guarantee bondholders their money back. What you need to know is whether the company insuring the bond is strong and solvent.

Often the insurance companies used for bond issues are large, publicly held companies. You can research these by applying many of the same techniques that are used to evaluate stocks. You could go to the library, phone the company and request an annual report, or review a value line on the company. Recently some insurance companies that reinsured municipal bonds failed. Exercise caution. If a bond has good insurance backing, chances are that Standard and Poors or Moody's will raise the rating of the bond.

Types of Bonds

The following are the different types of bonds you can choose to add to your investment portfolio.

Savings Bonds

Lately, Series EE government savings bonds have regained their popularity. You can buy these bonds for half of their value at maturity, and they are backed by the full faith and credit of the U.S. Government. While they do not pay current interest, the tax on the accrued earnings is deferred until you cash the bond.

Of course, at some point the tax must be paid. What some investors do is convert these savings bonds, upon their maturity, into HH bonds. This conversion avoids the big tax bite, because HH bonds pay current interest that is taxed. Usually, the HH bond does not enjoy as high an interest rate as EE bonds.

If you don't want or don't need current income, EE bonds might be a wise alternative to another secure "safe money" investment.

U.S. Treasury Bills, Notes, and Bonds

The biggest difference between a *bill* and a *bond* is the maturity. A Treasury bill usually matures at 30-, 60-, or 90-day intervals. A *note* has a maturity generally over one year, but less than 10 years. A Treasury bond can mature in anywhere from 10 to 30 years.

The other major difference is how the interest is paid. A Treasury bill is issued at a discount. Instead of paying $1,000 for a bond, you might pay $800 for a bill. When the bill matures, you will receive the full $1,000. A Treasury bond is issued for the full face value of $1,000 and will pay you (usually semiannually) at the current interest rate. U.S. Treasury obligations are free from all state tax.

Tax-Free Bonds

Investing in Treasuries can be accomplished easily and for little or no commission. The Treasury has a system called "Treasury Direct," in which you send them money directly to invest for you.

A *tax-free bond* is normally a bond issued by a municipality—a school district, city, or state. If you buy a tax-free municipal bond in the state where you live, it will customarily be free of any tax on the interest paid, both at the federal and state level. If you buy a tax-free municipal bond in a state that is not your principal residence, it is usually free from all federal taxes, but you will pay state taxes.

Just because a bond is tax-free, this does not mean that it is safe. For example, a bond could be tax-free and issued against a hospital in your state. Should that hospital fail, the bond could default and you could lose your money. Always check to determine whether the bond you are buying is insured and by whom. Also, be sure that you agree with the purpose of the bond.

In a broad sense, two major types of municipal bonds exist: *general obligation bonds* and *revenue bonds*. When purchasing a bond, it is important to distinguish the difference.

General obligation bonds are issued and backed by a municipality. For example, if California issues a general obligation bond, the chances are that it is backed by the full faith and credit of the state of California. In the past, this was considered to be very safe and secure. However, more and more people are justifiably concerned about the health and credit quality of certain states.

Revenue bonds are backed by the revenue a particular bond is offering to generate. For example, if you purchase a bond for the Buffalo County School District in New York, your bond is directed toward the financing of that school district. If the school district fails, so will your bond. Although this bond is still double-tax-free and a municipal bond, the State of New York has no obligation to back its bonds or to bail them out if a project fails. In essence, revenue bonds carry a higher degree of risk than general obligation bonds. To account for that, and to receive a higher rating, these bonds are frequently backed by private insurers that guarantee your principal.

Be careful when investing in municipal bonds. There seems to be more confusion and poor investment judgment in this category than in any other. Many people think their investments are insured and safe when they are not. In fact, many municipal bonds are considered "junk bonds" or not creditworthy.

As we have previously discussed, municipal bonds can be quite tricky. Just because it is a "municipal bond" does not mean it is safe. The risks are hidden in a myriad of different causes. First, you have to worry about the strength of the entity or municipality backing the bond. Second, there has been a rash of recent changes in the law. If there is even a hint that our tax code will change to represent something similar to a flat tax, or lower income taxes, municipal bonds will not be in nearly as much demand, and this will greatly affect the share price.

Corporate Bonds

The same concept applies here as discussed in tax-free bonds, but in this case you are lending money to a corporation. In other words, you are the bank. Thus, you will receive a specific interest rate and the return of your money upon maturity. Some corporations are considered extremely safe, while others are more risky. The more risk you take, the higher the interest rate.

In the past, bonds that were not rated BB or above have been termed "junk bonds." However, for the person who knows how to evaluate a company and who understands how to determine the level of risk, higher returns can be achieved. Remember, because you are a bondholder, your investment is different from owning stock. In every case, including bankruptcy, the bondholder is paid the interest first, before the shareholder receives dividends.

Before purchasing a corporate bond, ask several questions. Research the company to ascertain how much debt it carries. Should there be a high debt/asset ratio (such as 80 percent), how does the company plan to reduce it? Check not only whether profitability is increasing, but also whether an interest payment has ever been missed or defaulted upon.

Ginnie Mae, Fannie Mae, Freddie Mac

These funds include all types of securities issued by agencies of the government. Although not actually guaranteed by the full faith and credit of the U.S. Government, they are assumed to carry the same implied credit. A *Ginnie Mae* has the highest safety level, because it is an actual part of the government and has a AAA rating.

You must be careful when investing in these securities, because it is much more difficult to evaluate your investment. The attractive points include a better interest rate than a government bond, different maturities, and the safety of the government agency backing it. However, the maturity dates are not definite. Most of these securities are backed by pools of mortgages. Thus, if mortgage rates are lowered and many Americans refinance their home mortgages, your Ginnie Mae certificate could be paid off early. Additionally, portions of your principal will frequently be repaid over a period of years.

If that is the case, you will need to reinvest your money sooner than expected. Often, interest and principal are paid back on the same check.

In order to preserve your asset, you must be careful to reinvest the principal and use only the income from the Ginnie Mae. When the certificate is completely paid, you will have already received all of your interest, as well as the entire principal. Nothing will be left. If you hold the certificate with a broker, you might even consider asking the brokerage company to hold the principal payments and send you only the interest.

Zero-Coupon Bonds

An interesting twist to bond investments has been the concept of *zero-coupon bonds*. These do not pay interest; rather, you buy them at a deep discount (like a Series EE savings bond). The discount depends upon the date of maturity and the rating. At maturity, you will receive the full face value of the bond(s).

Many people think that there are only zero-coupon treasury bonds available, but this is not true. When you buy a zero-coupon bond, make sure you know who the issuer is: the government, a corporation, or another entity. Some investors question whether it makes sense to buy a bond that does not pay interest. Why buy it at a discount and wait for it to mature to face value? The reason that most people reject current interest is that the bond pays a higher rate than one that yields immediate, steady interest. Other investors like to use this method, knowing that a certain amount of money will be available on a particular date. For instance, it is an appropriate vehicle to fund a grandchild's education. Although you are not receiving current interest on a zero-coupon bond, you must report the taxable income every year, unless it is a tax-free zero-coupon.

Interest Rates and Prices When Buying a Bond

The average retiree's investment portfolio usually consists heavily of bonds, either through government mutual funds, income funds, or straight bonds. As advantageous as bonds might look, they do have disadvantages. Remember, when buying a bond, be cautious about the interest rate and the price of the bond.

If you buy a $1,000 bond with a stated interest rate of 8 percent and you pay $1,200, you have paid a $200 premium. In other words, you paid $200 more per bond than the amount the issuer will return to you when the bond matures, which is $1,000. This, of course, lowers what is termed the *yield to maturity*. Yes, you will receive the 8 percent interest. However, because you do not get your full $1,200 back, the actual yield you earn is only about 6 percent (depending upon the maturity). Unless the bond is a truly terrific deal (high yield to maturity), be careful of paying too much more than $1,000 per bond. Instead, try to pay less than $1,000 per bond, which means buying at a discount.

I am sure you have heard that investors buy at all the wrong times. Unfortunately, when the greed factor comes into play, this is sometimes true. For example, from 1990 to 1992, interest rates plummeted. At the end of that period, if you could find many bonds paying 8 percent, would you invest in these? If you said yes, you answered too quickly—I did not tell you the maturity. Those bonds were available at the end of 1992. The maturity dates were about 30 years. Many investors bought these bonds, and they may prove to be a very wise investment. Only time will tell, depending upon future interest rates.

If interest rates rise, the price of your bond will decrease. Conversely, if interest rates continue on a down trend, your bond price will go up until maturity.

If you own an individual bond, such as a government bond, and you intend to hold it to maturity, you should not care about the daily market price of your bond or the fact that other bonds are paying higher interest. You might read that bond prices are down and you may want to sell your bond, or that interest rates are going up and your bond will lose value. Why care about the price today if you hold it until maturity? You are guaranteed your full price at maturity.

Should interest rates rise and you need to sell your $1,000 bond before maturity, no one will give you full price. Why should anyone? If you bought a government bond yielding 8 percent, and two years later the same bond is yielding 9 percent, who would buy your old bond when the new one is paying 9 percent? In order to sell the bond, you will have to sell it at a discount. If you paid $1,000, you might have to sell it for $900.

It is important to remember that if you have already determined in your financial plan that your required return is 8 percent, your job should be to invest in as many 8-percent AAA-rated vehicles as possible. If your required return is truly only 8 percent, you do not have to worry about recessions, interest rates, or inflation. You have correctly completed your financial plan and know that, in order to live comfortably for the rest of your life, all you need is an 8-percent return.

However, trouble comes when you enter retirement based on the fact that you will be earning about 8 percent, but you are able to earn only 4 percent. Even worse, it may turn out that the 4-percent inflation rate you counted on has risen to 6 percent. Believe me, you are going to run out of money a lot sooner than you anticipated.

Perhaps one of the biggest risks associated with a bond, aside from the credibility or solvency of the issuer, is the interest rate. It is said that bonds are the greatest investment during periods of deflation, but during periods of high inflation, bonds will lose value. As in the previous example, if you buy a bond paying 8 percent today and next year the same bond is being offered at 9 percent, you will not be able to sell yours to buy the 9-percent bond without losing some money. If inflation rates rise to 6 percent and you buy 5-percent yielding bonds, you are losing money to the tune of 1 percent per year.

Throughout this book, I have been reminding you of something that you probably already know: *Everything runs in cycles.* If you are retiring during a period of low inflation, don't expect it to last indefinitely. Inflation will rear its ugly head again, and if you are not properly prepared, it might devastate you financially. An ironic fact is that many people think it is truly great when banks pay interest rates higher than 10 percent; however, with inflation at 12 percent, one is losing more money than one is earning.

Although there are many other types of bonds, the ones previously mentioned are the most common. Some people invest in a straight bond, while others invest in bond mutual funds or trusts. Again, it all depends on your particular needs.

How to Purchase Bonds

Usually you purchase a bond through a broker. You may purchase either a new bond or one existing in the aftermarket. The broker will probably add one or two percentage points to the wholesale price of the bond and sell it to you with his or her commission included, which is the retail price. Be sure to inquire about the amount of the commission. In addition, some companies issue bonds directly to the investor. You can phone the shareholder services of a company to find out whether such an option is available.

Stocks

A *stock* is simply an equity ownership in a corporation. If you own a share of McDonald's, you are, in fact, a part owner of the corporation. If the company does well, so will your stock. If the company does poorly, the stock will probably do likewise.

The prices of stocks vary from pennies per share to more than $1,000 per share. If the price of that $10-share increases to $11 per share, you just made 10 percent on your investment. That could happen in any period of time: an hour, a day, a week, or a year. Unfortunately, by the same token, the stock could decrease to $9 or less per share.

There are many kinds of companies in which you can buy stock. Small companies that are new usually start at a low share price, because the risk is greater. These are referred to as *small-cap* stocks. *Mid-cap* stocks consist of middle-sized companies. The larger companies are considered more safe and are sometimes called *blue chip* stocks.

The Stock Market

Many people refer to the stock market as simply "the market." However, it is important to discern which market they are referring to or whether they are talking about a particular index. Several companies are responsible for tracking the performance of stocks through indices. The most well-known include the following.

The Dow Jones Industrial Average

Perhaps the most popular index, the *Dow Jones Industrial Average* measures 30 large industrial stocks. You might ask how this can be a true measure of the stock market, because thousands of companies trade stock. This is the reason for different indices in which to track your area of interest. Each of the 30 stocks in the Dow are weighted differently, according to price and size of the company and quality of its stock.

Standard and Poors 500

The *Standard and Poors (S&P) 500* is a broad index that typically includes the 500 leading stocks. There are many other indices of this type, including the S&P 100, specialty utility indices, biotech, and others.

New York Stock Exchange

The *New York Stock Exchange (NYSE)* is both an actual market where stocks are traded and an index of all the stocks traded there. Although it remains very difficult to list with the NYSE, usually the larger companies trade on it.

Trading Stock

Many different methods and exchanges exist for trading stock. The name *Wall Street* has often symbolized the stock market. For many years the NYSE on Wall Street was the largest and most prestigious exchange "auction" in which to trade stock. This exchange is an actual physical location where people meet in an auction setting to trade stock.

Gaining greater popularity is an over-the-counter (OTC) exchange known as the *National Association of Securities Dealers Automated Quotation System (NASDAQ)*. There is no physical location for an OTC. Buys and sells on the NASDAQ are transacted by computer and executed without anyone ever having to go into a pit or special arena to trade.

Historically, smaller companies listed their securities on the over-the-counter exchange, because it was easier to be accepted for listing; thus, the popularity of the NASDAQ as an index for smaller cap stocks was established. However, the NASDAQ is gaining popularity with larger companies, as well.

Where and How Are Stocks Purchased?

A stock can be purchased by contacting a stockbroker, a financial planner, or the shareholder services department of the company. If you are just learning how to buy stocks, there is wisdom in phoning a broker or financial planner, because he or she will be prepared to offer you some good advice.

Many people ask, "Who determines the price of a stock?" The answer is, "You and I do." It's supply and demand. If I think a company is going to do well financially, I can call a broker and ask to buy the stock at the current price. At that point, I own the stock. I do not have to sell my stock until someone pays me the price I want. If someone buys my shares at my asking price, the new value, or new price of the stock, is established.

You have a choice of either receiving a certificate for the shares you buy or having it retained at the company or the brokerage firm. The benefit of the latter is that both the company and the firm are insured and liable for the certificate. Don't worry about whether a record of your owning the stock exists, because you will receive periodic statements and other information either directly from the company or the brokerage house where the shares were purchased. If you wish to take possession of the certificate, you will be responsible for its safekeeping.

Choosing Winning Stocks: An 11-Step Process

Generally, there are two types of stocks: preferred and common. *Preferred stocks* are in a preferred position to common stock because preferred shareholders are paid dividends first. If a company goes bankrupt, for example, the proceeds from the bankruptcy would first go to pay the *preferred* shareholders before the *common* shareholders. As a result, the price of the preferred stock is usually less volatile. Many people buy preferred stock to obtain a higher yield with greater stability of principal.

Some stocks, mostly preferred, pay a steady dividend, much like a bond. The investor also has the chance of having the stock increase in value as the company's profits increase. However, if the company does poorly, your share price could go down. But for the higher risk, you probably will enjoy a better *dividend* or interest rate on your money. If you are adept at picking a strong, solid company and need additional income, a preferred stock could be an excellent source of steady income as well as an opportunity for growth of your investment.

A *common stock* is generally just an equity, or ownership, position with a company. As this type of stock involves more risk, the share price will fluctuate more. Common stockholders usually have voting privileges, whereas only some preferred issues offer voting privileges. These privileges allow the investor to vote in elections for the company's board of directors and other important issues.

How Is the Price of a Stock Monitored?

There are many ways you can track the performance of your stock. Your broker, financial planner, shareholder services at the company where you are invested, or the financial section of your newspaper will quote current prices.

Before you invest, have your financial plan in place and know what you want to accomplish. Then you can determine the type of stock you want to buy. Next, review the asset allocation of your portfolio and decide how you want to fill the gaps that may exist in your investments.

How Is a Stock Selected?

There are many theories about how to choose stocks. Some theories concentrate on *dividend* theory, while others focus on *price-to-earnings (P/E)* evaluation. With so many ways to pick stocks, the important thing to remember is that none of them is foolproof. If there were a foolproof method, the market would compensate for it and it probably would not work any longer. Always be careful, and don't invest your money if you can't tolerate market fluctuations and possible losses.

In a broad sense, the two approaches to picking a stock are the *fundamental* and *technical* approaches. The fundamental approach entails watching the economy, market trends, and how well a particular company is positioned to perform in the marketplace against its immediate competition and the industry as a whole.

The technical approach involves researching a particular company's balance sheet, income statements, cash flow, book value, price-to-earnings ratio, and debt-to-equity ratio.

Questions for the Evaluation of a Stock

Before investing in a stock, evaluate it by asking the following questions. Careful consideration of these question and their answers will help you reduce your risk.

1. **Is the business of the company growing? How is the competition doing?**

2. **What is the company's price-to-earnings (P/E) ratio?**

   The P/E ratio gauges how expensive the stock is to buy. It is determined by dividing the most recent price of a share by the earnings per share. This indicates how many times the company's earnings the stock selling price may be. The higher the number, the more expensive the stock. For instance, if the P/E ratio of a company is 10, the stock is selling at 10 times the earnings. Usually, blue chip stocks will trade at a higher P/E ratio, because investors are willing to pay more for what they assume is a safer investment. Prices are higher for a more secure investment with a better chance for sound growth.

   New companies with lower P/E ratios sometimes interest investors who think the stock will rise dramatically. You might find a stock with a low P/E ratio, while all other stocks in that asset category are trading at higher P/E ratios. Research the company's history to determine whether there is a reason for their lower P/E. If you find no substantial explanation, it might simply be that analysts do not follow the stock and, therefore, offer no opinions that create demand. This could present a buying opportunity.

   Also, check the index of the stock you are thinking about buying. Take the average P/E ratio from that index. For example, if you buy into a Dow Jones stock and the Dow Jones stocks are averaging a 14-percent P/E, you might try to locate one trading for a little less.

3. **What are the company's earnings?**

   Are the earnings rising annually? If so, how many years have they risen? You can also look at revenue, which might be increasing every year. Nevertheless, if the earnings per share are not also increasing, why would it matter whether the company is bringing in more money?

4. **What is the debt structure of the company? How much is it leveraged?**

   If you own your home free and clear, there is little or no chance that a bank could take it away, even though your earnings are poor for a period of time. Conversely, if a company has borrowed a great deal of money and has a bad year, it might be in trouble when the bank comes to collect. For most stocks that the average mature American would be apt to consider, a good rule of thumb would be to stay with low- to no-debt companies.

5. What is the stock dividend yield? How much have the dividends increased or decreased since the company's beginning?

Often, the price of the stock is supported by the dividend the company pays the investor. If the dividend is cut or stopped, the stock could fall dramatically in price. Many investors use the dividend theory to select stocks. The theory is that stocks that have always increased their dividends and never decreased it over a period of time will perform better than the market average. Furthermore, the stock will not fall as much as other stocks when the market is down. Some people refine this theory by adding the following criteria: The stock cannot trade above two- or three-times the book value; the P/E ratio must be 10 percent less than the market average; earnings per share should be expected to increase in the next year.

These are a few examples of the guidelines investors might use to pick stocks. For the mature American who enjoys being a shareholder, the dividend theory seems to be a prudent way to invest. It may be a more cautious approach than monitoring the market average. However, over time, it holds positive potential for success. The easiest way to practice the dividend theory is to find the highest yielding stocks in the index that have the lowest prices.

6. What is the 200-day moving average of a stock?

If a stock has increased well above the moving average, you must ask yourself, "Why is the stock rising? How much further can it go past its average?" Some investors actually like to buy a stock after it dips below its moving average. Why? Perhaps the market dipped for some reason and the stock you are tracking dropped as well, but for no apparent reason other than a general market drop. This could be a buying opportunity.

7. What do the analysts say about the stock?

Do they like it? Why? What do they think the earnings per share will do over the next few years? You can receive information from the analysts by calling the company and asking them to send you reports that analysts have prepared on that company, or by asking for the names and phone numbers of those analysts and contacting them directly.

8. Based on today's economy, how will this company perform five or 10 years from now?

How would it do in a recession or expansion? Again, a stock selection is based on what you are trying to accomplish. Most mature Americans should not be taking excessive risk. If you like picking stocks, I believe you should proceed conservatively over a period of time. It's simply a matter of what criteria to use. The craze one year might be toy company stocks, but during a recession, toys are not a necessity. Along those same lines, think of industries that will always be in demand. Then choose a good, solid company in that arena.

9. Is the company environmentally friendly?

With the Clinton administration, major businesses have had to make many changes to help clean up the environment, and companies that had already done so did not have to bear such a large cost.

10. What is the momentum of the stock?

Are more investors and institutions buying the stock? Is this good, or is it artificially raising the stock price to higher levels than it should? Perhaps the reverse is true. Has there been some negative news that may have caused a selling frenzy at a lower price than the stock is actually worth?

11. Finally, are you willing to lose money?

Despite all the research and studying you might do, you can still lose money. You must be aware of this and be willing to take the risk.

The problem many investors have is that they don't buy or sell at the right time. Many investors buy too late, after a story on a particular company is already old. By then, this stock will be selling too high, and the sophisticated investor has already sold, driving the price down. The poor investor who bought late panics and sells low. Guess who's starting to buy again? If you hear about a good stock through a friend, it may be too late for you. Review the first 10 points on the preceding pages and, if the stock checks out, consider it, but only if it fits in with your financial plan.

Find a good company whose stock you are willing to hold for a long time. If the stock market takes a dive, and your stock in particular, you must treat that as a bonus—a buying opportunity. Now you can invest in that same stock at a discount. Just because Wall Street is foolish does not mean you can't be savvy and enjoy a buying opportunity.

You also must be ready to sell. If your stock is getting expensive, don't be afraid to continue selling at certain intervals. You will know whether it is overpriced by reexamining the previous 10 questions. After your stock goes up 20 percent, it is too expensive when earnings are not also up 20 percent. This is the time to sell the gain. After a rise of 50 percent, if the stock is too expensive, consider selling the rest. Remember, don't sell if the stock is up 50 percent but the earnings are equally up. Also, don't get emotional about your stock should the P/E ratio rise too drastically.

One of the best sources of stock tracking is *The Daily Graphs,* published by William O'Neil & Co., which includes a complete explanation on reading stock graphs.

Reading the Stock Page

Common stocks traded on the New York Stock Exchange (NYSE) or the American Stock Exchange (AMEX) are listed in the financial press in the following manner:

52-Week High	Low	Stock	Div	Yield %	P/E Ratio	Sales 100s	High	Low	Close	Net Change
36 3/8	25 3/8	ABC	1.16	3.7	9	60	32	31 3/8	31 3/8	+1/8
47½	28¼	DEF	.80	1.9	23	6	42	42	42	
37 7/8	18	XYZ	.40	1.3	11	1	30 7/8	30½	30 7/8	−¼

Reading from left to right, the columns are interpreted as follows:

52-Week High Low	This column lists the highest and lowest price for which the stock sold per share in the past 52 weeks. For example, this year's high for ABC is 36 3/8, or $36.375, whereas the year's low is 25 3/8, or $25.375. The year's high for DEF is 47½, or $47.50, whereas the year's low is 28¼, or $28.25.

Stock	This column lists the abbreviated name of the stock being reported.
Div	This column lists the annual cash per dividend share of stock based on the rate of the last quarterly payout. The dividend per share of ABC stock is $1.16; for DEF stock, the dividend per share is $.80; for XYZ, the dividend is $.40.
Yield %	This column represents the dividend yield, which is found by dividing the dollar amount of the dividend by the closing price of the stock. The result is then multiplied by 100 to produce the actual yield percentage. Dividend yield is a measure of the flow of income produced by an investment in a particular stock. The dividend yields for ABC, DEF, and XYZ are 3.7 percent, 1.9 percent, and 1.3 percent, respectively.
P/E Ratio	This column lists the price-earnings ratio of the stock, or the ratio of the latest closing price of the stock to the latest available annual earnings per share of the firm. The P/E ratio for ABC indicates that the stock is selling for 9-times the company's earnings. Earnings per share are calculated by dividing the closing price of the day being reported by the P/E ratio. For ABC, earnings per share are $3.49 ($31.375/9).
Sales Ratio	This data represents the volume of transactions (shares) bought and sold on the trading day considered. The entry is represented in the hundreds; that is, the entry must be multiplied by 100 to arrive at the actual volume of transactions. The number of shares traded for ABC, DEF, and XYZ are 6,000, 600, and 100, respectively.
High	This entry represents the highest selling price of one share of stock for the day considered. The highest selling prices for stocks ABC, DEF, and XYZ on the trading day considered are $32, $42, and $30.875, respectively.
Low	This entry represents the lowest selling price of one share of stock on the day considered. The lowest selling prices for ABC, DEF, and XYZ are $31.375, $42, and $30.50, respectively.

Close	This column lists the price of the last share of stock sold on the day considered. The prices of the shares sold for companies ABC, DEF, and XYZ are $31.375, $42, and $30.875, respectively.
Net Change	This column lists the net change between the closing price of the stock on the day considered and the closing price on the previous trading day. A plus sign preceding the number indicates that the closing price for the day considered is higher than the closing price for the previous trading day, whereas a minus sign indicates that the closing price is lower than on the previous day. The net change for ABC is +1/8, which indicates that the closing price for the previous day was 31¼ or $31.25 per share. There is no net change for DEF; this indicates that the closing price for the previous day was 42, or $42 per share. The net change for XYZ is −¼; this indicates that the closing price on the previous day was 31 1/8, or $31.125 per share.

Where to Find Stock Information

All the information we have discussed is readily available in the financial section of the newspaper and analysts use it every day. The following are suggestions for easy ways to obtain stock information.

1. **Use a broker.** A broker is paid a commission when you trade, so make sure he or she earns the money. If one calls to recommend a stock, don't do your own research. Ask the broker to send you the answers to your 10 questions.

   A discount broker will not give you as much information. You simply call a discount broker and tell him or her what trade you wish to make. You have to do your own research.

2. **Do research at the library.** The library usually subscribes to all of the material that would provide information for your research. *Value Line* is a publication that would answer most of the previous 10 questions. The library might also have *The Daily Graphs* and *Standard and Poors Stock Guides,* which are very helpful.

3. **Call the company.** The company's shareholder services department offers extensive financial assistance. You could inquire who the market maker is and ask for the phone number. The market maker is the person or company in charge of the whole stock underwriting. The market maker will send you any information you request.

4. **Obtain periodicals.** You can obtain, for a cost, literally hundreds of periodicals pertaining to anything from simple stock picks to complex graphs and projections. However, you don't have to spend any money; just go to a public library and cross reference all newsletters and periodicals that contain stock selection criteria.

Mutual Funds

Mutual funds are currently one of the most popular investment vehicles. They also happen to be among the easiest forms of investment. Of course, there is both good news and bad news associated with them. The good news is that it is easy for investors to get involved in a whole array of financial vehicles. The bad news is that because of the ease of investing, the results are often disappointing and misunderstood. Mutual funds in general are neither risky nor safe; it is the particular type of mutual fund that determines the risk.

When buying into a mutual fund, an individual pools his or her money with that of other individuals in order to buy more of several different investments. This provides greater diversification and allows the small investor an opportunity to invest in companies he or she could not afford alone. For every mutual fund there is a manager who is in charge of what the fund buys and sells. Good managers are very well-known and can be readily researched, together with the funds they manage.

A *mutual fund family* is a group of mutual funds with several different objectives all under one company. For example, the Franklin Fund Group is one large mutual fund family. Under the Franklin family, there are more than 30 different types of mutual funds from which to choose, depending upon investment needs.

The popularity of mutual funds is the consequence of many fine points of investing. It requires little effort to make an investment. Then, once in the fund, investors receive regular statements. Dividends may be reinvested or received on a routine, monthly basis. Those who have been in mutual funds for long periods of time and reinvest all of their dividends are often pleasantly surprised to see exactly how much the fund has grown in value.

Although there are many different funds, they all basically work in the same manner. You or your advisor send an application along with a check to the fund family. This application is found in the prospectus, which you should read and understand before investing. Sometimes, having an advisor fill out the forms for you makes sense because he or she is in a better position to know the optimal time to invest. It may also simplify the paperwork for you.

Once your money is received by the fund, the cost of a share is that day's closing price. If you invest in a growth fund and the market happens to be up on the day you invest, your fund is probably up too. Assuming that the price is $15 per share and you want to invest $20,000, you will have purchased 1,333.33 shares. Now, suppose that the growth fund you bought performs well and the share price rises to $20. Although you still have the same number of shares, you can now sell them back to the fund for $20 each. In that scenario you made a profit of $6,666.60.

If you were to invest in more of an income-type fund, such as a bond fund or U.S. Government fund, the rise in share price is usually secondary to the dividends you receive. Many people invest simply to receive the dividends on a monthly basis. That is their income, and hopefully, the share price will rise with the cost of living to maintain purchasing power. However, you do not have to take the dividends as income; you can always reinvest them and buy more shares.

What Types of Mutual Funds Are Popular with Retirees?

Depending upon the amount of homework you do, you can probably find the type of mutual fund that meets your objectives. Mutual funds range from those that will invest only in companies that are environmentally friendly, to those that will invest only in government bonds, Ginnie Maes, utilities, corporate bonds, or companies that are a part of the Dow Jones Industrial Average. There are funds that invest only in bonds of foreign countries. In essence, there is a different fund for almost every objective.

Even though there are hundreds of fund groups from which to choose, mature Americans can probably find what they need within a core group of possibly five funds in one family.

Remember, all investments involve risk. Be sure to read the prospectus and consult a professional before you invest.

Money Market Funds

Money market funds resemble passbook savings accounts held at a bank. The share price usually does not fluctuate. Typically, each share is bought and sold for a dollar per share. Most money markets invest in short-term instruments comprised of very safe securities, such as Treasury bills, overnight federal funds, and investments similar to those a bank might use for investing CD deposits. These funds generally offer free checking accounts and pay competitive interest rates. Some money markets are insured, while others are not. The main difference between a money market and a savings account is that a bank will normally use the money to invest in securities as short as two to 10 days. In contrast, a money market mutual fund might purchase securities with 30-day maturities. For the longer maturity, the yield is better and all the securities purchased in a money market are either government issued or insured. This is the safest type of fund. Most people use these as a liquid savings account.

Government Bond Funds

As the name implies, these funds customarily invest only in bonds that are either issued by the government or are backed by the government or one of its agencies. The first reason to invest in this type of fund is the safety factor. The second reason is the usually higher dividend. If a CD is paying 6 percent, these funds could be paying 8 percent.

The important point to remember is that these securities do, in fact, pay dividends. If you plan to keep this fund forever and use only the dividends, the share price is a secondary concern. However, *the share price does fluctuate*. Just because it is a government fund does not mean you cannot lose money. The biggest factor affecting the share price of a government fund is a change in the interest rate. For example, assume that you invest in a government bond fund paying a dividend of 8 percent. This sounds pretty good. If you invest $50,000 at a share price of $10, you have purchased 5,000 shares. Now, during the course of the year, you receive the 8 percent dividend for income, which is $4,000 for the year or $333 per month. This is not bad. However, throughout this time, interest rates rose and your share price dropped to $9.50. Now, at the end of the year you wish to sell the fund. Will you get your money back? At $9.50 per share, the 5,000 shares you own are worth only $47,500. Add to this figure the $4,000 of income the fund generated, for a total of $51,500. Over the year you made $1,500. This vividly illustrates the point that, although your dividend was 8 percent, your total return for the year was actually only 3 percent.

This example also illustrates why the share price is secondary if you plan to hold the fund forever. Don't forget that everything is cyclical. If you keep the fund for a long period of time, interest rates will periodically rise and fall and your share price will move with these market cycles. There will be times when you could sell the fund for more than you paid and other times when you would sell for less. Although history is no guarantee of future investment performance, it does show that, over time, the share price will probably slowly rise with the economic environment. If you desire additional income, your main concern should be that, without having to worry, you receive a competitive interest rate plus a check in your mailbox every month.

The most difficult part of investing is self-discipline. Most investors do not reap the benefits of worry-free dividend checks simply because they are preoccupied with the price per share of their fund during market cycles. Remember your objectives. Review your plan and stick to it. Also, try to dollar-cost average into the market whenever possible.

There are many types of government funds. As discussed earlier, when interest rates rise, the share price of most bond funds drop. Although most funds are liquid and you can sell them whenever you want, the maturity dates of the bonds in your fund vary. To earn the highest interest rate, some government funds buy long-term (as high as 30 years) government bonds, which receive the highest rates. Conversely, because the bonds are long-term, their share prices are most affected by interest rate fluctuations.

To stabilize the share price in a rising interest rate environment, you can purchase funds that invest only in short or intermediate maturity government bonds. Although the interest rate will probably not be as high as a long-term bond, the share price is much less volatile.

No one can predict when interest rates will rise or fall. Therefore, diversifying whenever possible is always advisable. For those dollars that may not be needed for a while, a long-term fund would protect current interest rates. For those assets that may be needed more quickly, a shorter maturity bond fund is advisable. The interest may not be as high, but the price per share is more stable.

Note: Be sure to read the fund's prospectus and ascertain the average maturity length of the portfolio holdings.

Tax-Free Mutual Funds

Although the merits and pitfalls of tax-free investing were examined in Chapter 6, *tax-free mutual funds* do serve their purpose among retirees. As with other types of funds, there are not only excellent, AAA-rated tax-free funds, but also junk tax-free funds. Do your homework. Know the average maturity of the bonds inside the fund, and make sure that a tax-free investment is right for you.

As discussed under the bonds section, most bonds issued by municipalities, states, and other agencies are tax-free. This means that the interest generated is free from all federal tax. In addition, if you purchase bonds in the state where you reside, the bonds are free from both federal and state taxes. This could be a benefit if you are in a high tax bracket and would like tax-free interest. The following are some precautions for tax-free investments.

♦ Because the bond is tax-free, the interest rate is lower than a taxable bond. You must figure out which bond or fund would yield a better return after deducting taxes and fees.

♦ Although the bonds are tax-free, some are AAA-rated and insured, while others are rated lower and noninsured. These bonds can default just like the bond of a private corporation. Many tax-free bond funds buy revenue bonds. For example, suppose a bond is financing a toll bridge. If no one uses the bridge, the bonds could default and you, the bondholder, will not receive the interest. You must be certain that the bond fund in which you decide to invest has the right risk for you. Be wary of too high a yield; it could be from one of the funds that does not invest in AAA-rated bonds.

♦ As with government funds, you have interest rate risk. If interest rates rise, your share price could drop in value. Know the maturity date of the bond to track its value.

♦ Of special significance to seniors is the fact that, although the interest is tax-free, the income generated from the fund must be calculated into your gross income for Social Security purposes. The result is that your adjusted gross income (AGI) is increased, which might increase your tax liability on Social Security benefits. In addition, tax-free bonds and bond funds are a preference item for the *alternative minimum tax (AMT)*. The AMT is an additional tax that you have to pay if your income falls into a certain category and you did not pay sufficient taxes on this income in relation to the type of income received.

Income Funds

An *income fund* invests primarily to generate income by way of dividends and to preserve the stability of the share price more than a growth fund. In order to accomplish this, the fund might purchase income-producing stocks (such as preferred or convertible) or stocks with high dividends (such as utilities). However, for the most part, these funds purchase government agency and corporate bonds.

These funds serve the purpose of providing income. What many people do is take only the income they need (such as the amount a CD would give them) and reinvest the rest. The funds usually will not experience growth like a growth fund, but they should experience some growth. Because the dividends are usually higher, reinvesting a portion enables the shares in the fund to build more quickly. This could be considered a good inflation-fighting technique. In any event, much like a bond or bond fund, if interest rates rise, share prices could drop.

Growth Funds

A *growth fund* rarely has a dividend or any source of income. Rather, the objective is to increase the value of the share price. Most investments are in stocks of various types, from aggressive to long-term growth funds. Although many mature Americans ask why they should be investing in growth, the answer is simple. people are living longer than ever before after retirement. To compensate for inflation, some growth is needed, not only to maintain the value of the principal, but also to increase it. Although high inflation has not existed for a while, everything is cyclical. It will return and rear its ugly head. A level as low as 4 to 5 percent could devastate a retirement unless the inflation factor is properly included in a financial plan.

The most common reason why people lose money in growth funds is the lack of discipline. Because everything is cyclical, there will be both up times and down times. Reconsider before selling your fund after the market drops and the share price goes down. Weigh the idea of averaging in more money at that point, when the price is low. If you are not a long-term or disciplined investor, a growth fund might not work for you.

The interesting fact is that most growth funds over any 10-year period have outperformed cash returns on savings or money market accounts. Then why do so many people lose money on growth funds? Again, the answer lies in lack of education, understanding, and discipline.

Investors sell after a market crashes when they probably should be buying, because they get emotionally frustrated in a bad economic period. Sometimes they are convinced by a broker to put their money elsewhere, or they forget that the fund was bought for long-term potential. Perhaps someone is touting a new investment at a time when their discipline level is at a low ebb, and they can be easily persuaded to switch investments.

There are only a handful of good reasons to sell a growth fund. None of the above are among them.

Growth and Income Funds

These funds are an interesting combination of both growth funds and income funds. In essence, they are a hybrid. As mature Americans realize they are living longer and will need more money than originally expected, these will, undoubtedly, become more popular.

A *growth and income fund* consists of traditional investments found in a growth fund, such as stocks, but the objective is to provide consistent monthly income, as well. The income is derived from the dividends earned by the bonds that are purchased inside the fund. Hopefully, the stocks will also appreciate in value, thereby increasing share prices.

The purpose of these funds is relevant, should you need both growth and income. If the income is the same as a CD rate, or better, and the growth from the share price is positive, then you are benefiting by achieving two goals: increasing your capital to keep up with inflation, and receiving the income you need.

Sector Funds

Sector funds are, in my opinion, volatile funds that should normally be avoided. A sector fund will invest in a specific asset class with a specific purpose. For example, there are sector funds that invest only in Mexican stocks or others that invest only in automobile stocks.

The scary thing about sector funds is that they can be the biggest winners one year, but the biggest losers the next. You are risking so much in one little sliver of the market that it almost defeats the purpose of the mutual fund: diversification. Wall Street might favor one class of stocks during the year and run prices up higher than the value should be. Then the market will realize that the prices are too high, and a large correction may erase much of the profit.

A utility mutual fund is one sector fund that I would consider, but only as part of a long-term strategy. Utility funds invest in stocks and bonds of public utility companies. Utility companies do not usually go out of business, so the degree of safety is higher. Be sure the fund is one that invests only in high-quality utilities, and avoid those that invest heavily in companies using nuclear power or other experimental sources of energy.

Utility funds generally grow with inflation and don't beat the market, but they also don't suffer as much when the market is down. In addition, utilities are a good source of income. Some pay 7 to 8 percent in dividends. A negative aspect is the fact that they are very interest-rate sensitive. If rates rise, the share price of the fund could decline.

Certain other sector funds might make sense as part of a diversification technique for an entire portfolio. If for some reason, you like a specific sector and want to invest in it, thoroughly research the industry, and limit your exposure to no more than the percentage of your portfolio you have already decided you could afford to lose.

Investing in sector funds is risky—period! Sector funds should only be used as part of an overall investment strategy. Utility funds have now lagged the Standard and Poors for a historically long time. Does that mean you should sell or not buy any now? A true contrarian would say the opposite—that now is the time to buy. As a believer in asset allocation, my fear is that someone hearing that utilities are a good, safe investment will then invest an extremely high percentage of his or her portfolio in utilities and then proceed to lose a great deal of investment principal.

Open-End Funds

Most investors tend to purchase *open-end funds*. These funds continually raise money and rarely close to new investors. Conceivably, such funds could continue unlimited growth in the number of investors and size of financial base. You buy shares of an open-end mutual fund directly from the mutual fund company, which issues the shares to you. When you sell, you sell shares back to the company, because they are never traded on the market like a stock. Here are some reasons that open-end funds are popular:

- It is advantageous for the company to advertise open-end funds and make investors aware of them on a continual basis.
- It is not necessary to go through a broker to buy and sell shares; you can deal directly with the mutual fund company.
- It is easy for the investor to obtain information, in addition to having greater flexibility in how and when to take income and other services that might be offered.

Closed-End Funds

Closed-end funds function much like stocks. In the money-raising stage, there are many advertisements and great publicity, similar to the *initial public offering (IPO)* of a stock. Unlike open-end funds, closed-end do not continually offer shares. Once the offering price is raised, the fund is closed to new investors.

Next, the fund resembles a stock and trades on an exchange, where buying and selling is very simple. At this point, it is usually necessary to go through a broker, unless that particular fund family has a system set up to buy or sell directly. The share price now becomes linked to supply and demand: When the number of shares are limited and the price rises, more investors will probably want to purchase some of that fund, driving the share price up even further. Here are some reasons that investors might prefer closed-end funds:

♦ If the fund cannot issue more shares, the demand for existing ones will rise faster, especially if the manager performs well (at least, that is the theory).

♦ A closed-end fund does not encounter a potential problem of an open-end fund. If an open-end mutual fund does well, and many people continually want to invest, the manager of that fund might not be able to manage the portfolio efficiently, no matter how good he or she may be. Imagine being the manager of a municipal bond fund that excels. Millions of dollars comes in every day for you to invest. The prospectus might permit you to hold only 10 percent of total assets in cash at any given time; thus, you must invest the excess amount. Yet, what if there are no excellent bond purchases at that time and you are forced to buy bonds? Here, the idea is that funds that continually issue new shares might get too big for their own good.

♦ When a new closed-end fund is in the stage of raising the money, the share price will be decided in advance. Figured into that offering price are usually the underwriting fees and the brokerage fee that entices brokers to sell it. Some people believe that if you wait until all the money is raised and the fund begins to trade on the market, the investor can purchase shares for less, because the price will be discounted by the amount of the fees. Although this does not always happen, it is worth considering.

The Importance of the Mutual Fund Prospectus

If you have ever studied investing in a mutual fund, you have heard the famous and faithful words, "Read the mutual fund prospectus." In all probability, if you have tried, you quickly discovered that you could read it three times and not understand anything because of the legal jargon. However, there is good information to be learned from it.

Before actually reading the prospectus, view the date on the document. If it is not recent, you might not be receiving all the critical, updated information. If the fund allows privileges, be sure you are allowed to write checks in denominations that are comfortable for you. Some might allow only one check a month of a $1,000 minimum to be written. Also find out the minimum amount required for an initial investment; if this is $5,000 and you want to invest $1,000, go no further.

What to Look for in the Prospectus

The following is the information you should expect to find in a mutual fund prospectus.

- **Required Statements.** Make certain that the prospectus has language similar to this (any representation to the contrary is a criminal offense): "These securities have not been approved or disapproved by the Securities and Exchange Commission (SEC), nor has the Commission passed upon the accuracy or adequacy of this prospectus."

  If the prospectus declares that the security has been approved by the SEC, this is false. The SEC does not approve or disapprove any security; it merely registers them. The prospectus should also indicate that you may obtain a copy of the Statement of Additional Information, which is essentially a continuation of the prospectus that goes into more detail. All investors are entitled to a copy upon request.

- **Fund Objective.** You should see some kind of statement outlining the objective of the fund. For example, a mutual fund might be named the ABC Dynamic Great Fund. Your friends have told you how wonderful it is, so you phone to request the prospectus. Under the fund objective, there might be a declaration describing it as an aggressive growth fund seeking high capital appreciation through investments in companies under $10 million in size. If you were not aware that you would be investing in an aggressive growth fund, this section of the prospectus clearly delineates the objective.

- **Fund Fee.** Within the first few pages of the prospectus you should find a fee table in which the fees are broken down. First, it should tell you the front sales charge, if any. The sales load is usually a one-time, up-front charge that is paid by the investor for buying the fund. The charge is expressed as a percentage of the amount invested. It would also tell you whether there is a charge or fee to sell the funds.

  The table further itemizes the annual expenses, such as management fees and 12b-1 fees. The total will tell you how much per year the fund is charging you. Finally, you should note any onetime fees, such as charges for switching funds into the family or wiring money to your bank.

- **Fund Performance.** Somewhat buried in the heart of the prospectus will be fund performance information, either explained or detailed in a graph. This might give you recent yield figures, performance on a year-to-year basis, and cumulative return since inception of the fund.

- **Fund Provisions and Policies.** In this section you will discover what the fund is and is not allowed to do. For example, if you purchase a government bond fund thinking the fund only invests in government bonds, this section of the prospectus will tell you exactly how much of the fund's total dollars actually must be invested in government bonds. You will learn whether the fund can invest in other types of bonds and whether these bonds are required to have certain maturities. Do you want a fund that can buy only bonds with maturities in excess of 20 years? What if the government bond fund you are researching needs to have only 30 percent of the portfolio in government bonds?

- **Fund Risk.** This is the section that will tell you the level of risk you are taking or the chances that you might lose money. It will categorize the risk into several areas. First, it might tell you the risk of the type of securities in the fund. Second, it might describe the risk regarding how the manager directs the fund. For example, the provisions of the prospectus might allow the manager of a particular fund to *Write Naked Options,* which generally increases risk. A third risk that could be detailed in the prospectus is economic risk and market cycle information.

- **Fund Family.** Somewhere in the prospectus you will find details about the mutual fund family that is offering a particular fund. The fund family is usually known as the *Investment Advisor.* In this section you should learn about how long the family has been in business, who is used for accounting, where the home office is located, and possibly telephone numbers to call. This information is helpful in judging how established the company may be.

- **Shareholder Rights.** Despite popular belief, the shareholder has rights as an investor. Almost without exception, the first is the right to vote. Normally you are allowed one vote for every share you own. You may vote on such issues as management compensation, investment policies, and the issuance of more shares. A complete breakdown of your voting rights can be found in this section. Also, your rights concerning complaints should be found here. The most common right is that you have the right to arbitration if a dispute arises.

♦ **Fund Earnings.** Many mutual funds, such as money market or Treasury funds, pay dividends to the shareholder. It is important to know how these dividends are declared and distributed. Many people want a fund that declares dividends daily and pays them monthly. A choice is available either to receive the dividends as a check or reinvest them in the fund to purchase more shares. Typically, growth funds do not declare dividends daily or pay them monthly.

♦ **Taxes of Funds.** If a mutual fund declares any kind of distribution, such as a dividend or capital gain, you, the shareholder, must report the amount you receive on your income tax return. Usually, you will know this amount through a 1099 tax statement that the mutual fund is required to send to you. Even tax-free returns should be noted on your tax return. There is a place on your tax return for this information.

♦ **Buying and Selling Shares.** This section informs you about the procedure to purchase and redeem shares. Should you call the company directly or go through a broker? When selling, are you required to write a letter, or can you liquidate by phone? Regardless, you should be aware before investing so there are no surprises later.

Of course, the prospectus goes into much greater detail than described here. You should read the entire document thoroughly. If you need further information or clarification, call the company or your financial advisor. Also, you can request a Statement of Additional Information.

Tips for Picking Great Mutual Funds

Unfortunately, most people do not receive the kinds of returns that many mutual funds quote. The reason is obvious: The average person does not know how to buy or sell a mutual fund correctly. Many newsletters and magazines offer opinions on which funds are the best—remember, publications can give you statistics on a particular fund, but they do not know what is right for you. Only you, your financial plan, and your advisors can ascertain that.

Selecting a mutual fund is not a simple task. Sometimes I wish it were as difficult to invest in a fund as it is to learn how to invest properly. Many people do not research sufficiently and, thus, make disappointing choices.

The 10-Point Checklist for Selecting a Mutual Fund

If you follow these basic 10 points for picking a mutual fund, and learn how to interpret the information you receive, the odds of your being pleased with your investment decision, or at least understanding what you are doing, are greatly enhanced.

1. **Your Objective.** One of the most important ingredients in picking a fund is to determine your objective. What are you trying to accomplish? Don't worry about what your neighbor, cousin, or friend is doing. Go back to square one and try to decide what goals you want to achieve. If you need only an 8-percent return, don't concern yourself with researching top performers, because they are usually the most risky. Forget what your friend says or what an advertisement proclaims. You should always know your objective first.

2. **Performance.** Don's just ask what the 1-, 3-, 5-, and 10-year annualized returns are, but also find out about performance during *every* year. How did the fund perform when the market did poorly? Good funds perform better than the market average in down years.

3. **Risk.** This is one of the most critical areas to research. Your fund might have returned 20 percent, but how much risk did you take? If you could have made *15 percent* with one-third the risk, which fund would you have used?

   Risk and volatility are measured by using *beta, alpha,* and *standard deviation.* The Standard and Poors 500 is the benchmark and is automatically assigned a beta of "1." If your fund has a beta greater than 1, your fund will be more volatile and possibly more risky than the S&P 500.

   For example, if the S&P 500 is down 10 percent and your mutual fund has a beta of 1.5 percent, your mutual fund could very well be down 15 percent when the market is down 10 percent. However, if your mutual fund has a beta of 5 percent and the market is down 10 percent, your fund might be down only 5 percent. Ideally, you would want to find a mutual fund with as low a beta as possible, but one that has returns as close to or better than the market average, especially if you are trying to achieve growth. While a government or similar bond fund might not yield the return of the market, it has very low beta.

The *alpha* is the measure of how your fund performed compared to the market. Suppose for a period of one year the market was flat, which means an investment of $10,000 was worth $10,000 12 months later. If your fund was also flat like the market, your fund would have an alpha of "0." The higher the alpha, the better your fund performed relative to the market.

Therefore, you want a high alpha. A negative alpha would indicate that your fund lost money when the market was flat; a positive alpha would indicate that your fund outperformed the market. Ideally, if you were evaluating mutual funds, you would want the highest alpha, with the lowest beta, and the best return.

4. **Top Fund Holdings.** Do you know which companies your fund owns and do you agree with these choices? Does the fund invest too much in a few select companies? If you don't like the companies, then reconsider whether you would want to invest in that fund.

5. **Prospectus Revisions.** When reading the prospectus (something you should always do), find out what the manager is allowed to do with your money. Does the fund have to be invested fully in stocks or bonds at all times, or can it simply hold cash? Can it buy options and future contracts? If so, does this lower or raise the risk of the fund?

6. **Fund Manager.** How long has the fund manager managed? Should a fund boast large returns, it does not mean much if the manager is brand new. What is the track record of the manager? How long has he or she been at the company and where did he or she manage previously?

7. **Fund Family.** Invest in a family of funds with many strong performers. People's goals change, and if you stay in one family, usually your fees are reduced and paperwork is simplified.

8. **Size of Fund.** Bigger funds are not necessarily better. Many funds get too large and cannot find a prudent way to invest all the money. I find this problem with many tax-free bond funds, which acquire so much money that all of it cannot be properly invested.

9. **Fund Expenses.** I like to know how much the fund is charging me. However, don't misunderstand me. Should I have a fund with expenses that are higher than average, this is all right if the yield is greater than other funds. If not, I select a fund with fewer expenses. First, I look at all the other criteria, then I check expenses. The bottom line is whether I will make more money after all the fees and charges.

   If you are a long-term investor, and a loaded fund (one that has a front charge) is superior to a no-load, don't worry about paying the load. Over a period of years, the fee becomes insignificant. Look first at which is the better fund.

10. **Market Interest Sensitive.** This indicates what will happen to the fund if the market drops or interest rates rise. In the first few years of the 1990s, interest rates dropped dramatically. Thus, the total return of many interest-sensitive funds (government, tax-free, or utilities) was very good. If interest rates begin to rise, these funds will probably not be able to maintain the same kind of returns. The fund might advertise that in the last few years the returns were very high. However, the reverse might occur in periods of rising interest rates.

It is apparent that picking a mutual fund is not easy. Your properly selecting a fund doesn't ensure that you will make money. Half the battle is picking the right fund, the other half is your investment disposition.

The important point is, after purchasing a fund, give it time to perform. If the market drops and your fund goes down, consider averaging in more money. Exercise discipline. Seriously review your decision before selling and taking a loss. Unless something fundamental changes in your plan, or in the particular fund in which you have invested, allow time to achieve your desired results. It is good to track your fund, and I would encourage graphing as well. However, if you watch it on a daily basis, it will probably drive you crazy.

Mutual Fund Comparison

In this section, we will be referring to two hypothetical mutual funds, ABC and XYZ. The ABC fund is more popular, praised in all the newspapers (hypothetically speaking). The obvious reason is because of its spectacular performance: over 10 years, 17.15 percent annualized; over five years, 26 percent; over three years, 27 percent. However, what risk did you take for that return? Notice under "Objective" that this is an aggressive growth fund. Also, notice under "Annual Total Returns" that it has returned as low as –18.93 percent.

In further reviewing the risk level of the fund, the beta and the alpha should be considered. The current beta of the ABC fund is 1.59, which means that if the Standard and Poors 500 beta is 1, this is more volatile. Thus, it has a greater propensity for risk than a fund with a beta of less than 1, which is the benchmark. The alpha compares fund performance with the market average, which results in the higher the alpha, the higher the beta. This particular fund's alpha is higher than the average of most aggressive growth funds. In addition, the standard deviation for performance ranking is quite high, indicating that there is much risk for the return that is generated.

A final step is to review the expenses of the fund. What are the net returns after the fees and loads have been deducted?

In comparing the XYZ fund, the same criteria must be evaluated. The performance figures are almost identical. Over the short term, ABC fund has outperformed XYZ fund. As a result, most investors may be inclined to purchase ABC first. However, XYZ is considered a long-term growth fund, not an aggressive growth fund. The lowest one-year performance (1987) was –8.27 percent.

The beta is almost identical to the benchmark S&P 500, thereby reducing risk and volatility. This is one reason the standard deviation is so much lower than the ABC fund, meaning the risk/reward ratio is more in line. (After all, you want a low standard deviation.) In addition, the alpha is higher than ABC, which means XYZ is performing better in a flat market.

Finally, consider the returns after all expenses and loads. Fund XYZ might not appear attractive because of its 3-percent load, but don't discount it. The ongoing expense ratios are lower, and the returns after all charges are not that much different.

Mutual Fund ABC

Objective	Aggressive growth
Address	123 Main St., Anytown, USA 10209
Telephone	(801) 555-1111, (800) 555-8282
Fund manager	Name of fund manager
NAV 02/26/96	$16.68
Fund symbol	ABC
Total net assets	$5,299,285,000
Year organized	1957

Fund Performance Summary
As of 2/26/96
(Based on NAV With Distribution Reinvested)
3 Months Total Return

	Total % return	Annualized % return	Performance ranking in the aggressive growth category (1 = top 10%; 10 = bottom 10%)
1 Year total return	–3.86	–3.86	9th Decile
3 Year total return	112.59	28.58	1st Decile
5 Year total return	183.86	23.20	1st Decile
10 Year total return	296.85	14.78	2nd Decile

Annual Total Returns

1986	26.28%	1991	13.32%
1987	–18.93%	1992	36.94%
1988	26.17%	1993	9.36%
1989	10.26%	1994	86.45%
1990	6.69%	1995	1.27%

Figure 20:
Mutual Fund ABC

Hypothetical $10,000 investment after maximum front-end load and distributions reinvested.

(As of 2/26/96)

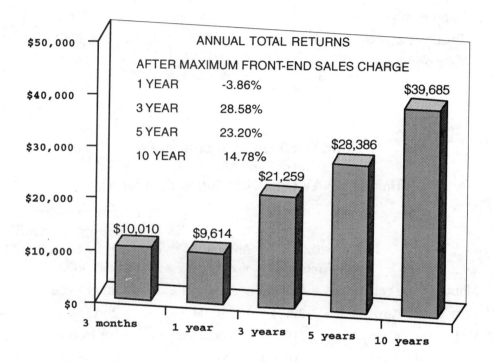

Minimum Investment	Initial 0	Subsequent Investment	$0
Maximum Front-End Load	0% (NL)	Maximum Back-End Load	(None)
12 B-1 Fees (12/31/93)	(Not Apr'd)	Expense Ratio (10/31/93)	1%
Turnover Ratio (12/93)	42 Average	Maturity	N/A
Alpha	0.57	Beta	1.57
Standard Deviation	7.62	Monthly Observations	36

Information contained herein is based on sources and data believed reliable, but is not guaranteed by the author and is not to be construed as a solicitation of an offer to buy or sell securities mentioned herein. Data quoted represents past performance. Investment values will fluctuate so that an investor's shares, when redeemed, may be worth more or less than their original cost.

Mutual Fund XYZ

Objective	Long-term growth
Address	82 Your St., Anytown, USA 10209
Telephone	(801) 555-1910, (800) 555-8888
Fund manager	Name of fund manager
NAV 02/26/96	$28.25
Fund symbol	XYZ
Total net assets	$1,974,200,000
Year organized	1963

Fund Performance Summary
as of 02/26/96
(Based on NAV with Distribution Reinvested)

	Total % return	Annualized % return	Performance ranking in the aggressive growth category (1 = top 10%; 10 = bottom 10%)
3 Months total return	6.55		2nd Decile
1 Year total return	13.34	13.34	2nd Decile
3 Year total return	100.48	26.09	1st Decile
5 Year total return	201.68	24.71	1st Decile
10 Year total return Total	389.56	17.21	1st Decile

Annual Total Returns

1986	23.28%	1990	−1.90%
1987	−8.27%	1992	43.15%
1988	27.06%	1993	3.94%
1989	13.32%	1994	54.92%
1991	21.02%	1995	15.89%

Figure 21:
Mutual Fund XYZ

Hypothetical $10,000 investment after maximum front-end
load and distributions reinvested.

(As of 2/26/96)

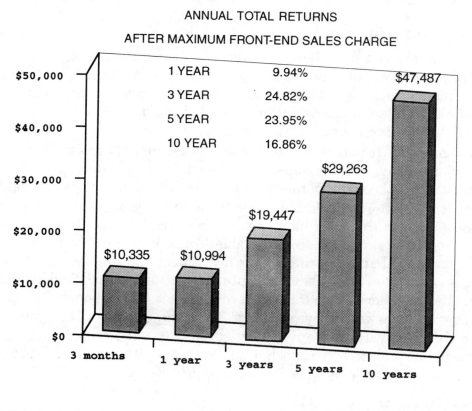

ANNUAL TOTAL RETURNS

AFTER MAXIMUM FRONT-END SALES CHARGE

1 YEAR	9.94%
3 YEAR	24.82%
5 YEAR	23.95%
10 YEAR	16.86%

	Minimum investment	Initial $0	Subsequent investment	$0
Maximum front-end load	3% (LL)	Maximum back-end load	(None)
12 B-1 Fees *(12/31/93)*	(Not Apr'd)	Expense ratio (10/31/93)	0.89%
Turnover ratio (12/93)	217	Maturity	N/A
Alpha	0.86	Beta	1.02
Standard Deviation	4.41	Monthly Observations	36

Information contained herein is based on sources and data believed reliable, but is
not guaranteed by the author and is not to be construed as a solicitation of an offer to
buy or sell securities mentioned herein. Data quoted represents past performance.
Investment values will fluctuate so that an investor's shares, when redeemed, may
be worth more or less than their original cost.

Annuities

For the mature American, a properly structured annuity could be an excellent investment that provides superior yields and guarantees. It is not only a terrific estate planning tool, but also a way to defer taxes. If my hunch is correct, annuities will soon be almost as common a financial vehicle as mutual funds are today. Of course, the key is your understanding of them to assure that they are properly structured on your behalf.

What Is an Annuity?

An *annuity* is a definition of a financial strategy. Just like a mutual fund, an annuity is neither bad nor good; rather, it is a particular type of investment. Depending upon the annuity, it presents the option of investing in many different assets, including mutual funds and guaranteed deposit funds similar to a certificate of deposit.

Usually the custodian of your money, or the *annuity issuer,* is an insurance company. Don't be confused. Although the investment might be in a mutual fund, the issuer of the annuity is always the insurance company.

As long as the funds remain inside the annuity, your money will grow tax-deferred. On the other hand, should you decide to take income from the interest, the earnings become taxable. Think of an annuity as an IRA. First, find one that offers the type of investment you are seeking. Next, place an amount of after-tax money into the contract, where dividends accumulate tax-deferred. Like an IRA, you cannot take money without a penalty until you are 59½ years of age. However, unlike an IRA, you are not required to withdraw any money at age 70½. You can continue the compounding as long as you wish. Usually an annuity is divided into two phases: an *accumulation phase* and an *annuitization phase.*

Accumulation Phase

The accumulation phase is the period of time in which your principal earns interest, which is tax-deferred. When you withdraw interest, you will be taxed. If you annuitize, you are no longer in the accumulation phase. Do not mistake the annuitization phase with simply taking income.

Annuitization Phase

This phase is mandatory with some companies; with others it is a choice. When you decide to annuitize, you relinquish all of your money to the insurance company. In return, you receive a guaranteed income for a specified period of time, determined by whatever annuity option you have selected—income either for the life of both you and a spouse, or for a guaranteed number of years. This income is usually partially tax-free.

In addition to these two phases, two major types of annuities exist: fixed and variable.

Fixed Annuity

A *fixed annuity* is insured and pays you a guaranteed rate of return. The guarantee and insurance is offered by the insurance company issuing the annuity. Here are some guidelines to refer to when considering the purchase of a fixed annuity.

1. **Decide whether you believe in the insurance company.** Ask for the rating. AAA by Standard and Poors is among the highest. In addition, inquire where your funds will be deposited. When you invest in a bank CD and ask where your money will go, I'm not sure whether you will get a good answer. However, when investing in an annuity, you will be told explicitly where the funds are invested.

    While some insurance companies place your money only in U.S. Government-backed instruments, others will place them in various vehicles. Incidentally, this is one reason the interest rates vary so greatly. If you are confident about the size and quality of the insurance company backing your deposit, you might not be worried about where your funds are invested. Otherwise, find out.

    I have never been in a bank or savings and loan and heard customers ask where their CD money will be invested. Yet look at what happened. Many banks invested in questionable real estate or other poor instruments and are now in trouble. When you invest in an annuity, you will probably get a higher interest rate than at a bank, but it is not FDIC insured. Therefore, it is important to ask where your money is being invested.

2. **Ask whether your money is kept in a separate account.** Because investors are getting smarter, issuers of annuities are making their investments better. If the issuer of the annuity states that funds are kept in a separate account, this means that your money is not commingled with the general assets of that insurance company. Should the company fail, your assets cannot be combined with all the other bad assets or be bait for creditor claims.

3. **Find out how interest is credited and how long it is guaranteed.** You might see an advertisement for an annuity guaranteeing a higher interest rate than you might expect. Often the rate will be guaranteed for one year, after which it will drop to a much lower rate set by the insurance company. You cannot simply withdraw your money, because you will incur a penalty for a certain number of years (usually between five and 10).

   If you do invest in this type of annuity, ask for a log of interest rates the issuer has paid to investors in the past, after the first year. Feel reassured if a credible rate was maintained. If not, then reconsider. Incidentally, the "lingo" used by insurance companies is "old money/new money." When you first deposit, your money is new, earning a better rate. Subsequently it is old, earning the lower rate.

   Other annuities have no old money/new money policy. This means that, whatever the new investor receives in interest, the old investor also receives. Usually these annuities readjust their interest rates up or down every quarter, depending on the prevailing rates. They probably will not pay as high a first-year rate, but chances are, over the term of the contract, you will receive more competitive interest rates. The reason for this is that new investors receive the same rate that you are earning. To attract new investors, it had better be good. Also, know in advance what the absolute lowest rate paid is should interest rates plummet. Annuities generally have a minimum rate.

4. **Ask what the penalty is for early withdrawal.** Similar to a CD-type account, if you withdraw early, you will pay a penalty fee. Ask whether there are any charges up front. In addition, if you decide to take interest, how often is it paid? Monthly? Quarterly? Semiannually? Is there a charge for this service?

5. **Understand the terms of the annuitization.** Are you required to annuitize and, if so, when? Is it set by number of years, or your age? If you must annuitize, is there a "bailout option" allowing you to withdraw your money free of penalty before that date? I prefer companies that never make an investor annuitize. While annuitizing might make sense for you, it should be a choice, not a requirement.

Variable Annuity

A *variable annuity* will have most of the characteristics of a fixed annuity with a few major differences. One difference is that the interest rate is not fixed; you choose the investment.

What has been happening lately is that popular mutual fund companies have been teaming up with certain insurance companies to issue variable annuities. The advantage of this is that you can invest with your favorite mutual fund company inside a variable annuity.

Advantages of a Variable Annuity

A variable annuity offers several advantages, including the following.

1. **Tax-deferred growth of your mutual funds.** Assume that you invest in a growth and income mutual fund that averages 10 percent per year in total return (part dividend and part capital gain), and you have been reinvesting for 10 years. You originally started with $10,000. You now have $26,000. However, if your investment is outside an annuity, it is taxed every year (you receive a 1099 tax statement). In addition, you will pay taxes on the stock capital gain the year in which you sell. Assume that after the 10th year you sell and pay the tax. After all is said and done, your after-tax proceeds were about $20,000.

   Now assume you invested in the same fund inside an annuity. In 10 years you would have the same $26,000, but you did not pay taxes every year on the reinvested dividends. Assume you are pleased with the investment, have made enough money and decide to sell the fund, transferring the proceeds to the money market inside the variable annuity. All the taxable gain is completely deferred.

   Even if you sold the annuity and paid the tax, chances are you would have more money. In the first example, outside the annuity, your fund generated dividends and although you reinvested them, you received a 1099 tax form every year and paid taxes. Depending on the amount of dividends paid, this could take a 10-percent return down to a true 8.5-percent return. The difference of 1.5 percent compounded over 10 years is dramatic.

   Inside the annuity, all the dividends are tax-deferred until you withdraw, earning you the true 10-percent return. Imagine you own a government bond mutual fund that is mostly dividends and little capital gain. If you make 9 percent per year in that fund and 8 percent is dividend, your return after taxes could be reduced by more than 2 percent every year. If you do not need the money, consider this tax-deferral technique.

Another point to consider is for those investors who try to beat the market and use "timed" switches between growth accounts and markets in their mutual funds. If they are doing well, the capital gains could be tremendous. Why not defer all taxes under the umbrella of an annuity?

2. **A variable annuity simplifies your investments.** You might find an annuity that offers several different popular mutual fund families. Instead of receiving numerous statements from numerous companies, you will receive one consolidated statement.

3. **Assets should be held in a separate account.** As in the case of the fixed annuity, make certain your assets are kept in a separate account, which means that the funds are either at the mutual fund company, or in a completely separate account from the issuer of the annuity. Should the company fail, you don't want your funds to be a part of it.

4. **Most variable annuities offer a guarantee.** The guarantee states that if you invest in a mutual fund and subsequently pass away, your beneficiary(ies) is guaranteed your original investment at the least. This means that if you invested $10,000 and the fund lost money and dropped to $8,000 before you died, your beneficiary(ies) is guaranteed the original $10,000.

Advantages and Disadvantages of Both Types of Annuities

If you are an investor in CDs or mutual funds, and if your money is continually rolled over or reinvested, you pay taxes on the return every year. Tax-deferral could be a better alternative. Even if you invest in tax-free accounts, the interest earned is still computed into your gross income for Social Security purposes and will affect the amount of tax paid on Social Security benefits.

Should you have a problem with taxation on your Social Security, the income earned in an annuity is not figured into the gross income calculation for Social Security.

Other advantages of annuities were discussed in Chapter 4. Technically, the annuity is issued by an insurance company, thereby providing a beneficiary. The beneficiary will receive this asset free of probate.

Although the money will be received free of probate by a beneficiary, it will not be free of taxes forever. When the beneficiary sells the annuity, he or she will pay a capital gain on the difference of the original contribution and the value at the time of sale. Annuities will not receive a step-up in basis like many other investments that are properly structured to do so.

Another disadvantage is the fact that you will probably incur a tax penalty if you withdraw prior to age 59½. Make sure that this is long-term money and that the company issuing the annuity is solid.

Annuitization

For those of you who own an annuity, do the following: Get your policy and read the first page. Note the *annuity date* or *retirement date,* then read the definition in your policy under annuitization.

Say the annuity is in the accumulation phase. You are probably allowed to add to it, take out funds (with or without a penalty), and possibly have dividends paid to you instead of being reinvested. In the annuitization phase, the company that issued the annuity gives you a guaranteed income for a period of time—for one lifetime, your lifetime and your spouse's, or a guaranteed number of years.

You must realize that once you annuitize, you lose control of your money. It now becomes the property of the company. If you do close the annuity and withdraw all your money before the annuity date, the contract will not automatically annuitize.

As much as I like annuities, annuitizing rarely works to the investor's benefit. Several companies are now offering annuities that you never have to annuitize. I like these over companies that require you to annuitize.

Annuitizing an annuity might proceed as follows: You originally invested $10,000, it is now worth $50,000, and your annuity date is next month. The company sends you a document that reads, "We will be annuitizing your annuity; which option would you prefer? (1) Income for the rest of your life equal to $500 per month, or (2) Income for the remainder of your life and your spouse's life equal to $450 per month?"

Let's say you and your spouse are both 70 years of age in fairly good health. Which option should you take?

First, the one option not mentioned was to liquidate your money; close the annuity and have them send you a check for $50,000. This option often makes the most sense.

The second option of $500 per month for life sounds wonderful, because it seems to be a return of more than 12 percent. But think about it. The company issuing the annuity is assuming that you won't live past 90. If it pays you $500 per month, which is $6,000 per year for the next 20 years, you will have received a total of $120,000. Sounds terrific! However, when compounded, the return is under a 5-percent annualized interest rate. Actually it is even less, because the company had the use of your money during the 20 years. Remember, you never have access to your principal again.

The same scenario is true for the final option. Obviously, these numbers are extreme, but they illustrate how one can make a bad decision simply because he or she did not run the numbers.

Do the Numbers—They Don't Lie

In all fairness, situations do exist when annuitization makes sense. Three of these times might be as follows:

1. **Receiving tax-free income.** When you annuitize, much of the income you receive is tax-free, because part of it represents your after-tax principal The company making the annuity payments shows on your 1099 tax form the portion that is actually your principal being returned that is not taxable. Be sure to figure in the tax benefits when deciding whether you should annuitize.

2. **Avoiding creditor claims.** Sometimes you can annuitize to avoid creditor claims. If you don't have access to the money, neither do your creditors. They might, however, garnish the income.

3. **Making income endure.** If your estate is extremely large and subject to high estate taxes and you can find no other solution, you may benefit by annuitizing the money and making the income last as long as possible (taking a guaranteed 30-year income option). Your beneficiaries will receive the income as well, even after you have passed away.

Chapter 16

Understanding Portfolio Risk and Volatility

Understanding portfolio risk and volatility is the last component of the investment process. Your financial plan should already be in place, and you should have a fairly good understanding of investments. When deciding exactly how to diversify your portfolio, you must have the answers to a great many questions. The following is some good advice you can follow when you plan your investments.

- **Don't change your portfolio without good reason.** Once you allocate and diversify your portfolio in the way that best represents your needs, seriously deliberate before making any changes to the portfolio, unless your goals change or something is seriously wrong with an investment you have chosen.

- **Be wary of recommendations.** Don't invest based only on a friend's recommendation; it is not advisable to invest in something recommended by anyone who does not know your portfolio.

- **Don't borrow money to invest.**

- **Never invest in something you don't understand.** If you can't describe the investment in three minutes or less, forget it. Many other investments exist that you probably understand better.

- **Remember that everything is cyclical.** Don't sell simply because something is down; if you are diversified correctly, something in your portfolio may always be down.

- **Think of investing as smart shopping.** Investing is like buying clothes. If you see something on sale and know it is worth more than the sale price, buy it. If you like a pair of jeans and buy them, don't return them if they go on sale— buy another pair!

- **Don't try to guess the high and low price.** Never put all your money in one stock at one time. Too many people say, "I'll wait until interest rates rise (or fall)," or "I'll wait until the market is cheaper before I invest." The problem with this approach is that you might never get the price you want and thus lose the many benefits of long-term investing.

If you are a long-term investor (as all investors should be), had you bought on the worst conceivable day every year, your return would still be better then a savings account over a 10-year period. Use the dollar-cost averaging approach as much as possible. Great investors don't risk money they can't afford to lose, do not put all their eggs in one basket, and often don't "make a killing" in the market. A simple, methodical strategy usually wins out.

Always review the objectives that you are trying to accomplish: *control, maximization,* and *preservation.*

Let's assume you review your financial plan and decide that, to be safe, your portfolio needs a 9-percent return. Assume that both you and your spouse are going to be retired for another 35 years, and you would like to avoid using principal as much as possible; you want the principal to go to your grandchildren's education. It does not matter how much money you have to invest in deciding how to allocate; what matters is the 9-percent return.

If you allocated correctly, you should be able to answer these questions:

- What is my risk level on the entire portfolio?
- Will I earn my required rate of return?
- What changes should be made as economic environments change?
- How can I earn the return I need with the lowest risk?

Portfolio Risk and Asset Allocation

You may hear people say, "It doesn't matter if the market is high or low, just invest. If you are a long-term investor, the markets move up over time and you will probably be better off than just parking the money in the bank." There is some truth to that statement. However, that could also invite more risk than necessary to accomplish the same return. Further, which markets and investments should you choose?

In allocating a portfolio, I would follow these rules:

♦ **Look for value.** Regardless of whether the company grows next year or whether or not earnings are expected to improve dramatically, ask yourself, Is the stock undervalued based on the current market conditions?

♦ **Try to keep your beta below the market beta,** but try to beat the return of the market. (See the next section for further explanation.)

♦ **Avoid overheated markets.** Markets tend to get overheated and move up too fast. Look back at the speed at which the technology market moved up during the first half of 1995. These stocks could rise even higher than they are today, but because they ran up so fast, a short-term sell-off is more probable than continued appreciation.

♦ **Broadly diversify your portfolio** in many different markets and asset categories. Diversifying is not simply owning five different growth funds; these might all invest in the same type of U.S. stocks, bonds, foreign investments, and real estate. A properly diversified portfolio is "asset allocated" to provide the highest return with the lowest risk. You might currently have a portfolio that makes 10 percent per year—but you might be taking a great deal of risk for that 10 percent. Wouldn't you rather get 10 percent with less risk? This is what is known as *portfolio optimization* and proper asset allocation of your portfolio. Once your assets are properly allocated you'll need to rebalance your portfolio periodically. If your portfolio had 15 percent in a blue chip stock fund, and blue chips had a great year and rose 30 percent, you might consider selling some of that segment of your portfolio and investing more in the markets that did more for your portfolio last year. If your foreign holdings were down last year and now appear undervalued, it might be time to use those profits to increase your foreign holdings.

When assessing portfolio risk, consider that you face two broad types of risk: diversifiable risk and undiversifiable risk. The diversifiable risk is the risk you can diversify away from. However, you cannot control the markets. The stock market could drop and you and your stock could go down with it. This is an undiversifiable risk. The best way to decrease the risk to your portfolio is to have many different investments in different markets. Then, if one of the markets does have a correction and your investment goes down, invest more. As long as it is still a good investment, and that particular investment has not changed (except that it's cheaper), invest more while it is on sale!

Which of the following portfolios is more aggressive: one that just buys an index mutual fund in the S&P 500, or one that invests a portion in the S&P 500 Index fund, a little in the International Index fund, and some more in small-cap stocks? Consider Figure 22 on page 232. This clearly illustrates that tested over a period of time, the broadly diversified portfolio earns more money with less risk.

Determining if a Market Is Overvalued

Many different indicators are used to determine if a certain market segment is overvalued or undervalued. If you go back in time and study the trends in the market (Standard and Poors 500 or Dow Jones Industrial Average), you will see that if more people are buying more stocks than ever before, we are close to a market peak. The reason is most investors are usually wrong and tend to buy investments too late and sell investments too early.

Another indicator is the advance/decline line indicator. The advance/decline line shows how many more stocks are up than down. An index such as the Dow Jones may be up because of a few stocks, but the overall market may actually be doing poorly. This is a bearish signal that should be considered if the market is overvalued.

Some analysts study interest rates. As interest rates rise, the stock market tends to not perform as well, because investors can get a decent interest rate in bonds with less risk than stocks. The less money flowing into stocks, the harder it is for the stock market to increase.

Other analysts decide if a market is overvalued or undervalued by determining how low or high the yields are on stocks. The argument is that gains in the market are actually due to the dividends that stocks pay. Historically, when yields (the percent of dividends) are very low, the stock market will correct to bring yields higher.

Analysts study a myriad of economic indicators, such as the inflation indicators as measured by the Producer Price Index or the Consumer

Price Indicator. If inflation is rising, interest rates might rise, which is often not good for stocks. Also, look at housing costs and unemployment to determine if we are in a recession or heading toward one. This could be both negative and positive for the market. If we are heading toward a recession, but interest rates are low, some companies may actually be very profitable—especially if they are selling necessary items.

Figure 22:
Traditional Portfolio vs. Broadly Diversified Portfolio

Asset Mix Comparison

Investment Policy Allocation Asset Classes	Traditional	Percentage Allocation	
		Portfolio	Broadly Diversified Portfolio
10% short-term debt investments	Treasury bills	10%	10%
40% long-term debt investments	Long-term corporate bonds	40%	20%
50% equity investments	International bonds	0%	20%
	S&P 500	50%	15%
	Small stocks	0%	5%
	International stocks	0%	15%
	Equity REITS	0%	15%

Comparative Investment Performance

	16-year period ending 1998	
Compound return	13.9%	15.3%
Standard Deviation (risk)	12.0%	11.2%
Return per unit of risk*	1.2%	1.4%
Compound return	9.9%	12.3%
Standard Deviation (risk)	12.4%	11.5%
Return per unit of risk*	.8%	1.1%

*Calculated by dividing the compound return by the corresponding standard deviation.

Average Return and Beta Coefficient

First, learn how to figure your portfolio's *average expected return* and your *beta coefficient*. When creating or reviewing your portfolio, if you do not know the weighted average expected return, you're investing without knowing what you wish to accomplish. The weighted average expected return tells you very clearly what your portfolio is positioned to return to you periodically. This is important, because you could be earning a very low portfolio return while taking on much risk. If half of your money is in growth mutual funds and half is in the bank, your portfolio might return only 8 percent annually. However, you are taking on more risk than if you simply bought a U.S. government bond paying the same 8 percent, because the growth part of your portfolio could lose.

Calculate the weighted average expected return by determining the proportion of each investment to the total portfolio value. The expected return on each investment is multiplied by its respective weight in the portfolio. The weighted average expected returns are then added together to reach the total weighted average expected return for the portfolio.

For example, assume you own XYZ stock. The current market value is $6,000 with an expected return of 11 percent. Your other stock, ZZZ, has a current market value of $4,000 with an expected return of 14 percent.

Figure 23:
Weighted Average Expected Return

Stock	Current Market Value	Expected Return	Weighted Average Expected Return		Percent of Portfolio
XYZ	6,000	11%	.60 x .11 =	.066	60%
ZZZ	+ 4,000	14%	.40 x .14 =	+.056	40%
	10,000		Total Portfolio:	.122	
				or 12.2%	
		12.2 % is the Average Expected Return			

First, add the $6,000 and $4,000 to total $10,000. Then, divide each number by the total ($6,000 divided by $10,000 and $4,000 divided by $10,000). The expected return for the $6,000 invested was 11 percent, so multiply the .60 by .11. Do the same for the $4,000 investment. Now, add the two and you have the weighted average expected return. Convert the decimals to percents, and the sum is the average expressed as a percentage. Once you calculate this for your portfolio, you will see how investments such as money markets bring your average way down, yet highly speculative investments don't bring it way up. When figuring what average return to use, try to get the average performance of the investment over the last 10 years.

Beta Coefficient and Portfolio Risk

A *beta* is often referred to as the level of risk or volatility. Normally, the benchmark used is the S&P 500, which has a beta of "1." If your investment has a beta greater than "1," your investment is probably more volatile (price swings are greater) than the market. This means that your investment could be either higher or lower than the market. The rule of thumb is, the greater the beta, the greater the risk. For instance, if your investment has a beta of 2 and the market was down 10 percent, your investment might be down 20 percent. However, if the market was up 10 percent, you could be up 20 percent. Ideally, if you have a growth portfolio, you would want to have a beta equal to or less than the market, with as good or better a return than the market.

If all you want is steady income and minimal principal fluctuations, you might look for the highest yielding fund with a beta of .15. To find a beta of .15, seek high quality income investments, such as intermediate government and tax-free bonds.

Whatever the objective of your portfolio, the beta will help you determine whether your portfolio is being maximized. If your required rate of return is 8 percent, a good exercise would be to study all the mutual funds that have returned 8 percent over the last 10 years, then find the one with the lowest beta. Compute the beta for your entire portfolio; your beta should be on the low end, or you could be taking too much risk.

Your job is to calculate your portfolio beta coefficient by averaging all the betas of your different investments. As shown in Figure 24, assume that you have two mutual funds called ABC and XYZ.

Figure 24:
How to Calculate the Beta Coefficient

	Amount Invested	Weight in Portfolio*	Beta	Weighted Beta Co-efficient**
ABC Mutual Fund	$ 5,000	.25	1.2	.3
XYZ Mutual Fund	+15,000	.75	.8	.6
Total:	20,000			.9

*5,000/20,000 = .25; 15,000/20,000 = .75

**.25 x 1.2 = .3; .75 x .8 = .6

This portfolio has an average beta factor of .9.

Finding the beta of any individual investment should be one of the criteria you look for before investing. This information can be found by calling the company, asking your broker, or checking the *Value Line Reports* for stocks and *Lipper* or *Morningstar* in the library for mutual funds. This is a key criteria and should not be overlooked.

In my opinion, a mature American will probably, on average, strive to achieve around an 8 to 10 percent true rate of return. Based on risk vs. reward, the average portfolio beta, to earn 8 to 10 percent, should be no more than .6 to .7. As mentioned earlier, it is prudent to create your financial plan using only 90 percent of your true investable dollars. The remaining 10 percent of your assets are not included in your portfolio beta average. That 10 percent could be invested.

Sample Portfolio

Assume that in creating your financial plan and studying your situation, you have determined that you need a 9-percent return and should do it with a beta of .6 or less. Next, assume that over the last few years there has been a recession, interest rates are low, and the global economy is rather unstable, but the U.S. economy is beginning to show signs of improvement. Stock and bond markets are reaching new highs, and many people believe they are overvalued.

The only way to be a successful investor is to remember one thing: The only constant is change. As long as you live, there will be pessimists, doomsayers, and uncertainties. You must be prepared to invest wisely. Although there are numerous types of investments, they really fit into four categories: stocks, bonds, real estate, and cash. All others are primarily different ways to own these core holdings.

Further assume that you want a moderate, but limited, involvement in managing your portfolio. By this I mean that you will watch it but want the freedom to take a three-month vacation. You would like a professional co-managing with you. Now that these parameters are established, how best to allocate your assets must be decided.

Your financial plan has already revealed that a 9-percent return on your money is required. Presume that you only need 7 percent in income to live, with 2 percent going back into the estate for "extras": nursing home costs, grandchildren's education fund, inflation, etc. Based on the economy and the understanding that interest rates might go up, Figure 25 on page 236 shows a sample portfolio.

Figure 25:
Managing Your Portfolio (Sample Allocations)

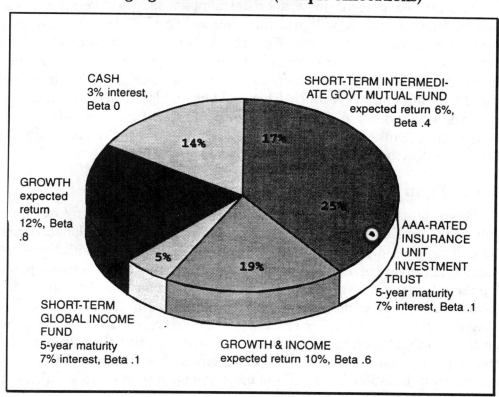

CASH
3% interest,
Beta 0

SHORT-TERM INTERMEDI-
ATE GOVT MUTUAL FUND
expected return 6%,
Beta .4

GROWTH
expected
return
12%, Beta
.8

AAA-RATED
INSURANCE
UNIT
INVESTMENT
TRUST
5-year maturity
7% interest, Beta .1

SHORT-TERM
GLOBAL INCOME
FUND
5-year maturity
7% interest, Beta .1

GROWTH & INCOME
expected return 10%, Beta .6

14%   17%   25%   5%   19%

Unit Investment Trust

Allocate 25 percent in a fixed AAA-rated, insured Unit Investment Trust (UIT) paying 7 to 8 percent. Although the price will fluctuate, it provides sufficient income and you are guaranteed interest, plus principal upon maturity. You should not allocate more, because this is a long-term maturity that you will want to hold the entire time. However, that doesn't matter unless inflation gets out of control, since you are receiving your required return.

Although you need an average of only 7 percent in income from the whole portfolio, you take the full 8 percent (if you can get it) as income, in order to allow one of your other investments to reinvest in an effort to grow.

Should you wish to diversify this 25 percent further, you could allocate 15 percent in the UIT and 10 percent in a long-term government fund. With a government mutual fund, you have a probability that the share price, over time, will rise, acting as an inflation hedge. You can also diversify this 25 percent in tax-free municipal bond funds, if you feel that you need the tax free income.

Short-Term/Intermediate Government Mutual Fund

Allocate 20 percent in a short-term/intermediate government-type mutual fund. This fund will probably yield only 5 to 6 percent, depending upon interest rates at the time of purchase. The reason for the lower yield is because these are short-term obligations of the government. As interest rates rise, so should the interest rate on this fund, and the principal should not fluctuate very much. This could be an ideal place for funds that you still want access to if you need them, but it will give you a better return than a bank. Some call this the "CD alternative." Leave only the least essential in the bank and 20 percent in a fund.

Short-Term Global Income Fund

Based on the economic situation discussed in the preceding example, you might consider 5 percent in a high-quality, short-term global income fund. This should give you an overall yield of between 7 and 9 percent (depending upon current rates). The bonds of many foreign nations pay a higher interest rate. In addition, historically, foreign countries have followed our interest cycle. As rates stabilize and rise in the United States, they usually begin to fall overseas. If you purchase a fund before rates decline, you will receive a good interest rate and, when they drop, an increase in your share price as well. The increase in share price will, again, act as your inflation hedge. Remember, when interest rates fall, bond share prices rise.

A good case in point is the state of the economy during the years from 1991 to 1993. U.S. government bond funds, on the average, performed extremely well between 1991 and 1992. As a result of interest rate declines, these share prices increased. However, it was very difficult for the share prices to continue rising on these funds unless rates dropped further. Yet how far could they drop?

In the beginning of 1993, record numbers of dollars poured into these U.S. government funds. At the same time, disgruntled investors liquidated their investments in global government bond funds. Why? Globally, interest rates were still high, while American rates were low. Statistics show that foreign rates will usually decline following the United States. However, more money went into U.S. bond funds with record low rates, and investors were selling global bond funds with higher rates. If rates decline globally, the share prices have a propensity to rise. If they remain at the status quo, then rates overseas will probably remain higher for a longer time period than in the United States. This is the scientific or technical aspect of investing. Timing is the artistic aspect of investing.

Investing in foreign countries may involve more risk, and you will need to exercise caution in finding investments that will minimize your risk exposure. Seek investments that invest only in government bonds of leading nations and only on a short-term basis. Make sure the manager has a good track record and is well-respected. Should global economies become unstable, be certain that you can withdraw your funds whenever you wish to.

Growth and Income Fund

Now, 20 percent of the portfolio should be positioned for both growth and income. When attempting to obtain both objectives, for safety reasons it is better not to seek the highest income and the highest growth. In a conservative investment, the interest is usually higher than a CD rate, and the growth is more limited than a risky growth stock, which means it probably will not decline as dramatically as the market. The following are some good ideas to keep in mind when seeking both growth and income.

- ◆ **Invest in one, two, or three growth-and-income or straight income funds.** Take the income dividends generated by the fund and reinvest the capital gains. The income should average between 4 and 5 percent. Obviously many mutual funds brag about much higher percentages, but an investor should take a conservative approach. Because you took more income on previous investments, you can afford less income on this investment, and you need the growth. Remember, if this part of your portfolio receives 5-percent growth, it is on only 15 percent of the portfolio. You will still need more growth to maintain purchasing power. When selecting these funds, try to keep the beta low (preferably under .6) and the alpha high. If you can find one that has never lost money, that would be another plus.

- ◆ **Invest in individual stocks.** Here's how to do this. Do your stock research, and then pick five stocks you like. Make sure they all pay dividends of at least 5 to 6 percent. Be sure that the companies you select have a history of paying their dividends regularly. Try to find those that have rarely or never cut dividends, but rather have always increased them. Most dividends are paid quarterly, but many firms work from different quarters. Therefore, stagger the dividends of the stocks you buy to arrive in different months in order to maintain a consistent monthly income, as opposed to receipt of a huge check every three months.

◆ **Keep the beta of the portfolio at about .6.** To receive that dividend, your five investments will probably consist of utility stocks, preferred stocks of major blue chip companies and possibly a convertible bond. A good rule of thumb is that, if you cannot buy at least 100 shares per stock, the costs are too high and the diversification is not as great.

◆ **Do your homework on how to pick a stock.** Determine that the companies you choose typically do well in the market. Look for stock growth that is in line with, or better than, inflation. Also, look at the stock performances in the years that the market was down and select those that do not lose money in such an environment. Don't invest completely in utilities, as they are interest-sensitive and rates could rise, causing a decline in share prices. Pick a couple of high-quality blue chips with very strong dividends. Now you will hopefully be getting the income of 6 percent along with growth of at least 4 percent per year. As a result of the price of your stock rising, plus our dividend, you receive an overall return of 10 percent.

Growth Fund

About 15 percent of a portfolio is usually growth. Obviously, many kinds of growth potential exist, and I encourage you to review your financial plan in order to evaluate them. If all you need is the return from growth and income, with less risk, then perhaps you should increase the allocation on growth and income. However, if you primarily need growth, the best way is to seek stocks with the highest return and the lowest risk. Before actually investing, determine your risk tolerance.

For example, suppose that you do not want a fund with a beta more than .8 and an alpha under .45. If you research long-term growth funds, I can assure you that your list will be reduced to only a handful.

One comment about growth is often overlooked: If you are successful, it will increase your taxes. Should your income rise, your Social Security may be taxed. Two prudent ways to avoid this possibility are to place your growth assets either in your IRA or a variable annuity for tax deferral.

It always amazes me to look at a portfolio and see an investor's account comprised of stock in a liquid account and the IRA in a bank CD. That seems backward to me, because the IRA is not taxed on a capital gain. If you are doing any mutual fund switching or timing, do it inside your IRA, where growth is not figured into your gross income (which determines whether you have to pay taxes on your Social Security) until you withdraw.

I'm sure your next question is, "Do we need the IRA for money because the income from our other investments is not enough?" My answer is another question—"Which is better: using IRA money and paying the taxes, or using after-tax principal from your other investments?"

I prefer taking principal from one of my other investments to live on, rather than my IRA. The reason is simple. When I use my principal, I am not taxed on it as income. Thus, I do not increase my tax burden and do not increase my income, which might result in my having to pay Social Security taxes.

If you plan your estate correctly, by the time you are required to withdraw from the IRA, your income should be in the lowest bracket. Because that money compounded for so long at a tax-deferred rate, even if taxes are high, the difference on the tax-deferred compounding is significant.

As noted in the variable annuity discussion, many annuities allow you to invest in the most popular mutual funds. You neither have to lose control of your money nor begin withdrawing at age 70½, as with an IRA. Many have no front-end commissions, although most have a penalty for early withdrawal. However, this vehicle allows you to realize no taxable gain until funds are withdrawn.

If you are successful with the growth portion of your portfolio, you incur capital gains. However, inside an IRA or annuity, you can sell a mutual fund, place the proceeds in a money market inside the annuity, and avoid all capital gains. Then your income would be reduced, lowering your taxes and protecting you from Social Security taxes.

Finally, don't forget that you can find growth investment in places other than American stocks. It is always interesting when someone asks me what I think of the market. I always ask, "Which one?" There is the domestic stock market, bond market, overseas equities, overseas debt, real estate market, plus others. Usually, markets work very much like the principles of physics. When there is an action, there is a reaction. If one market goes up, another goes down. Should interest rates begin to rise domestically, they may still be declining overseas. If the United States is experiencing a recession, perhaps another country is in an expansion/growth phase, and you could probably find a mutual fund investing there. Should the United States start to experience high inflation, bonds probably will perform poorly, but real estate will generally appreciate. Recently, real estate has been depressed and not fashionable, while stocks have been doing very well. Soon the tables will be turned. The bottom line is, *don't have tunnel vision.* Look at the future, not at the past, and broaden your horizons when considering growth.

Cash

Leave the final 15 percent in cash. Although some investors may feel that this is an excessive amount, you will need liquid cash to make your plan successful. The reason is the averaging effect. I repeat, everything is cyclical. You might average more into a mutual fund or stock if your plan calls for it, only to find the next day that negative economic news forces your investment lower. However, while it may have been dragged down with the rest of the market, it may still be a viable investment. The way to take advantage of a depressed price is by systematically averaging more into the asset. By all means, don't frivolously sell your investment; rather, have cash ready to purchase more. This strategy is known as dollar-cost averaging and is one of the best ways to reduce risk and increase portfolio return. Then, when one investment is "overbought" and it's time to sell, you can replenish your cash.

How to Monitor the Plan

Obviously the investment plan has to be continually monitored. However, when you monitor your plan, *don't make changes unless it is absolutely necessary*. Or, make changes, but the right ones. A common mistake might pertain to your long-term growth fund that starts declining for a long period of time (one year or more). The account should not be sold. Use your cash reserves to average more, or average the profits from another account, should that account now be overvalued. If you did your homework and know that the fund is good and that this is simply a correction, then take advantage of the opportunity to buy some shares on sale.

Also, look at your profits. If you have made the return you wanted, don't be afraid to sell. It's often said that the easy part is buying; the hard part is selling. Simply revert to your plan. If you expected your growth account to make 20 percent, and this was accomplished in two months, perhaps you should take a profit and wait for a correction (if you feel it is overvalued).

Another excellent example is what happened with bond funds in the early 1990s. The funds not only paid the dividends expected, but for the most part, had an excellent appreciation of the shares. The reason was the lowering of interest rates. You must say to yourself, "This is an economic cycle. How much further can interest rates drop? Is the probability greater that they will rise or drop even lower?"

If you think rates might rise and you have a handsome profit, again consider selling. Take the profit and find an alternative investment in the same asset class. Consider the percentage (rate of return) you will make from selling (after paying the tax). Even if you had to place the funds in a short-term government account for up to a year, earning a dividend of 1 percent less than your other investments, will making the switch and capturing the profit still be worth it?

With respect to economic cycles, watch the global markets. If domestic interest rates have continually been dropping, often foreign rates will follow the trend. Without seriously increasing your risk, you might want to average into a foreign bond fund to take advantage of the declining interest rates as experienced with domestic rates.

When monitoring your portfolio, you must be a forward thinker and be patient. Economic cycles could last three, five, or even more years. How will your plan be affected if interest rates rise? How will your plan be affected if inflation takes off? What usually happens during the first few years when a Democrat takes office? Is your portfolio properly diversified to take advantage of it? If you look at the next four years, you might say, "Okay, a Democrat is in office, taxes have a propensity to rise, as does inflation. More environmental programs will begin, and with all this might come higher interest rates. We are in a fairly strong, but nervous, recovery period." So, what should you do? Perhaps you could allocate a portion of your portfolio to whatever should do well if interest rates rise, but not suffer if they don't. Find some tax-advantaged investments, and possibly look at stocks, bonds or funds that might do well under a Democratic leadership, such as those that help build our infrastructure or support environmentally friendly companies. Also, take profits on investments that did well in declining interest rate cycles, and look globally to see if there is any value in that arena.

Remember, your retirement should be a long and happy one. Once you set the plan for the long haul, you can fine-tune it as market conditions fluctuate, but the overall allocation should be retained, unless your needs change. Be diligent not to stray from your plan or make any unnecessary modifications. Think like a technician and try to avoid emotional decisions.

Dollar-Cost Averaging

Since I have referred to this strategy repeatedly, a further definition is warranted. *Dollar-cost averaging* is a systematic savings plan that helps to reduce not only the price paid for investments but also the risk, while hopefully increasing the return. The old saying of "buy low and sell high" is not that easy to do. However, if you can make a commitment to add to your stock the same amount of money, at the same time every month (or quarter), you will take advantage of all the highs and the lows and reduce your average cost per share. In rising market environments you will be purchasing fewer shares and, during declining markets, more shares.

For instance, assume you invest $1,000 per month for nine consecutive months at different market prices. Over nine months you invest $9,000. Now take a hypothetical example to see whether your money is still worth $9,000.

Figure 26:
Portfolio Growth

($1,000 per month investment)

Months	Share Price	No. Shares Purchased w/$1,000	Cum. Market Value
1	8	125	$1,000
2	10	100	2,250
3	8	125	2,800
4	5	200	2,750
5	4	250	3,200
6	5	200	5,000
7	8	125	9,000
8	10	100	12,250
9	8	125	10,800

Figure 26 shows that your portfolio has grown to $10,800. You invested a total of $9,000.

Note: *Cumulative Market Value* is found by adding the number of shares owned in total for that period and multiplying it by the share price for that period. Thus, in period three, you already owned a total of 350 shares, the current price is $8 per share, which amounts to a dollar value of $2,800.

Conclusion

This book has discussed many issues pertaining to financial investments, estate planning and health care. For your purposes, focus on just one aspect at a time in order to get your plan in place and your life more organized. You have the power to control maximize and preserve what you have worked so hard for. You decide if you will reduce your taxes; you decide who will inherit your asset; you decide to not go broke because of creditor claims, medical costs, and all of the other obstacles waiting to bring you down in retirement. Get proactive. Act as opposed to react. Create a plan, seek competent advice and make your retirement all that you wish it to be. And remember the three main objectives you are striving to accomplish with your estate and financial plan: *control, maximization,* and *preservation.*

Miscellaneous Charts

Life Expectancy Table I

Minimum Distribution Incidental Benefit Table
(Joint Life With Non-spouse More Than 10 Years Younger

Age		Divisor				Age		Divisor
70	....	26.2				93	....	8.8
71	....	25.3				94	....	8.3
72	....	24.4				95	....	7.8
73	....	23.5				96	....	7.3
74	....	22.7				97	....	6.9
75	....	21.8				98	....	6.5
76	....	20.9				99	....	6.1
77	....	20.1				100	....	5.7
78	....	19.2				101	....	5.3
79	....	18.4				102	....	5.0
80	....	17.6				103	....	4.7
81	....	16.8				104	....	4.4
82	....	16.0				105	....	4.1
83	....	15.3				106	....	3.8
84	....	14.5				107	....	3.6
85	....	13.8				108	....	3.3
86	....	13.1				109	....	3.1
87	....	12.4				110	....	2.8
88	....	11.8				112	....	2.6
89	....	11.1				113	....	2.4
90	....	10.5				114	....	2.2
91	....	9.9				115	....	2.0
92	....	9.4		15 and older			....	1.8

Life Expectancy Table II

Minimum Distribution Incidental Benefit Table
(Joint Life With Non-spouse More Than 10 Years Younger)

Age		Divisor				Age		Divisor				Age		Divisor
5	... ...	76.6				42	... ...	40.6				79	... ...	10.0
6	... ...	75.6				43	... ...	39.6				80	... ...	9.5
7	... ...	74.7				44	... ...	38.7				81	... ...	8.9
8	... ...	73.7				45	... ...	37.7				82	... ...	8.4
9	... ...	72.7				46	... ...	36.8				83	... ...	7.9
10	... ...	71.7				47	... ...	35.9				84	... ...	7.4
11	... ...	70.7				48	... ...	34.9				85	... ...	6.9
12	... ...	69.7				49	... ...	34.0				86	... ...	6.5
13	... ...	68.8				50	... ...	33.1				87	... ...	6.1
14	... ...	67.8				51	... ...	32.2				88	... ...	5.7
15	... ...	66.8				52	... ...	31.3				89	... ...	5.3
16	... ...	65.8				53	... ...	30.4				90	... ...	5.0
17	... ...	64.8				54	... ...	29.5				91	... ...	4.7
18	... ...	63.9				55	... ...	28.6				92	... ...	4.4
19	... ...	62.9				56	... ...	27.7				93	... ...	4.1
20	... ...	61.9				57	... ...	26.8				94	... ...	3.9
21	... ...	60.9				58	... ...	25.9				95	... ...	3.7
22	... ...	59.9				59	... ...	25.0				96	... ...	3.4
23	... ...	59.0				60	... ...	2.2				97	... ...	3.2
24	... ...	58.0				61	... ...	23.3				98	... ...	3.0
25	... ...	57.0				62	... ...	22.5				99	... ...	2.8
26	... ...	56.0				63	... ...	21.6				100	... ...	2.7
27	... ...	55.1				64	... ...	20.8				101	... ...	2.5
28	... ...	54.1				65	... ...	20.0				102	... ...	2.3
29	... ...	53.1				66	... ...	19.2				103	... ...	2.1
30	... ...	52.2				67.00	... ...	18.4				104	... ...	1.9
31	... ...	51.2				68.00	... ...	17.6				105	... ...	1.8
32	... ...	50.2				69.00	... ...	16.8				106	... ...	1.6
33	... ...	49.3				70.00	... ...	16.0				107	... ...	1.4
34	... ...	48.3				71.00	... ...	15.3				108	... ...	1.3
35	... ...	47.3				72.00	... ...	14.6				109	... ...	1.1
36	... ...	46.4				73.00	... ...	13.9				110	... ...	1.0
37	... ...	45.4				74	... ...	13.2				111	... ...	0.9
38	... ...	44.4				75	... ...	12.5				112	... ...	0.8
39	... ...	43.5				76	... ...	11.9				113	... ...	0.7
40	... ...	42.5				77	... ...	11.2				114	... ...	0.6
41	... ...	41.5				78	... ...	10.6				115	... ...	0.5

Life Expectancy Table II (page 1)

	35	36	37	38	39	40	41	42	43	44	45	46	47	48	49	50	51	52	53	54
35	54	53.5	53	52.6	52.2	51.8	51.4	51.1	50.8	50.5										
36	53.5	53	52.5	52	51.6	51.2	50.8	50.4	50.1	49.8										
37	53	52.5	52	51.5	51	50.6	50.2	49.8	49.5	49.1										
38	52.6	52	51.5	51	50.5	50	49.6	49.2	48.8	48.5										
39	52.2	51.6	51	50.5	50	49.5	49.1	48.6	48.2	47.8										
40	51.8	51.2	50.6	50	49.5	49	48.5	48.1	47.6	47.2										
41	51.4	50.8	50.2	49.6	49.1	48.5	48	47.5	47.1	46.7										
42	51.1	50.4	49.8	49.2	48.6	48.1	47.5	47	46.6	46.1										
43	50.8	50.1	49.5	48.8	48.2	47.6	47.1	46.6	46	45.6										
44	50.5	49.8	49.1	48.5	47.8	47.2	46.7	46.1	45.6	45.1										
45	50.2	49.5	48.8	48.1	47.5	46.9	46.3	45.7	45.1	44.6	44.1	43.6	43.2	42.7	42.3	42	41.6	41.3	41	40.7
46	50	49.2	48.5	47.8	47.2	46.5	46.9	45.3	44.7	44.1	43.6	43.1	42.6	42.2	41.8	41.4	41	40.6	40.3	40
47	49.7	49	48.3	47.5	46.8	46.2	45.5	44.9	44.3	43.7	43.2	42.6	42.1	41.7	41.2	40.8	40.4	40	39.7	39.3
48	49.5	48.8	48	47.3	46.6	45.9	45.2	44.5	43.9	43.3	42	42.2	41.7	41.2	40.7	40.2	39.8	39.4	39	38.7
49	49.3	48.5	47.8	47	46.3	45.6	44.9	44.2	43.6	42.9	41.6	41.8	41.2	40.7	40.2	39.7	39.3	38.8	38.4	38.1
50	49.2	48.4	47.6	46.8	46	45.3	44.6	43.9	43.2	42.6	41.3	41.4	40.8	40.2	39.7	39.2	38.7	38.3	37.9	37.5
51	49	48.2	47.4	46.6	45.8	45.1	44.3	43.6	42.9	42.2	41	41	40.4	39.8	39.3	38.7	38.2	37.8	37.3	36.9
52	48.8	48	47.2	46.4	45.6	44.8	44.1	43.3	42.6	41.9	40.7	40.6	40	39.4	38.8	38.3	37.8	37.3	36.8	36.4
53	48.7	47.9	47	46.2	45.4	44.6	43.9	43.1	42.4	41.7	40.4	40.3	39.7	39	38.4	37.9	37.3	36.8	36.3	35.8
54	48.6	47.7	46.9	46	45.2	44.4	43.6	42.9	42.1	41.4	40.2	40	39.3	38.7	38.1	37.5	36.9	36.4	35.8	35.3
55	48.5	47.6	46.7	45.9	45.1	44.2	43.4	42.7	41.9	41.2	40	39.7	39	38.4	37.7	37.1	36.5	35.9	35.4	34.9
56	48.3	47.5	46.6	45.8	44.9	44.1	43.3	42.5	41.7	40.9	39.7	39.5	38.7	38.1	37.4	36.8	36.1	35.6	35	34.4
57	48.3	47.4	46.5	45.6	44.8	43.9	43.1	42.3	41.5	40.7	39.6	39.2	38.5	37.8	37.1	36.4	35.8	35.2	34.6	34
58	48.2	47.3	46.4	45.5	44.7	43.8	43	42.1	41.3	40.5	39.4	39	38.2	37.5	36.8	36.1	35.5	34.8	34.2	336
59	48.1	47.2	46.3	45.4	44.5	43.7	42.8	42	41.2	40.4	39.2	38.8	38	37.3	36.6	35.9	35.2	34.5	33.9	33.3
60	48	47.1	46.2	45.3	44.4	43.6	42.7	41.9	41	40.2	39.1	38.6	37.8	37.1	36.3	35.6	34.9	34.2	33.6	32.9
61	47.9	47	46.1	45.2	44.3	43.5	42.6	41.7	40.9	40	38.9	38.4	37.6	36.9	36.1	35.4	34.6	33.9	33.3	32.6
62	47.9	47	46	45.1	44.2	43.4	42.5	41.6	40.8	39.9	38.8	38.3	37.5	36.7	35.9	35.1	34.4	33.7	33	32.3
63	47.8	46.9	46	45.1	44.2	43.3	42.4	41.5	40.6	39.8	38.7	38.1	37.3	36.5	35.7	34.9	34.2	33.5	32.7	32
64	47.8	46.8	45.9	45	44.1	43.2	42.3	41.4	40.5	39.7	38.6	38	37.2	36.3	35.5	34.8	34	332	32.5	31.8
65	47.7	46.8	45.9	44.9	44	43.1	42.2	41.3	40.4	39.6	38.5	37.9	37	36.2	35.4	34.6	33.8	33	32.3	31.6
66	47.7	46.7	45.8	44.9	44	43.1	42.2	41.3	40.4	39.5	38.4	37.8	36.9	36.1	35.2	34.4	33.6	32.9	32.1	31.4
67	47.6	46.7	45.8	44.8	43.9	43	42.1	41.2	40.3	39.4	38.4	37.7	36.8	36	35.1	34.3	33.5	32.7	31.9	31.2
68	47.6	46.7	45.7	44.8	43.9	42.9	42	41.1	40.2	39.3	38.3	37.6	36.7	35.8	35	34.2	33.4	32.5	31.8	31
69	47.6	46.6	45.7	44.8	43.8	42.9	42	41.1	40.2	39.3	38.2	37.5	36.6	35.7	34.9	34.1	33.2	32.4	31.6	30.8
70	47.5	46.6	45.7	44.7	43.8	42.9	41.9	41	40.1	39.2	38.2	37.4	36.5	35.7	34.8	34	33.1	32.3	31.5	30.7
71	47.5	46.6	45.6	44.7	43.8	42.8	41.9	41	40.1	39.1	38.1	37.3	36.5	35.6	34.7	33.9	33	32.2	31.4	30.5
72	47.5	46.6	45.6	44.7	43.7	42.8	41.9	40.9	40	39.1	38.1	37.3	36.4	35.5	34.6	33.8	32.9	32.1	31.2	30.4
73	47.5	46.5	45.6	44.6	43.7	42.8	41.8	40.9	40	39	38.1	37.2	36.3	35.4	34.6	33.7	32.8	32	31.1	30.3
74	47.5	46.5	45.6	44.6	43.7	42.7	41.8	40.9	39.9	39	38	37.2	36.3	35.4	34.5	33.6	32.8	31.9	31.1	30.2
75	47.4	46.5	45.5	44.6	43.6	42.7	41.8	40.8	39.9	39	38	37.1	36.2	35.3	34.5	33.6	32.7	31.8	31	30.1
76	47.4	46.5	45.5	44.6	43.6	42.7	41.7	40.8	39.9	38.9	38	37.1	36.2	35.3	34.4	33.5	32.6	31.8	30.9	30.1
77	47.4	46.5	45.5	44.6	43.6	42.7	41.7	40.8	39.8	38.9	37.9	37.1	36.2	35.3	34.4	33.5	32.6	31.7	30.8	30
78	47.4	46.4	45.5	44.5	43.6	42.6	41.7	40.7	39.8	38.9	37.9	37	36.1	35.2	34.3	33.4	32.5	31.7	30.8	29.9
79	47.4	46.4	45.5	44.5	43.6	42.6	41.7	40.7	39.8	38.9	37.9	37	36.1	35.2	34.3	33.4	32.5	31.6	30.7	29.9
80	47.4	46.4	45.5	44.5	43.6	42.6	41.7	40.7	39.8	38.8	37.9	37	36.1	35.2	34.2	33.4	32.5	31.6	30.7	29.8
81	47.4	46.4	45.5	44.5	43.5	42.6	41.6	40.7	39.8	38.8	37.9	37	36	35.1	34.2	33.3	32.4	31.5	30.7	29 8
82	47.4	46.4	45.4	44.5	43.5	42.6	41.6	40.7	39.7	38.8	37.8	36.9	36	35.1	34.2	33.3	32.4	31.5	30.6	29.7
83	47.4	46.4	45.4	44.5	43.5	42.6	41.6	40.7	39.7	38.8	37.8	36.9	36	35.1	34.2	33.3	32.4	31.5	30.6	29.7
84	47.4	46.4	45.4	44.5	43.5	42.6	41.6	40.7	39.7	38.8	37.8	36.9	36	35.1	34.2	33.2	32.3	31.4	30.6	29.7
85	47.4	46.4	45.4	44.5	43.5	42.6	41.6	40.7	39.7	38.8	37.8	36.9	36	35.1	34.1	33.2	32.3	31.4	30.5	29 6
86	47.3	46.4	45.4	44.5	43.5	42.5	41.6	40.6	39.7	38.8	37.8	36.9	36	35	34.1	33.2	32.3	31.4	30.5	29 6
87	47.3	46.4	45.4	44.5	435	42.5	41.6	40.6	39.7	38.7	37.8	36.9	35.9	35	34.1	33.2	32.3	31.4	30.5	29 6
88	47.3	46.4	45.4	44.5	43.5	42.5	41.6	40.6	39.7	38.7	37.8	36.9	35.9	35	34.1	33.2	32.3	31.4	30.5	29 6
89	47.3	46.4	45.4	44.4	435	42.5	41.6	40.8	39.7	38.7	37.8	36.9	35.9	35	34.1	33.2	32.3	31.4	30.5	29 6
90	47.3	46.4	45.4	44.4	43.5	42.5	41.6	40.6	39.7	38.7	37.8	36.9	35.9	35	34.1	33.2	32.3	31.3	30 5	29 6
91	47.3	46.4	45.4	44.4	43.5	42.5	41.6	40.6	39.7	38.7	37.8	36.8	35.9	35	34.1	33.2	32.2	31.3	30 4	29 5
92	47.3	46.4	45.4	44.4	43.5	42.5	41.6	40.6	39.7	38.7	37.8	36.8	35.9	35	34.1	33.2	32.2	31.3	30 4	29 5

Life Expectancy Table II (page 2)

	55	56	57	58	59	60	61	62	63	64	65	66	67	68	69	70	71	72	73	74
55	34.4	33.9	33.5	33.1	32.7	32.3	32	31.7	31.4	31.1										
56	33.9	33.4	33	32.5	32.1	31.7	31.4	31	30.7	30.4										
57	33.5	33	32.5	32	31.6	31.2	30.8	30.4	30.1	29.8										
58	33.1	32.5	32	31.5	31.1	30.6	30.2	29.9	29.5	29.2										
59	32.7	32.1	31.6	31.1	30.6	30.1	29.7	29.3	28.4	28.6										
60	32.3	31.7	31.2	30.6	30.1	29.7	29.2	28.8	27.8	28										
61	32	31.4	30.8	30.2	29.7	29.2	28.7	28.3	27.3	27.4										
62	31.7	31	30.4	29.9	29.3	28.8	28.3	27.8	26.9	26.9										
63	31.4	30.7	30.1	29.5	28.9	28.4	27.8	27.3	26.4	26.4										
64	31.1	30.4	29.8	29.2	28.6	28	27.4	26.9	26	26.9										
65	30.9	30.2	29.5	28.9	28.2	27.6	27.1	26.5	25.6	25.5	25	24.6	24.2	23.8	23.4	23.1	22.8	22.5	22.2	22
66	30.6	29.9	29.2	28.6	27.9	27.3	26.7	26.1	24.9	25.1	24.6	24.1	23.7	23.3	22.9	22.5	22.2	21.9	21.6	21.4
67	30.4	29.7	29	28.3	27.6	27	26.4	25.8	24.6	24.7	24.2	23.7	23.2	22.8	22.4	22	21.7	21.3	21	20.8
68	30.2	29.5	28.8	28.1	27.4	26.7	26.1	25.5	24.3	24.3	23.8	23.3	22.8	22.3	21.9	21.5	21.2	20.8	20.5	20.2
69	30.1	29.3	28.6	27.8	27.1	26.5	25.8	25.2	24	24	23.4	22.9	22.4	21.9	21.5	21.1	20.7	20.3	20	19.6
70	29.9	29.1	28.4	27.6	26.9	26.2	25.6	24.9	23.8	23.7	23.1	22.5	22	21.5	21.1	20.6	20.2	19.8	19.4	19.1
71	29.7	29	28.2	27.5	26.7	26	25.3	247	23.5	23.4	22.8	22.2	21.7	21.2	20.7	20.2	19.8	19.4	19	18.6
72	29.6	28.8	28.1	27.3	26.5	25.8	25.1	24.4	23.3	23.1	22.5	21.9	21.3	20.8	20.3	19.8	19.4	18.9	18.5	18.2
73	29.5	28.7	27.9	27.1	26.4	25.6	24.9	24.2	23.1	22.9	22.2	21.6	21	20.5	20	19.4	19	18.5	18.1	17.7
74	29.4	28.6	27.8	27	26.2	25.5	24.7	24	23	22.7	22	21.4	20.8	20.2	19.6	19.1	18.6	18.2	17.7	17.3
75	29.3	28.5	27.7	26.9	26.1	25.3	24.6	23.8	22.8	22.4	21.8	21.1	20.5	19.9	19.3	18.8	18.3	17.8	17.3	16.9
76	29.2	28.4	27.6	26.8	26	25.2	24.4	23.7	22.7	22.3	21.6	20.9	20.3	19.7	19.1	18.5	18	17.5	17	16.5
77	29.1	28.3	27.5	26.7	25.9	25.1	24.3	23.6	22.6	22.1	21.4	20.7	20.1	19.4	18.8	18.3	17.7	17.2	16.7	16.2
78	29.1	28.2	27.4	26.6	25.8	25	24.2	23.4	22.4	21.9	21.2	20.5	19.9	19.2	18.6	18	17.5	16.9	16.4	15.9
79	29	28.2	27.3	26.5	25.7	24.9	24.1	23.3	22.3	21.8	21.1	20.4	19.7	19	18.4	17.8	17.2	16.7	16.1	15.6
80	29	28.1	27.3	26.4	25.6	24.8	24	23.2	22.3	21.7	21	20.2	19.5	18.9	18.2	17.6	17	16.4	15.9	15.4
81	28.9	28.1	27.2	26.4	25.5	24.7	23.9	23.1	22.2	21.6	20.8	20.1	19.4	18.7	18.1	17.4	16.8	16.2	15.7	15.1
82	28.9	28	27.1	26.3	25.5	24.6	23.8	230	22.1	21.5	20.7	20	19.3	18.6	17.9	17.3	16.6	16	15.5	14.9
83	28.8	28	27.1	26.3	25.4	24.6	23.8	23	22	21.4	20.6	19.9	19.2	18.5	17.8	17.1	16.5	15.9	15.3	14.7
84	28.8	27.9	27	26.2	25.4	24.5	23.7	22.9	22	21.3	20.5	19.8	19.1	18.4	17.7	17	16.3	15.7	15.1	14.5
85	28.8	27.9	27	26.2	25.3	24.5	23.7	22.8	21.9	21.3	20.5	19.7	19	18.3	17.6	16.9	16.2	15.6	15	14.4
86	28.7	27.9	27	26.1	25.3	24.5	23.6	22.8	21.9	21.2	20.4	19.6	18.9	18.2	17.5	16.8	16.1	15.5	14.8	14.2
87	28.7	27.8	27	26.1	25.3	24.4	23.6	22.8	21.8	21.1	20.4	19.6	18.8	18.1	17.4	16.7	16	15.4	14.7	14.1
88	28.7	27.8	26.9	26.1	25.2	24.4	23.5	22.7	21.8	21.1	20.3	19.5	18.8	18	17.3	16.6	15.9	15.3	14.6	14
89	28.7	27.8	26.9	26.1	25.2	24.4	23.5	22.7	21.8	21.1	20.3	19.5	18.7	18	17.2	16.5	15.8	15.2	14.5	13.9
90	28.7	27.8	26.9	26.1	25.2	24.3	23.5	22.7	21.8	21	20.2	19.4	18.7	17.9	17.2	16.5	15.8	15.1	14.5	13.8
91	28.7	27.8	26.9	26	25.2	24.3	23.5	22.6	21.7	21	20.2	19.4	18.6	17.9	17.1	16.4	15.7	15	14.4	13.7
92	28.6	27.8	26.9	26	25.2	24.3	23.5	22.6	21.7	21	20.2	19.4	18.6	17.8	17.1	16.4	15.7	15	14.3	13.7
93	28.6	27.8	26.9	26	25.1	24.3	23.4	22.6	21.7	20.9	20.1	19.3	18.6	17.8	17.1	16.3	15.6	14.9	14.2	13.6
94	28.6	27.7	26.9	26	25.1	24.3	23.4	22.6	21.7	20.9	20.1	19.3	18.5	17.8	17	16.3	15.6	14.9	14.2	13.6
95	28.6	27.7	26.9	26	25.1	24.3	23.4	22.6	21.7	20.9	20.1	19.3	18.5	17.8	17	16.3	15.6	14.9	14.2	13.5
96	28.6	27.7	26.8	26	25.1	24.2	23.4	22.6	21.7	20.9	20.1	19.3	18.5	17.7	17	16.2	15.5	14.8	14.2	13.5
97	28.6	27.7	26.8	26	25.1	24.2	23.4	22.5	21.7	20.9	20.1	19.3	18.5	17.7	17	16.2	15.5	14.8	14.1	13.5
98	28.6	27.7	26.8	26	25.1	24.2	23.4	22.5	21.7	20.9	20.1	19.3	18.5	17.7	16.9	16.2	15.5	14.8	14.1	13.4
99	28.6	27.7	26.8	26	25.1	24.2	23.4	22.5	21.7	20.8	20	19.2	18.5	17.7	16.9	16.2	15.5	14.7	14.1	13.4
100	28.6	27.7	26.8	26	25.1	24.2	23.4	22.5	21.7	20.8	20	19.2	18.4	17.7	16.9	16.2	15.4	14.7	14	13.4
101	28.6	27.7	26.8	25.9	25.1	24.2	23.3	22.5	21.7	20.8	20	19.2	18.4	17.7	16.9	16.1	15.4	14.7	14	13.3
102	28.6	27.7	26.8	25.9	25.1	24.2	23.3	22.5	21.7	20.8	20	19.2	18.4	17.6	16.9	16.1	15.4	14.7	14	13.3
103	28.6	27.7	26.8	25.9	25.1	24.2	23.3	22.5	21.7	20.8	20	19.2	18.4	17.6	16.9	16.1	15.4	14.7	14	13.3
104	28.6	27.7	26.8	25.9	25.1	24.2	23.3	22.5	21.6	20.8	20	19.2	18.4	17.6	16.9	16.1	15.4	14.7	14	13.3
105	28.6	27.7	26.8	25.9	25.1	24.2	23.3	22.5	21.6	20.8	20	19.2	18.4	17.6	16.8	16.1	15.4	14.7	13.9	13.3
106	28.6	27.7	26.8	25.9	25.1	24.2	23.3	22.5	21.6	20.8	20	19.2	18.4	17.6	16.8	16.1	15.3	14.6	13.9	13.3
107	28.6	27.7	26.8	25.9	25.1	24.2	23.3	22.5	21.6	20.8	20	19.2	18.4	17.6	16.8	16.1	15.3	14.6	13.9	13.2
108	28.6	27.7	26.8	25.9	25.1	24.2	23.3	22.5	21.6	20.8	20	19.2	18.4	17.6	16.8	16.1	15.3	14.6	13.9	13.2
109	28.6	27.7	26.8	25.9	25.1	24.2	23.3	22.5	21.6	20.8	20	19.2	18.4	17.6	16.8	16.1	15.3	14.6	13.9	13.2
110	28.6	27.7	26.8	25.9	25.1	24.2	23.3	22.5	21.6	20.8	20	19.2	18.4	17.6	16.8	16.1	15.3	14.6	13.9	13.2
111	28.6	27.7	26.8	25.9	25	24.2	23.3	22.5	21.6	20.8	20	19.2	18.4	17.6	16.8	16.1	15.3	14.6	13.9	13.2
112	28.6	27.7	26.8	25.9	25	24.2	23.3	22.5	21.6	20.8	20	19.2	18.4	17.6	16.8	16.1	15.3	14.6	13.9	13.2

Life Expectancy Table II (page 3)

	75	76	77	78	79	80	81	82	83	84	85	86	87	88	89	90	91	92	93	94
75	16.5	16.1	15.8	15.4	15.1	14.9	14.6	14.4	14.2	14										
76	16.1	15.7	15.4	15	14.7	14.4	14.1	13.9	13.7	13.5										
77	15.8	15.4	15	14.6	143	14	13.7	13.4	13.2	13										
78	15.4	15	14.6	14.2	13.9	13.5	13.2	13	12.7	12.5										
79	15.1	14.7	14.3	13.9	135	13.2	12.8	12.5	12.3	12										
80	14.9	14.4	14	13.5	13.2	12.8	12.5	12.2	11.9	11.6										
81	14.6	14.1	13.7	13.2	12.8	12.5	12.1	11.8	11.5	11.2										
82	14.4	13.9	13.4	13	12.5	12.2	11.8	11.5	11.1	10.9										
83	14.2	13.7	13.2	12.7	12.3	11.9	11.5	11.1	10.8	10.5										
84	14	13.5	13	12.5	12	11.6	11.2	10.9	10.5	10.2										
85	13.8	13.3	12.8	12.3	11.8	11.4	11	10.6	10.2	9.9	9.6	9.3	9.1	8.9	8.7	8.5	8.3	8.2	8	7.9
86	13.7	13.1	12.6	12.1	11.6	11.2	10.8	10.4	10	9.7	9.3	9.1	8.8	8.6	8.3	8.2	8	7.8	7.7	7.6
87	13.5	13	12.4	11.9	11.4	11	10.6	10.1	9.8	9.4	9.1	8.8	8.5	8.3	8.1	7.9	7.7	7.5	7.4	7.2
88	13.4	12.8	12.3	11.8	11.3	10.8	10.4	10	9.6	9.2	8.9	8.6	8.3	8	7.8	7.6	7.4	7.2	7.1	6.9
89	13.3	12.7	12.2	11.6	11.1	10.7	10.2	9.8	9.4	9	8.7	8.3	8.1	7.8	7.5	7.3	7.1	6.9	6.8	6.6
90	13.2	12.6	12.1	11.5	11	10.5	10.1	9.6	9.2	8.8	8.5	8.2	7.9	7.6	7.3	7.1	6.9	6.7	6.5	6.4
91	13.1	12.5	12	11.4	10.9	10.4	9.9	9.5	9.1	8.7	8.3	8	7.7	7.4	7.1	6.9	6.7	6.5	6.3	6.2
92	13.1	12.5	11.9	11.3	10.8	10.3	9.8	9.4	8.9	8.5	8.2	7.8	7.5	7.2	6.9	6.7	6.5	6.3	6.1	5.9
93	13	12.4	11.8	11.3	10.7	10.2	9.7	9.3	8.8	8.4	8	7.7	7.4	7.1	6.8	6.5	6.3	6.1	5.9	5.8
94	12.9	12.3	11.7	11.2	10.6	10.1	9.6	9.2	8.7	8.3	7.9	7.6	7.2	6.9	6.6	6.4	6.2	5.9	5.8	5.6
95	12.9	12.3	11.7	11.1	10.6	10.1	9.6	9.1	8.6	8.2	7.8	7.5	7.1	6.8	6.5	6.3	6	5.8	5.6	5.4
96	12.9	12.2	11.6	11.1	10.5	10	9.5	9	8.5	8.1	7.7	7.3	7	6.7	6.4	6.1	5.9	5.7	5.5	5.3
97	12.8	12.2	11.6	11	10.5	9.9	9.4	8.9	8.5	8	7.6	7.3	6.9	6.6	6.3	6	5.8	5.5	5.3	5.1
98	12.8	12.2	11.5	11	10.4	9.9	9.4	8.9	8.4	8	7.6	7.2	6.8	6.5	6.2	5.9	5.6	5.4	5.2	5
99	12.7	12.1	11.5	10.9	10.4	9.8	9.3	8.8	8.3	7.9	7.5	7.1	6.7	6.4	6.1	5.8	5.5	5.3	5.1	4.9
100	12.7	12.1	11.5	10.9	10.3	9.8	9.2	8.7	8.3	7.8	7.4	7	6.6	6.3	6	5.7	5.4	5.2	5	4.8
101	12.7	12.1	11.4	10.8	10.3	9.7	9.2	8.7	8.2	7.8	7.3	6.9	6.6	6.2	5.9	5.6	5.3	5.1	4.9	4.7
102	12.7	12	11.4	10.8	10.2	9.7	9.1	8.7	8.2	7.7	7.3	6.9	6.5	6.2	5.8	5.5	5.3	5	4.8	4.6
103	12.6	12	11.4	10.8	10.2	9.7	9.1	8.6	8.1	7.7	7.2	6.8	6.4	6.1	5.8	5.5	4.2	4.9	4.7	4.5
104	12.6	12	11.4	10.8	10.2	9.6	9.1	8.6	8.1	7.6	7.2	6.8	6.4	6	5.7	5.4	5.1	4.8	4.6	4.4
105	12.6	12	11.3	10.7	10.2	9.6	9	8.5	8	7.6	7.1	6.7	6.3	6	5.6	5.3	5	4.8	4.5	4.3
106	12.6	11.9	11.3	1.7	10.1	9.6	9	8.5	8	7.5	7.1	6.7	6.3	5.9	5.6	5.3	5	4.7	4.5	4.2
107	12.6	11.9	11.3	10.7	10.1	9.5	9	8.5	8	7.5	7.1	6.6	6.2	5.9	5.5	5.2	4.9	4.6	4.4	4.1
108	12.6	11.9	11.3	10.7	10.1	9.5	9	8.5	8	75	7	6.6	6.2	5.8	5.5	5.2	4.9	4.6	4.3	4.1
109	12.6	11.9	11.3	10.7	10.1	9.5	9	8.4	7.9	7.5	7	6.6	6.2	5.8	5.5	5.1	4.8	4.5	4.3	4
110	12.6	11.9	11.3	10.7	10.1	9.5	9	8.4	7.9	7.5	7	6.6	6.2	5.8	5.4	5.1	4.8	4.5	4.3	4
111	12.5	11.9	11.3	10.6	10.1	9.5	8.9	8.4	7.9	7.4	7	6.5	6.1	5.7	5.4	5.1	4.8	4.5	4.2	3.9
112	12.5	11.9	11.3	10.6	10.1	9.5	8.9	8.4	7.9	7.4	7	6.5	6.1	5.7	5.4	5	4.7	4.4	4.2	3.9
113	12.5	11.9	11.2	10.6	10	9.5	8.9	8.4	7.9	7.4	6.9	6.5	6.1	5.7	5.4	5	4.7	4.4	4.2	39
114	12.5	11.9	11.2	10.6	10	9.5	8.9	8.4	7.9	74	6.9	6.5	6.1	5.7	5.3	5	4.7	4.4	4.1	3.9
115	12.5	11.9	11.2	10.6	10	9.5	8.9	8.4	7.9	7.4	6.9	6.5	6.1	5.7	5.3	5	4.7	4.4	4.1	3.9

Compounding Interest Chart

Years	4	4.5	5	5.5	6	6.5	7	7.5	8	8.5	9	9.5	10	10.5	11	11.5	12
1	1.04	1.05	1.05	1.06	1.06	1.07	1.07	1.08	1.08	1.09	1.10	1.10	1.10	1.11	1.11	1.12	1.12
2	1.08	1.09	1.10	1.11	1.12	1.13	1.14	1.16	1.17	1.18	1.19	1.20	1.21	1.22	1.23	1.24	1.25
3	1.12	1.14	1.16	1.17	1.19	1.21	1.23	1.24	1.26	1.28	1.30	1.31	1.33	1.35	1.37	1.39	1.40
4	1.17	1.19	1.22	1.24	1.26	1.29	1.31	1.34	1.36	1.39	1.41	1.44	1.46	1.49	1.52	1.55	1.57
5	1.22	1.25	1.28	1.31	1.34	1.37	1.40	1.44	1.47	1.50	1.54	1.57	1.61	1.65	1.69	1.72	1.76
6	1.27	1.30	1.34	1.38	1.42	1.46	1.50	1.54	1.59	1.63	1.68	1.72	1.77	1.82	1.87	1.92	1.97
7	1.32	1.36	1.41	1.45	1.50	1.55	1.61	1.66	1.71	1.77	1.83	1.89	1.95	2.01	2.08	2.14	2.21
8	1.37	1.42	1.48	1.53	1.59	1.65	1.72	1.78	1.85	1.92	1.99	2.07	2.14	2.22	2.30	2.39	2.48
9	1.42	1.49	1.55	1.62	1.69	1.76	0.84	1.92	2.00	2.08	2.17	2.26	2.36	2.46	2.56	2.66	2.77
10	1.48	1.55	1.63	1.71	1.79	1.88	1.97	2.06	2.16	2.26	2.37	2.48	2.59	2.71	2.84	2.97	3.11
11	1.54	1.66	1.71	1.80	1.90	2.00	2.10	2.22	2.33	2.45	2.58	2.71	2.85	3.00	3.15	3.31	3.48
12	1.60	1.70	1.80	1.90	2.01	2.13	2.25	2.38	2.52	2.66	2.81	2.97	3.14	3.31	3.50	3.69	3.90
13	1.67	1.77	1.89	2.01	2.13	2.27	2.41	2.56	2.72	2.89	3.07	3.25	3.45	3.66	3.88	4.12	4.36
14	1.73	1.85	1.98	2.12	2.26	2.41	2.58	2.75	2.94	3.13	3.34	3.56	3.80	4.05	4.31	4.59	4.89
15	1.80	1.94	2.08	2.23	2.40	2.57	2.76	2.98	3.17	3.40	3.64	3.90	4.18	4.47	4.78	5.12	5.47
16	1.87	2.02	2.18	2.36	2.54	2.74	2.95	3.18	3.43	3.69	3.97	4.27	4.59	4.94	5.31	5.71	6.13
17	1.95	2.11	2.29	2.48	2.69	2.92	3.16	3.42	3.70	4.00	4.33	4.68	5.05	5.46	5.90	6.36	6.87
18	2.03	2.21	2.41	2.62	2.85	3.11	3.38	3.68	4.00	4.34	4.72	5.12	5.56	6.03	6.54	7.09	7.69
19	2.11	2.31	2.53	2.77	3.03	3.31	3.62	3.95	4.32	4.71	5.14	5.61	6.12	6.67	7.26	7.91	8.61
20	2.19	2.41	2.65	2.92	3.21	3.52	3.87	4.25	4.66	5.11	5.60	6.14	6.73	7.37	8.06	8.82	9.95
21	2.28	2.52	2.79	3.08	3.40	3.75	4.14	4.57	5.03	5.55	6.11	6.73	7.40	8.14	8.95	9.83	10.80
22	2.37	2.63	2.93	3.25	3.60	4.00	4.43	4.91	5.44	6.02	6.66	7.36	8.14	8.99	9.93	10.97	12.10
23	2.46	2.75	3.07	3.43	3.82	4.26	4.74	5.28	5.87	6.53	7.26	8.06	8.95	9.94	11.03	12.23	13.55
24	2.56	2.88	3.23	3.61	4.05	4.53	5.07	5.67	6.34	7.08	7.98	8.83	9.85	10.98	12.24	13.63	15.18
25	2.67	3.01	3.39	3.81	4.29	4.83	5.43	6.10	6.85	7.69	8.62	9.67	10.83	12.14	13.59	15.20	17.00
26	2.77	3.14	3.56	4.02	4.55	5.14	5.81	6.56	7.40	8.34	9.40	10.59	11.92	13.41	15.08	16.95	19.04
27	2.88	3.28	3.73	4.24	4.82	5.48	6.21	7.05	7.99	9.05	10.25	11.59	13.11	14.82	16.74	18.90	21.32
28	3.00	3.43	3.92	4.48	5.11	5.83	6.65	7.58	8.63	9.82	11.17	12.69	14.42	16.37	18.58	21.07	23.88
29	3.12	3.58	4.12	4.72	5.42	6.21	7.11	8.14	9.32	10.65	12.17	13.90	15.86	18.09	20.62	23.49	26.75
30	3.24	3.75	4.32	4.98	5.74	6.61	7.61	8.75	10.06	11.56	13.27	15.22	17.45	19.99	22.89	26.20	29.96
31	3.37	3.91	4.54	5.26	6.09	7.04	8.15	9.41	10.87	12.54	14.46	16.67	19.19	22.09	25.41	29.21	33.55
32	3.51	4.09	4.76	5.55	6.45	7.50	8.72	10.12	11.74	13.61	15.76	18.25	21.11	24.41	28.21	32.57	37.58
33	3.65	4.27	5.00	5.85	6.84	7.99	9.33	10.88	12.68	14.76	17.18	19.98	23.23	26.97	31.31	36.31	42.09
34	3.79	4.47	5.25	6.17	7.25	8.51	9.98	11.69	13.69	16.02	18.73	21.88	25.55	29.81	34.75	40.49	47.14
35	3.95	4.67	5.52	6.51	7.69	9.06	10.68	12.57	14.79	17.38	20.41	23.96	28.10	32.94	38.57	45.15	52.80

Directory of Agencies for the Aging

Each state has its own laws and regulations governing all types of insurance. The insurance offices listed in the left column of this directory are responsible for enforcing the laws as well as providing the public with information about insurance. The middle column lists the telephone numbers to call for insurance counseling service; calls to 800 numbers are toll-free when made within the state. The agencies on aging, listed in the right column, are responsible for coordinating services for older Americans.

Insurance Departments	Insurance Counseling	Agencies for the Aging
Insurance Department 135 South Union Street Montgomery, AL 36130-3401 (205) 269-3550	**Alabama** (800) 242-5463	Commission on Aging 770 Washington Ave., Suite 470 Montgomery, AL 36130 (800) 243-5463, (205) 242-5743
Division of Insurance 800 E. Diamond, Suite 560 Anchorage, AK 99515 (907) 349-1230	**Alaska** (907) 563-5654	Older Alaskans Commission P.O. Box C MS 0209 Juneau, AK 99811 (907) 465-3250
Insurance Department Consumer Affairs/Invest. Div. 3030 N. Third Street Phoenix, AZ 85012 (602) 255-4783	**Arizona** (800) 432-4040	Dept. of Economic Security Aging & Adult Administration 1789 W. Jefferson Street Phoenix, AZ 85007 (602) 542-4460

Insurance Departments	Insurance Counseling	Agencies for the Aging
Insurance Department Seniors Insurance Network 1123 S. University 400 University Tower Building Little Rock, AR 72204 (501) 686-2900	**Arkansas** (800) 852-5494	Division of Aging & Adult Services Donaghey Plaza South 7th and Main Streets, Suite 1417 P.O. Box 1417, Slot 1412 Little Rock, AR 72203-1437 (501) 682-2441
Insurance Department Consumer Services Division 3450 Wilshire Blvd. Los Angeles, CA 90010	**California** (800) 927-4357	Department of Aging 1600 K. Street Sacramento, CA 95814 (916) 322-3887
Insurance Division 1560 Broadway, Suite 850 Denver, CO 80202 (303) 894-7499	**Colorado** (303) 894-7499	Department of Social Services 1575 Sherman Street, 10th Floor Denver, CO 80823-1714 (303) 866-3851
Insurance Department 153 Market Street P.O. Box 816 Hartford, CT 06142-0816	**Connecticut** (800) 443-9946	Department on the Aging 175 Main Street Hartford, CT 06106 (800) 443-9946 (203) 566-7772
Insurance Department 841 Silver Lake Blvd. Dover, DE 19901 (302) 739-4251	**Delaware** (800) 851-3535	Division of Aging Dept. of Health & Human Services 11901 DuPont Highway New Castle, DE 19720 (302) 577-4660
Insurance Department 613 G. Street, NW, Room 638 P.O. Box 37200 Washington, DC 20001-7200 (202) 727-8009	**District of Columbia** (202) 724-5626	Office on Aging 1424 K. Street, NW, 2nd Floor Washington, DC 20005 (202) 724-5626 (202) 724-5622
Department of Insurance State Capitol, Plaza 11 Building 2, Room 323 Tallahassee, FL 32399-0300 (800) 342-2762; (904) 922-3100	**Florida** (904) 922-2073	Office on Aging & Adult Services 1317 Winewood Blvd. Tallahassee, FL 32399-0070 (904) 488-8922
Insurance Department 2 Martin L. King, Jr., Drive Room 716, West Tower Atlanta, GA 30334 (404) 656-2056	**Georgia** (404) 894-5333	Office of Aging Department of Human Resources 88 Peachtree St., NE, Room 632 Atlanta, GA 30309 (404) 894-5333
Dept. of Consumer Affairs Insurance Division P.O. Box 3614 Honolulu, HI 96811 (808) 586-2790	**Hawaii** (808) 586-0100	Executive Office on Aging 335 merchant Street, Room 241 Honolulu, HI 96813 (808) 586-0100

Insurance Departments	Insurance Counseling	Agencies for the Aging
Insurance Division Consumer Services Division 280 Friend Street Boston, MA 02114 (617) 727-7189	**Massachusetts** (617) 727-7750	Executive Office of Elder Affairs Ashburton Place, Fifth Floor Boston, MA 02108 (800) 882-2003 (617) 727-7750
Insurance Department P.O. Box 30220 Lansing, MI 48909 (517) 373-0220	**Michigan** (517) 373-8230	Office of Services to the Aging 611 W. Ottawa Street P.O. Box 30026 Lansing, MI 48909 (517) 373-8230
Insurance Department Department Of Commerce 133 E. Seventh Street St. Paul, MN 55101-2362 (612) 296-4026	**Minnesota** (800) 392-0343	Board on Aging Human Services Building 44 Lafayette Road St. Paul, MN 55155-3843 (612) 296-2770
Department of Insurance Consumer Services Division P.O. Box 79 Jackson, MS 39205 (601) 359-3569	**Mississippi** (Counseling services are not provided at this time.)	Council on Aging 455 Lamar Street Jackson, MS 39202 (800) 345-6347 (601) 359-6770
Consumer Assistance Division P.O. Box 690 Jefferson City, MO 65102-0690 (800) 726-7390 (314) 751-2640	**Missouri** (800) 726-7390	Division of Aging Department of Social Services P.O. Box 1337 615 Howerton Court Jefferson City, MO 65102-1337 (314) 751-3082
Insurance Department 126 N. Sanders, Mitchell Bldg., Rm. 270 P.O. Box 4009 Helena, MT 59604 (800) 332-6148; (406) 444-2040	**Montana** (800) 332-2272	The Governor's Office in Aging State Capitol Building, Room 219 Helena, MT 59620 (800) 332-2272 (406) 444-3111
Insurance Department Terminal Building 941 O Street, Suite 400 Lincoln, NE 68508 (402) 471-2201	**Nebraska** (402) 471-4887	Department on Aging State Office Building 301 Centennial Mall South Lincoln, NE 68509-5044 (402) 486-3545
Department of Insurance Consumer Services 1665 Hot Springs Road Capitol Complex Carson City, NV 89701 (712) 687-4270; (800) 992-0900	**Nevada** (702) 687-4270	Dept. of Health & Human Services Division of Aging Services 340 N. 11th Street, Suite 114 Las Vegas, NV 89101 (702) 486-3545

Insurance Departments	Insurance Counseling	Agencies for the Aging
Insurance Department Life and Health Division 169 Manchester Street Concord, NH 03301 (603) 271-2261; (800) 852-3416	**New Hampshire** (603) 271-4642	Division of Elderly & Adult Services 6 Hazen Drive Concord, NH 03301 (603) 271-4680
Insurance Department 20 W. State Street Roebling Building Trenton, NJ 08625 (609) 292-5390	**New Jersey** (800) 792-8820	Department of Community Affairs Division on Aging S. Broad & Flint Streets, CN 807 Trenton, NJ 08625-0807 (800) 792-8820, (609) 292-0920
Insurance Department P.O. Box 1269 Santa Fe, NM 87504-1269 (505) 827-4500	**New Mexico** (800) 432-2080	Agency on Aging La Villa Rivera Building, 1st Floor 224 E. Palace Avenue Santa Fe, NM 87501 (800) 432-2080, (505) 827-7640
Insurance Department 160 W. Broadway New York, NY 10013 (212) 602-0203; (800) 342-3736	**New York** (800) 342-9871	State Office for the Aging 2 Empire State Plaza Albany, NY 12223-0001 (800) 342-9871; (518) 474-5731
Insurance Department Seniors Health Insurance Information Program (SHIIP) P.O. Box 26387 Raleigh, NC 27611 (919) 733-0111 (SHIIP) (800) 662-7777	**North Carolina** (800) 443-9354	Department of Human Resources Division of Aging 693 Palmer Drive Raleigh, NC 27626-0531 (919) 733-3983
Insurance Department Capitol Building, Fifth Floor 600 E. Boulevard Bismarck, ND 58505-0320 (800) 247-0560 (701) 224-2440	**North Dakota** (800) 247-0560	Department of Human Services Aging Services Division State Capitol Building Bismarck, ND 58507-7070 (701) 224-2577
Insurance Department Consumer Services Division 2100 Stella Court Columbus, OH 43266-0566 (800) 686-1526 (614) 644-2673	**Ohio** (800) 686-1578	Department of Aging 50 W. Broad Street, 8th Floor Columbus, OH 43266-0501 (614) 466-1221
Insurance Department P.O. Box 53408 Oklahoma City, OK 73152-3408 (405) 521-2828	**Oklahoma** (405) 521-6628	Department of Human Services Aging Services Division 312 NE 28th Street Oklahoma City, OK 73125 (405) 521-2327

Insurance Departments	Insurance Counseling	Agencies for the Aging
Department of Insurance Insurance Div. Consumer Advocacy 440 Labor & Industries Building Salem, OR 97310 (503) 378-4484	**Oregon** (503) 378-4484	Dept. of Human Resources Senior Services Division 500 Summer St. NE, 2nd Floor Salem, OR 97310 (800) 232-3020, (503) 378-4728
Insurance Department Consumer Services Bureau 1321 Strawberry Square Harrisburg, PA 17120 (717) 787-2317	**Pennsylvania** (717) 783-8975	Department of Aging 231 State Street Barto Building Harrisburg, PA 17101 (717) 783-1550
Insurance Division 233 Richmond St., Suite 233 Providence, RI 02903-4233 (401) 277-2223	**Rhode Island** (800) 322-2880	Department of Elderly Affairs 160 Pine Street Providence, RI 02903 (401) 277-2858
Insurance Department Consumer Assistance Section P.O. Box 10015 Columbia, SC 29202-3105 (803) 735-0210; (800) 768-3467	**South Carolina** (800) 896-9095	Commission on Aging 400 Arbor Lake Drive, Suite B-500 Columbia, SC 29223
Insurance Department Enforcement 910 E. Sioux Avenue Pierre, SD 57501-3940 (605) 733-3563	**South Dakota** (605) 773-3656	Agency on Aging Richard F. Kneip Building 700 Governors Drive Pierre, SD 57501-2291 (605) 773-3656
Dept. of Commerce & Insurance Insurance Assistance Office, 4th Floor 400 James, Robertson Parkway Nashville, TN 37243 (800) 525-2816; (615) 741-4955	**Tennessee** (800) 525-2816	Commission on Aging 706 Church Street, Suite 201 Nashville, TN 37243-0860 (615) 741-2056
Department of Insurance Complaints Resolution, MC 111-1A 333 Guadalupe St., P.O. Box 149091 Austin, TX 78714-9091 (512) 463-6515; (800) 252-3439	**Texas** (800) 252-9420	Department on Aging P.O. Box 12786 Capitol Station 949 U.S. Route 35 South Austin, TX 78741 (512) 444-2727
Insurance Department Consumer Services 3110 State Office Building Salt Lake City, UT 84114 (800) 439-3805 (801) 538-3805	**Utah** (801) 538-3910	Division of Aging & Adult Services 120 North 200 West P.O. Box 45500 Salt Lake City, UT 84103 (801) 538-3910

Insurance Departments	Insurance Counseling	Agencies for the Aging
Dept. of Banking & Insurance Consumer Complaint Division 89 Main Street, Drawer 20 Montpelier, VT 05602-3101 (802) 828-3301	**Vermont** (800) 642-5119	Office on Aging Waterbury Complex 103 S. Main Street Waterbury, VT 05671-2301 (802) 241-2400
Insurance Department Consumer Services Division 700 Jefferson Building P.O. Box 1157 Richmond, VA 23209 (804) 786-7691	**Virginia** (800) 552-4464	Department for the Aging 700 Centre, 10th Floor 700 E. Franklin Street Richmond, VA 23219-2327 (800) 552-4464 (804) 225-2271
Insurance Department Insurance Building AQ21 P.O. Box 40255 Olympia, WA 98504-0255 (800) 562-6900 (206) 753-7300	**Washington** (800) 562-6900	Aging/Adult Services Administration Dept. of Health & Human Services 12th & Jefferson Streets Mail Stop OB-44-A Olympia, WA 98504 (206) 586-3786
Insurance Department 2019 Washington Street E. Charleston, WV 25305 (304) 348-3386; (800) 642-9004 (800) 435-7381 (Hearing Impaired)	**West Virginia** (304) 558-3317	Commission on Aging State Capitol Complex Holly Grove Charleston, WV 25305 (304) 558-3311
Insurance Department Complaints Department P.O. Box 7873 Madison, WI 53707 (800) 236-8517; (608) 266-0103	**Wisconsin** (800) 242-1060	Bureau on Aging Dept. of Health & Human Serv. P.O. Box 7851 217 Hamilton St., Suite 300 Madison, WI 53707 (608) 266-2536
Insurance Department Hemher Building 122 W. 25th Street Cheyenne, WY 82002 (800) 442-4333; (307) 777-7401	**Wyoming** (800) 442-4333 ext. 6888	Division on Aging Hathaway Building 2300 Capitol Avenue Room 139 Cheyenne, WY 82002 (800) 442-2766 (307) 777-7986

Index